THE BIG ILLUSTRATED BOOK OF
TRANSPORT

Funded by a
grant from
ConocoPhillips

THE BIG ILLUSTRATED BOOK OF
TRANSPORT

ALL ABOUT SHIPS, TRAINS, CARS AND FLIGHT WITH 1000 PHOTOGRAPHS
AND ILLUSTRATIONS AND 50 STEP-BY-STEP PROJECTS AND EXPERIMENTS!

EDITOR: CHRIS OXLADE

southwater

CONTENTS

THE NEED FOR TRAVEL.....6

SHIPS

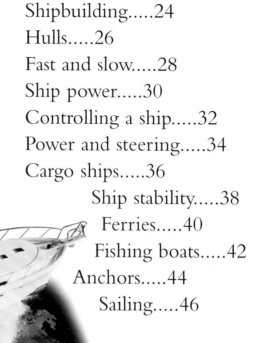

TRAINS

CARS

AIRCRAFT AND FLIGHT

THE NEED FOR TRAVEL

Imagine a world without cars, ships, trains or planes. It would be a very small world compared with the one you know today. Its limits would be defined by how far you could walk. Moving house would be impossible without trucks to transport your belongings, and you would have to rely on food that you could find nearby to survive.

This is what it was like for our early ancestors, who hunted wild animals and gathered wild plants to eat. Even such a simple life had its transportation problems. After a successful hunt, heavy animal carcasses had to be hauled back to a cave. If drought or cold weather killed off the local plants, people had to trek long distances to find new sources of food. If there was

Finding a way of travelling over water enabled people to fish away from the shore. Looking for easier ways of travelling over difficult terrain also meant that early humans could look for richer lands in their search for food.

a fast-flowing river or a vast lake blocking the way, they were stuck – unless someone could work out a way to get across.

The fact that someone did shows how the earliest methods of transportation grew from solving such problems as these.

As the lifestyle of the solitary prehistoric family group was very basic, people did not need to develop new methods of transportation. Gradually, families banded together to form clans and tribes, and life grew more complicated. Settlements made greater demands on the land, and a move to fresh

The early Native Americans came from the northernmost part of Asia to North America. They came on foot, as the two continents were once connected. They may have been seeking a warmer climate and more plentiful supplies of food.

territory was a major event. Animal hides and shelters, pots, pans, and primitive tools were loaded on to simple frameworks or sleds.

To cross rivers and lakes, humans adapted what they saw in the natural world to their own needs. A floating log or raft of reeds carried on the spring meltwater might have been the first form of water transportation. But this basic idea was soon improved upon. Early humans lashed branches together into rafts – the ferries and cargo vessels of their day – and hollowed out logs to make dugout canoes.

None of these early methods of transportation was up to extreme conditions or long-distance travel. Tribal communities were still very limited to areas over which they could travel easily by foot, and to coastal waters. It took a momentous change in the way people lived to trigger the next leap forward in transportation history.

The challenge of civilization

In various fertile river valleys in different parts of the world, some people decided to settle down. They learned to cultivate plant crops and no longer moved around to forage for food. Their hunting ancestors had tamed some animals, such as sheep, goats, and oxen, instead of killing them for the next meal. This opened up new horizons for humankind, because the stronger animals could be used to carry heavy packs. Then, about 6,000 years ago in the

Canoes made from solid logs were the simplest boats. People used fire or stone axes to make small hollows in the logs for somewhere to sit and to make the canoes float better. When people began to make floating shells from scratch, by stretching animal skins over wooden frames, they had boats that were lighter, faster, and easier to control.

steppelands of central Asia, Mongolian tribes applied what they had learned about handling animals to the horse. This swift and powerful pack animal needed only the poorest of grass diets to survive, but played a huge part in transportation history. Harnessed to a plow, the horse transformed farming. Over the centuries, it was to carry people rich and poor, in peace and war, for work, and for pleasure. A fine horse hitched to a personal carriage or cart could also show off personal status and wealth – rather

The wild ox was one of the first animals to be domesticated, along with sheep and goats. At first, animals were tamed to provide milk and to be bred for ongoing supplies of meat. It was not long before the stronger animals were used to carry packs or for plowing.

like stylish cars can do today. But the taming of the horse came sometime before the cart – and the wheel was yet to be invented.

The need for an easier life drove people of the early civilizations in Mesopotamia, northern India, Egypt, and China, to invention. The first, solid-wheeled carts appeared some 3,250 years ago. Imagine the change in peoples' lives! A wheeled vehicle drawn by an animal meant faster and better sowing and harvesting, and the ability to travel farther, faster, and with a lot more baggage.

Swap shop

One effect of successful farming was that for the first time in human history people produced more food than they needed for themselves. They traded leftovers for other goods they needed, or even for luxuries from faraway countries. As civilizations developed and empires grew, people traveled greater distances to trade with their neighbors and expand into new territories. At the same time, they devised ever-more efficient and specialized ways of travel and transportation. Competition for land led to conflict and warfare, which provided another boost to the

Heavy wooden ships propelled by sails or crews of powerful oarsmen were able to cross the world's seas and oceans with ease. Up until the 1400s, most European ships were square-rigged, like this one, which meant they could only sail with the wind behind them. Ships called caravels were then developed with triangular, or 'lateen', sails. With these sails, caravels could sail directly into the wind.

development of transportation. One of the ways to win a war is to have the fastest horses, chariots, or the most maneuvrable and well-armed ships.

Trade and exploration spurred people who lived by the sea or on the banks of rivers to put sails on their ships to harness wind power. The Phoenicians of the eastern Mediterranean, whose trading empire was at its peak in 1400BC, built boats that combined sails with banks of oars, and braved the high seas of the Atlantic Ocean. The ancient Egyptians sailed around the southernmost tip of Africa to the Indian Ocean in the quest for new trading opportunities and colonies.

Over the centuries, sail power was adapted to various conditions of water and weather, and boats were built for many different purposes. On land, however, methods of transportation were founded on the same basic principles for hundreds of years – there were just lots of variations on the animal and chariot theme. In the 1800s, however, the Industrial Revolution brought about completely new forms of transportation.

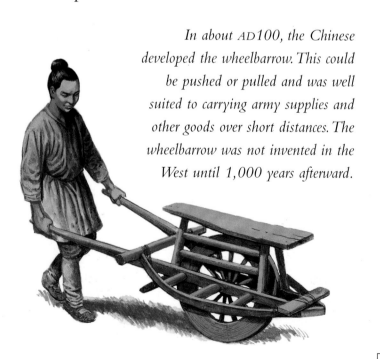

In about AD100, the Chinese developed the wheelbarrow. This could be pushed or pulled and was well suited to carrying army supplies and other goods over short distances. The wheelbarrow was not invented in the West until 1,000 years afterward.

Steaming ahead

In the late 1700s, the harnessing of steam power to make working engines heralded the start of the Industrial Revolution. It was some time before a steam-powered ship could better the time of the sleek, sail-powered clippers carrying tea from China to England. By the early 1900s, however, sailing ships were mostly relegated to the worlds of sport and leisure.

Change was more rapid on land and had an enormous impact on everyday life. The Stockton–Darlington line in northeast England was the world's first railroad to carry passengers when it opened in 1825. Railroads soon transformed the lives of ordinary people. Food and fuel could be distributed rapidly throughout a country, bringing a wider range of cheaper supplies to more people.

Trains brought travel and transportation for the masses. The development of the first usable internal combustion engine in 1860 paved the way for a personal and independent method of travel – the motor car.

The ancient Greeks made the first railed tracks by cutting grooves into rocky ground. Iron rails were not developed until the middle of the 17th century.

The concentrated power of combustion engines also made powered flight possible, and American brothers Wilbur and Orville Wright built the first heavier-than-air aircraft in 1903.

Today, people can travel when and where they want in their cars, and fly all over the world quickly and comfortably. Unlike our ancestors, they may not always need to do so. The incentive behind developing new methods of transportation is now more to do with convenience than with survival. There is also a price to pay. Our fast, fuel-burning motor vehicles and planes, and the sheer numbers of them, damage and pollute our world. The challenge for the future of transportation is to find ways of reducing that damage.

Traffic congestion is a sign that transportation has got out of control. As with all other fuel-powered means of transportation, the waste gases from burning fuel cause dangerous and unhealthy levels of pollution in the atmosphere.

SHIPS

*For centuries, those who were masters of sea travel
were masters of the world. Countries with fast and
reliable ships were the most successful traders,
explorers and conquerors. The story of waterborne
vessels starts several thousand years ago and has, in
many ways, shaped the course of civilization.
Most of the basic design principles of keeping a vessel
afloat have remained the same from the days of the
dug-out canoe and the first sailing boats. What you
will discover here, though, is the enormous variety of
ships that has evolved through the ages. Some were
built for special jobs, such as ramming enemy ships or
transporting heavy loads. Others took advantage of
new technology, such as steam power. You will find out
about all sorts of ships, past and present, from simple
rafts, small leisure craft, and rescue boats to
streamlined racing yachts, hovercraft, and supertankers.*

AUTHOR
Chris Oxlade
CONSULTANT
Trevor Blakeley

WHAT IS A SHIP?

PEOPLE HAVE used rafts, boats and ships to travel across water for many thousands of years. At its simplest, a ship is any craft that travels on water, but ships have developed from simple log rafts to vast oil tankers. This development has affected life on land, in shipbuilding yards and at ports where hundreds of people work loading and unloading cargo. The difference between a ship and a boat is not very clear. Generally, ships are larger and travel across seas and oceans. Boats are smaller and usually travel on rivers, lakes and coastal waters. Ships and boats come in a huge variety of shapes and sizes and have a wide range of uses from simple rowing boats to massive cruise liners. The selection of ships and boats shown here illustrates the wide range of jobs they do, and their importance for transportation, commerce, leisure, exploration and combat. Simple projects will help you understand the technical side of ships – how they float and how they are powered and controled.

Boats on inland waters
Two types of boat common on rivers and canals are shown here. In the foreground is a very simple row boat. It has many uses – transportation, fishing and ferrying from ship to shore. It is usually propelled by oars, but it can be fitted with sails or an outboard motor. Behind is a narrow, flat-bottomed canal boat. It is used for transporting cargo.

Parts of a ship
This fishing trawler looks similar to many other ships and boats. The body of the boat is called the hull. The backbone of the hull is the keel. The bow (front) is sharply pointed to cut easily through the water. A deck provides a watertight covering for the crew to work on. An engine-driven propeller pushes the ship along. The rudder at the stern (back) is used for steering.

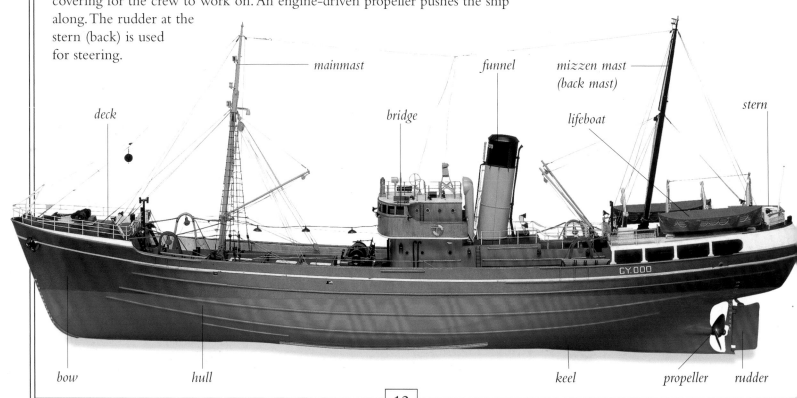

mainmast

deck

bridge

funnel

mizzen mast (back mast)

lifeboat

stern

CY.000

bow

hull

keel

propeller

rudder

Fishing boats

One of the earliest uses of boats was fishing. Today there are fishing boats designed to catch different fish in all sorts of conditions – from calm lakes to the deep oceans. Fishing trawlers drag nets through the water behind them.

Cargo carriers

The largest moving machines ever built are big cargo ships. There are several types designed to carry different types of cargoes. The one pictured here is a container ship, which carries different cargoes packed in large metal boxes.

Fast and fun

The fastest boats are racing powerboats. They are just one of many different types of boats used for having fun on the water. Their hulls are designed to rise out of the water and skim the surface at high speed. The deep V-shape of the hull helps the bow to lift clear of the water and slice through the waves.

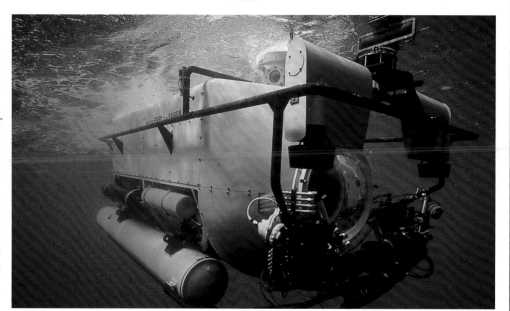

Under the water

Submersibles and submarines are the only types of boat designed to travel under the water as well as on the surface. The submersible shown here is just breaking the surface of the water. Submersibles are small craft used for underwater research, exploration and repairs to seabed pipes and cables. Submarines are usually larger and most are for military purposes. They are used to launch missiles and sink ships. Most submersibles can dive much deeper than a military submarine.

13

HOW DO SHIPS FLOAT?

SHIPS AND all other objects that float can do so because the water they are floating in pushes upward against them. This pushing force is called upthrust. An object will float if the upthrust of the water is great enough to overcome the downward push of the object's weight. The size of the upthrust depends on how much water the object pushes out of the way. When you put an object in water and let it go, it settles into the water, pushing liquid out of the way. The farther it goes in, the more water it pushes away and the more upthrust acts on it. When the upthrust becomes the same as the object's weight, the object floats. If, when the object is fully underwater, its weight is bigger than the upthrust, however, it will sink. The simplest boats, such as rafts, float because the material they are made of is less dense (lighter) than water. Heavy metal ships float, because they are specially designed to displace (push aside) a large weight of water. Not all water has the same density. Salt water is denser than fresh water and gives a stronger upthrust. Ships float higher in salty seawater than in fresh lake water.

fresh water *salt water*

Measuring density
The density of water is measured with a hydrometer. Make a simple hydrometer by putting non-hardening modeling material on the end of a straw. Put it in a glass of water. Mark the water level with tape. Put the straw in an equal amount of salty water. What happens?

TESTING UPTHRUST

You will need: two polystyrene blocks (one twice the size of the other), wooden block, marble.

1 Put the two polystyrene blocks into a tank of water. They will float well, because their material, polystyrene, is so light. Only a small amount of upthrust is needed.

2 Push the blocks under water. Now you are pushing lots of water aside. Can you feel upthrust pushing back? The bigger block will experience more upthrust.

3 A wooden block floats deeper in the water, because wood is more dense (heavier) than polystyrene. A marble sinks, because the upthrust on it is not as great as its weight.

PROJECT

HOLLOW HULLS

You will need: *scissors, aluminum foil, ruler, marbles.*

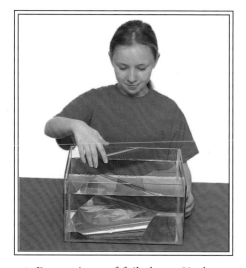

1 Put a piece of foil about 8in by 6in into a tank of water. With only a slight push, it will sink. This is because it does not displace much water so there is little upthrust.

2 Lift the sheet of foil out of the water. Now mold it into a simple boat shape with your fingers. Take care not to tear the foil.

3 Put your foil boat back into the tank of water. It should now float. Its shape pushes aside much more water than it did when it was flat, so the upthrust is greater.

4 Try filling your foil boat with small objects such as marbles, for cargo. As you put more marbles in it will float lower and lower. How many marbles can your boat hold before it sinks?

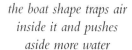

the boat shape traps air inside it and pushes aside more water

Foil float

This simple foil boat works like a real ship's hull. Even though it is made of metal, it is filled with air. This gives the hull shape a much lower overall density.

THE FIRST BOATS

NOBODY KNOWS exactly when people first started using craft to travel on water, but it must have been tens of thousands of years ago. The first craft were probably extremely simple – perhaps just a log, an inflated animal skin, or a bundle of reeds tied together. People discovered that craft like these, made from what was available close by, could help them to cross a stretch of water more easily. These craft probably developed into early simple boats, such as dug-out canoes and skin-covered boats, in which a person could sit while fishing or traveling along a river. The basic designs are still in use in many areas of the world today and have many advantages over modern boats. They are simple to make from cheap local materials. Although they are not very long-lasting, there are no high-tech materials to mend or engine parts to replace. The simplest boats do not use up expensive fuel or hard-to-find equipment such as batteries.

Simple raft
A raft like this one from Australia can be built with very basic tools. It is used in shallow water and propelled along with a long stick pushed into the riverbed. Rafts are probably the oldest form of water transportation. Aboriginals may have used sea-going rafts to first reach Australia around 55,000 years ago.

Dug-out canoe
A dug-out canoe is made by hollowing out a thick tree trunk to leave a thin wooden hull. The hull is smoothed and shaped so that it moves easily through the water. Dug-out canoes are fairly heavy boats and sit low in the water.

FACT BOX
• In 1970, Norwegian Thor Heyerdahl built a large Egyptian-style reed boat called *Ra II*. He sailed it from Africa to the Caribbean. This proved the Egyptians would have been able to reach America more than 4,000 years ago.

• One of the greatest sea battles of all time took place at Salamis, off Greece, in 480BC. In the battle, 380 Greek triremes defeated an invading fleet of around 1,000 Persian ships.

Yak-skin boat
This strange-looking boat was photographed on a river in Tibet, now part of China. It is made by stretching yak hides (a type of ox skin) over a wooden framework. The hide is then treated to make it waterproof.

Inuit kayak

The kayak was developed by the Inuit people of the Arctic. It is also a hide boat, made from sealskin stretched over a driftwood frame. Kayaks were used as fast hunting craft for harpooning seals, fish and walruses. Boats like this work well in rough seas. A skilled paddler can turn the kayak upright if it capsizes (rolls over).

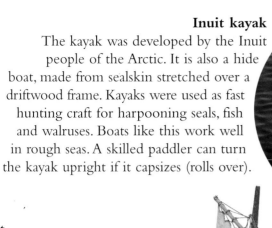

Nile boat

A model boat from an ancient Egyptian tomb shows the type of craft used on the river Nile about 5,000 years ago. Boats like these were the first to use a simple sail. The boat was propelled with oars when there was no wind or the wind was in the wrong direction. It was steered using a long oar hanging over the stern.

square sail

rigging (ropes and poles)

a tiller (handle) was used to move the steering oar

steering oar

the helmsman steered the boat

a crew raised and lowered the mast, or rowed the boat

shallow-scooped, wooden hull

oar

passenger

Greek warship

This is a full-scale replica of an ancient Greek trireme. A trireme was a warship with three banks of oars operated by about 170 men. Triremes attacked other ships by ramming them. Soldiers were also transported on deck.

Roman galley

A Roman mosaic from Tunisia, made around AD200, shows that Roman warships were very similar to earlier Greek ships. In the stern they often had wooden towers painted to look like stone. Underneath the high bow was a ram.

MAKE SIMPLE BOATS

YOU CAN build your own models of ancient types of boats that are still in use today. Instructions for making a model reed boat are given in the first project. Reed boats are made by tying thousands of river reeds together into huge bundles. The bundles themselves are then tied together to make hull shapes. Small reed boats are still built in southern Iraq and on Lake Titicaca in South America. In ancient Egypt, quite large boats were made like this from papyrus reeds. Some historians believe that Egyptians may have made long ocean crossings in papyrus craft. The model in the second project is of a craft called a coracle. This is a round boat made by covering a light wooden frame with animal hides. Like reed boats, coracles are still made, but today builders use a covering of canvas treated with tar instead of hide. They were small enough for one person to paddle along a river and were used for fishing. Look for pictures of other simple craft and try making working models of them, too.

Chariots, boats and bladders
A stone carving from 860BC shows Assyrian soldiers crossing the river Tigris. They are transporting a war chariot in their coracle-like boat. Assyrian soldiers also used inflated pig's bladders as buoyancy aids to help them swim across wide rivers.

MAKE A REED CRAFT

You will need: *large bunch of raffia, scissors, ruler.*

1 Make bundles of raffia by tying a few dozen strands together with a short length of raffia. You will need two bundles about 8in long and two more about 10in long.

2 Tie the two long bundles and the two short bundles together. Tie the short bundles on top of the long ones. Fix a strand between each end to make the ends bend up.

3 Gently lower the reed boat onto the surface of a tank of water. How well does it float? Does it stay upright? Try leaving it in the water to see if it becomes waterlogged.

PROJECT

MAKE A CORACLE

You will need: *scissors, craft cane, string, dark cotton cloth, white glue, paint brush.*

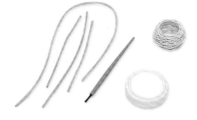

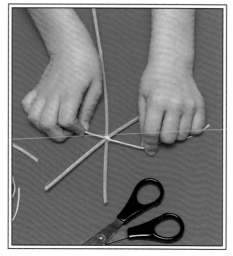

1 Cut one long and three short pieces of cane. Using short lengths of string, tie all three short pieces to the long piece to make a triple-armed cross.

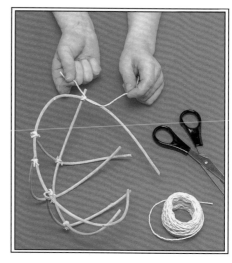

2 Cut a much longer piece of cane. Form it into a loop and tie it to all the ends of the triple cross shape. Bend the ends of the cross up as you tie them to form a dish shape.

— *waterproof covering*

lightweight frame

Model of an ancient craft

The design of the coracle has not changed in thousands of years. Early Britons used them 9,000 years ago. They are light to carry, easy to maneuvre and stable enough to fish from.

3 Cut pieces of cotton cloth about 6in by 2in. Apply glue to the outside of the frame and put the pieces over it. Glue the pieces to each other where they overlap.

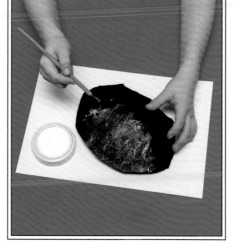

4 Glue down the cloth where it folds over the top of the frame. Put two coats of glue on the outside of the cloth to waterproof it. Leave the glue to dry completely.

5 When dry, put the finished coracle into a tank of water. How well does it float? Why not try making a person from modeling clay to sit in your model coracle?

THE AGE OF SAIL

Sails capture the wind and use it to push ships and boats along. As far as experts can tell, sails first appeared on ships on the river Nile in about 3500BC. These ships had just one simple square sail on a single mast. They were only useful when the wind was blowing in the same direction that the crew of the ship wanted to go. If the wind was blowing in another direction, such as from their destination, the crew had to row there instead. Viking boats in the AD600s used square sails to sail the coasts of Scandinavia. Later, large coastal Viking ships crossed the Atlantic to reach North America. In the Middle Ages, the lateen (triangular) sail was invented by the Chinese and Arabs. The lateen sail allowed ships to be sailed with the wind from the side. From the 1100s, European sailors began building fully rigged ships with a combination of square and lateen sails. This allowed them to make the maximum use of the wind. Their boats also had sturdy, seaworthy hulls. In ships like these, European sailors began long voyages of exploration.

Viking sails

A stone carving from Sweden that dates from the AD700s shows a Viking merchant boat with a simple square sail. The sail was made from cloth reinforced with diagonal strips of leather. Sails like this helped the crew sail downwind.

Chinese way ahead

The Chinese developed multi-masted ships called junks. These used triangular sails several centuries before they were introduced to Europe. This modern junk has sails that hang from poles that are hauled up the mast. The sails can swivel around the mast to take advantage of wind from behind or the side. They are made of cloth stiffened with bamboo poles. The poles keep the sails flat, make it easy to fold up the sails and provide a handy ladder for the crew.

Triangular sails

This fishing boat on the river Nile is called a felucca. Its design has been in use for 1,000 years and is most often seen on Arab trading vessels called dhows. The single triangular sail is an example of a lateen sail.

Men-of-war
These French ships are typical of the men-of-war (warships) that developed by 1700. They had many rows of cannons and hulls that were richly carved and gilded.

A mixture of sails
This painting shows ships off the coast of Portugal in the 1520s. The large ships are heavily armed carracks, a design that used both square and triangular sails. Smaller carracks were used as merchant vessels. The flagship *Santa Maria*, which took Columbus to the New World in 1492, was probably a small carrack.

Life onboard
A cartoon shows sailors celebrating victory in battle with Admiral Nelson in 1798. Hundreds of men were needed to sail a man-of-war. They lived in cramped conditions on the gun decks. Tables and hammocks were suspended between the guns.

The golden age of sail
By the 1850s, sleek, fast and efficient ships called clippers carried cargo such as tea and wool around the world. They represented the peak of sailing ship design and were the largest wooden vessels ever built. Larger merchant ships with iron hulls and up to seven masts were built up to the 1930s.

STEAM POWER

THE FIRST steam engines were developed in the early 1700s for pumping water out of mines. By the end of the century they had become small and more efficient and engineers began to use them in trains and ships. Steam power meant that a ship could keep going even if the wind was in the wrong direction, or not blowing at all. The first craft to use steam power was a small river boat called the *Charlotte Dundas*, launched in 1802. At sea, steamships carried sails to save fuel when the wind was blowing in the right direction. Early steamships used paddles, but propellers gradually proved to be more efficient. After the 1850s, shipbuilders began to use iron instead of wood. The superior strength of iron meant that much larger ships could be built, which could also be fitted with more powerful steam engines.

Stoking the boilers
To create steam, stokers constantly fed the fire boxes under a ship's boilers with coal. It was hot, unpleasant work in the stokehole.

Crossing the Atlantic
The huge *Great Eastern* was built in 1858. Steamships arrived at a time when crossing the Atlantic Ocean was becoming more popular. Steam power allowed faster and more reliable crossings, which people were willing to pay for. The *Great Eastern* could carry 4,000 passengers. It was the only ship to have both paddles and a propeller. Passengers did not entirely trust steam, however, so it was also equipped with sails.

An iron monster
This print shows the construction of the *Great Eastern's* central compartment. At 700ft long and 32,000 tons, it was by far the largest ship in the world at its launch in 1858. It was the last of three revolutionary ships designed by British engineer Isambard Kingdom Brunel. The *Great Eastern's* design was copied on other steamships for several decades. The hull was divided into ten watertight compartments, with double iron plating from the keel to the waterline. It took three months and seven attempts to finally launch the *Great Eastern*. Unfortunately, it had a pronounced roll in heavy seas, which passengers did not like. The ship was sold for scrap in 1888.

Paddle-powered riverboats on the Mississippi

On the shallow rivers of the southern United States, steam powered riverboats with huge paddles were developed. Here, two riverboats are racing each other on the Mississippi River in about 1850. Riverboats had flat, shallow hulls and no keel. Paddlewheels were mounted on each side, or at the stern.

Steaming to war

Steam power and iron construction gave warships much greater speed, maneuvrability and strength. *Dreadnought,* built in 1906, was the fastest battleship of its day and became the model for the period.

Tramp steamer

A typical cargo ship was known as a three-island steamer. This was because it had three raised decks, or islands. They were also called tramp steamers if they sailed from port to port with no fixed route.

Luxury travel

As transatlantic travel grew, shipping companies built large, luxurious ships called liners. This 1920s poster is from the golden age of the liner. Rival companies competed to provide the quickest crossing.

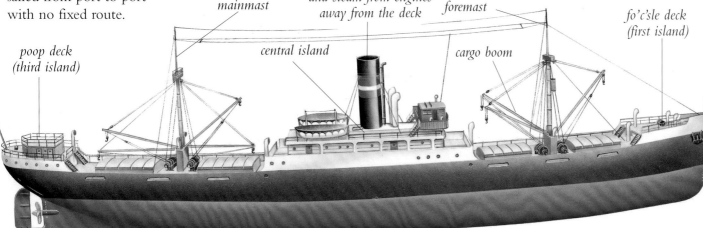

poop deck (third island)

mainmast

central island

a funnel carries smoke and steam from engines away from the deck

foremast

cargo boom

fo'c'sle deck (first island)

SHIPBUILDING

HIPS ARE constructed in a shipyard. Large ships are usually made from steel. Generally, the hull is built first by welding pieces of steel together. Often the hull is built in large sections that are then welded together. When the hull is finished, the ship is launched onto the water, where the rest of the ship is completed. Dozens of different tradespeople, such as welders, crane drivers, painters, electricians and carpenters work in shipyards. Boatbuilding takes place in smaller boatyards. Boats are usually made from wood or fiberglass.

Shipbuilding methods have changed as new materials have become available. Originally all ships were made from wood. A skeleton hull was made, then covered with planks. Steel ships are built with the metal skin forming part of the structure. New ships are designed on computer and models of them are tested before being built.

Viking boatbuilders
This image from the Bayeux Tapestry shows Norman shipwrights building the fleet that invaded England in 1066. The Normans were descended from the Vikings and shared many of the same boatbuilding techniques. They used special tools, such as axes and augers (hole borers), to shape the hull of a ship. Slender, Viking war boats were called longships.

FACT BOX
• The size of a ship is given in gross registered tonnage (g.r.t.). This is not a measure of its weight, but of the space inside it. One ton is equal to 9 cubic feet.

• The displacement of a ship is equal to the weight of the water that it pushes out of the way when it floats. This is usually equal to the weight of the ship and everything on it.

• The deadweight of a ship is the difference between the ship's displacement when empty and when it is full. It measures the weight of the cargo and passengers.

Wooden ribs
Here, the ribs of a wooden boat are being attached to the central keel. The timbers form a skeleton frame to which the planks of the hull and deck will be attached.

Covering the hull
Planks are attached edge to edge to the ribs of a wooden boat to make a smooth hull. The tight-fitting planks will be given several coats of paint or varnish to make a completely watertight finish.

Naval architects

Just as there are architects who design buildings, there are naval architects who design ships. These architects are planning the deck layouts of the cruise liner *Oriana*.

Shipbuilding shed

This picture shows the bow section of the cruise liner *Oriana* under construction. You can see the steel decks, bulkheads (watertight walls and doors) and skin. The ship is being built in a huge construction shed, where its progress is unaffected by the weather.

Float out

Once the hull has been completed, the floor of the construction shed is flooded so that the entire hull can be floated out. Here *Oriana* is being floated out at its launch. Smaller ships are built on slipways and then launched by sliding them down into the water.

Fitting out

Work on electrical equipment, lighting, pipes and other fixtures and fittings is completed after the ship is launched. This process is called fitting out. After fitting out, the ship will undergo sea trials.

HULLS

THE MAIN part of a ship is the hull, which sits in the water. The hull does four things. It provides the strong, rigid shape that makes the structure of the ship. It is a waterproof skin that stops water getting in. It supports all the equipment in the ship, such as the engines, and it provides space for the cargo. The shape of the hull also lets the ship slide easily through the water. The hull shape of a ship or boat depends on what that ship or boat is designed to do. Long, thin hulls are designed for traveling at high speed, while broad hulls are designed to carry as much cargo as possible. Wide, shallow hulls float high in the water and are good for traveling on shallow lakes, rivers and canals. The hull shape also dictates the stability of the ship, or how easily it tips from side to side. Inside the hull, solid walls called bulkheads make the hull stiffer and divide it into a number of watertight compartments.

Hulls for floating
Try pushing a light ball underwater. It will spring back up. Upthrust from the water makes a hollow hull float in the same way.

Multihulls
This canoe will not tip over because it has outriggers. The outriggers work like small hulls on each side of the canoe, making it a very stable vessel. Catamarans (boats with two hulls) and trimarans (three hulls) work in the same way. Boats with only one hull are called monohulls.

Plastic hulls
A whitewater canoe has a one-piece hull made of tough, rigid plastic. Its materials are strong enough to resist bumping against rocks and the riverbed. The hull's long, thin shape is designed for speed, slicing through the rough water. The canoeist sits in a sealed cockpit, which prevents water getting in. This not only keeps the canoeist dry, but means that the canoe remains buoyant (afloat).

Hulls in halves

Here, two halves of a yacht hull are made from fiberglass. Fiberglass is made by filling molds with layers of glass fiber and glue. It is light but strong and has a smooth finish.

Points and bulbs

While a fishing boat is in dry dock it enables us to see the parts of the hull usually underwater. The bulb shape at the bottom of the bow helps the boat to slip more easily through the water.

Changing shape

If you could cut through a ship and look at the cut ends, you would see a cross-section of its hull. Here you can see how the cross-section of a container ship's hull changes along its length.

Overlapping planks

This is a head-on view of the bow of a 1,000-year-old Viking ship. The hull is made from a shell of overlapping planks, hammered together with nails and strengthened by internal ribs. Hulls constructed of overlapping planks are called clinker built.

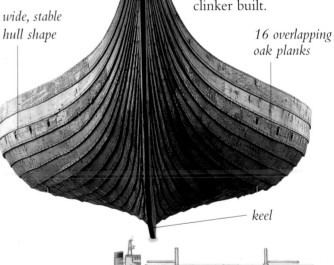

stempost

ocean-going high bow

wide, stable hull shape

16 overlapping oak planks

keel

Stern cross-section
The sides curve inward to make the bottom narrower than the deck.

Central cross-section
The hull is almost square. This allows the maximum space for cargo.

Bow cross-section
Just behind the sharp bow the bottom is very narrow and the sides are high.

FAST AND SLOW

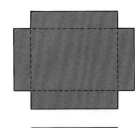
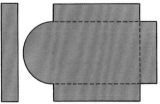
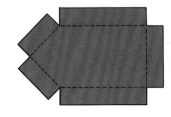

WHENEVER AN object such as a ship moves through the water, the water tries to slow it down. The push that the water makes against the object is called water resistance, or drag. The faster the object moves, the bigger the water resistance gets. If you look around a busy harbor, you will see dozens of different hull designs. Sleek, narrow hulls with sharp bows cause less resistance than wide hulls with square bows, so they can move through the water faster. You can test how the shape of a bow affects the speed of a ship in the project below. The deeper a hull sits in the water, the more resistance there is. Some hulls are designed to just touch the water. For example, a small speedboat has a flaring, V-shaped hull designed to skim across the surface. A cargo ship, however, has a more square-shaped hull that sits lower in the water. Speed is not as important for the cargo ship as it is for the speedboat. Instead, the cargo ship is designed for stability and to carry the maximum amount of cargo.

TESTING HULL SHAPES

You will need: colored stiff cardboard, pen, ruler, scissors, sticky tape, aluminum foil, paper clips, non-hardening modeling material, scales, string, watering can, long plastic tray, three equal wooden blocks.

Templates
Use these three templates to help you cut out and make the three boat shapes in this project. Their dimensions are roughly 6in long, by 4in wide. Make the sides of each boat shape about 1¼in deep.

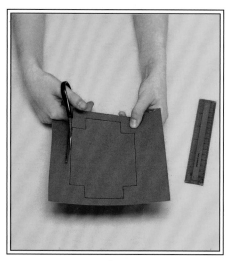

1 Use a ruler to draw out the three templates shown above on sheets of stiff cardboard. Make sure the corners are square and the edges straight. Cut out the shapes.

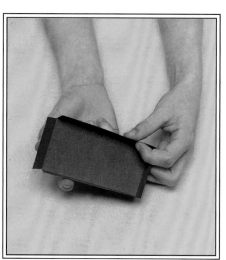

2 Using scissors, score along the lines inside the bottom of each shape (shown as broken lines above). Bend up the sides and use sticky tape to fix the corners together.

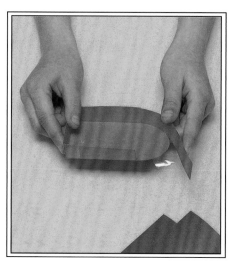

3 Make the round-ended and pointed boats in the same way as the first boat. Use a separate piece of cardboard to make the round bow and tape to the bottom in several places.

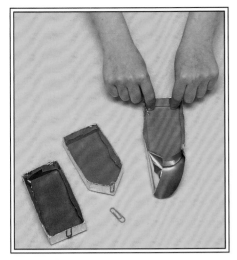

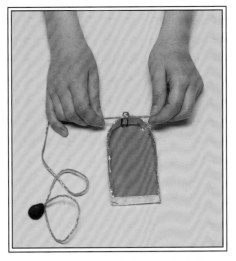

4 Now cover the outside of each shape with foil, neatly folding the foil over the sides. This will make the shapes more waterproof. Attach a paper clip to the bow of each boat.

5 Roll out three balls of modeling material to the size of a walnut. Weigh the balls to make sure they are the same weight. Attach a ball to the bow of each boat with string.

6 Put a large plastic bowl or long tub on a table or a strong box. Fill the tub with water to about ½in from the top of the tub.

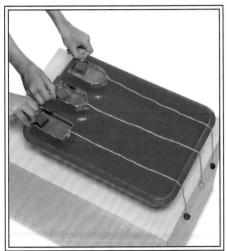

Try timing the boats with a stopwatch. You could find the difference between the fastest and slowest boats.

8 Release the boats all at the same time. The weighted strings will pull them along down the length of the tub. Which one wins the race to the other end of the tub?

7 Line up the boats at one end of the tub. Hang the strings and modeling material balls down over the other end of the tub. Put a wooden block inside each boat.

The shapes being tested
Boats' hulls are usually pointed to help them cut through the water. Energy is wasted pushing a flat end through the water, which makes a boat slower.

SHIP POWER

Punting

In a punt, a person stands on the back of the boat to push down on a long pole against the bottom of the river. Each push propels the boat forward. The pole is also used to steer the punt and keep it straight.

THERE ARE many different ways of propelling boats and ships through the water. The most basic, such as rowing and paddling, are human-powered. Oars and paddles work by pushing against the water. Today, they are only used in small vessels. Sails harness the natural power of the wind to propel a boat or ship. Engines convert the energy stored in fuel into the movement of a propeller. As the propeller spins, its blades force water to rush backward, which thrusts the boat or ship forward. Most engines used in boats and ships are diesel engines. Other types of marine engine are petrol engines, gas turbine engines and steam turbine engines. Some short-distance ferries move by pulling themselves along a wire or chain attached to the bank on the other side of a lake or river. Other craft, such as hovercraft, have aircraft-like propellers. These are useful in very shallow or plant-filled water where an underwater propeller could be easily damaged.

FACT BOX

• In 1845, there was a tug-of-war between a ship with a propeller and a ship with paddlewheels. The ship with the propeller won easily.

• In future boats may lift up out of the water altogether. Wingships use air pressure to skim above the water's surface. They can fly along about 6ft above the waves.

• In the swamps of the South, people travel in swamp skimmers pushed along by a huge fan at the back.

Rowing with oars

An oar is a long pole with a flattened blade at one end. It is fixed to a pivot on the edge of the rowboat, called a oarlock. The rower faces backward and propels the boat forward with a continuous cycle of strokes. Rowing a boat using a pair of oars is called sculling.

Paddles

A dragon boat from Hong Kong is propeled by a team of paddlers. A paddle is a short pole with a flat blade at one end used to propel a canoe. Paddles are easier to maneuvre than oars, but they are not as efficient.

Propeller power

A propeller is made up of several angled blades (usually between two and six) attached to a central hub. The enormous propeller being checked here will be one of a pair used on a large cruise liner. Its blades are specially curved to cut down turbulence as water is drawn past the hull. Each propeller will be driven by an electric motor.

pits on the surface of the blades help with water flow

Capturing the wind

Sails catch the wind and push a boat along. The sailors adjust the position of their sails to make the best use of the wind. These yachts have the wind blowing from behind and are using large sails called spinnakers for extra speed.

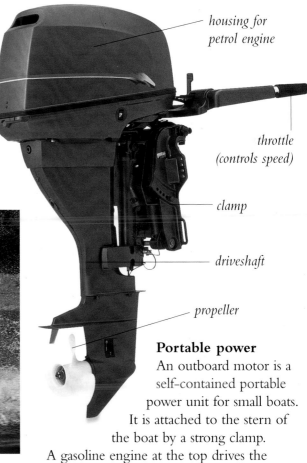

housing for petrol engine

throttle (controls speed)

clamp

driveshaft

propeller

Portable power

An outboard motor is a self-contained portable power unit for small boats. It is attached to the stern of the boat by a strong clamp. A gasoline engine at the top drives the propeller via a driveshaft. Twisting the throttle controls the speed of the propeller. Moving it from side to side changes the direction of the boat. When not in use, the whole engine can be unclamped and taken away.

Jet propulsion

A jet ski has no propeller. Instead, its engine sucks in water and pumps it out of the back of the ski in a powerful jet. The jet of water shooting out backward pushes the ski forward. Boats powered by waterjets can reach much higher speeds with less wear and tear than those with propellers.

CONTROLLING A SHIP

A LL SHIPS and boats have simple controls for
steering. Usually this is a rudder at the stern. The
rudder is controled by a tiller (handle) or wheel. The
rudder only works when the boat or ship is moving
through the water. Powered craft also have engine
controls for adjusting speed. Many boats have twin
propellers and can also be steered by running the
engines at different speeds or in different
directions (forward or reverse). Large ships may
also have bow and stern thrusters, which are used
in port to push the ship sideways or rotate it on
the spot. On modern cruise liners, which often have
to enter a different dock every night of the cruise, the ship
can be moved by means of a small joystick on the bridge. Large
modern ships have a computerized autopilot like that on
an aircraft. This automatically adjusts the rudder and
engine speed to follow a set course.

Simple rudder

The rudder on a Norman ship from
the Bayeux Tapestry is a single oar.
The long oar is set on the right side
of the ship at the stern. Many early
boats were steered with simple side
rudders like this.

flow of water   *boat goes straight*

rudder

How a rudder works

The rudder works by cutting
into the flow of water. With
the rudder in the center, water
flows past each side and the
boat goes in a straight line.

flow of water is deflected left

rudder is turned to left

When the rudder is turned
to the side, the flow of water
is deflected away to that side.

boat turns to the left

The water pushes against the
blade of the rudder. This
makes the stern go to the
right, swinging the bow left.

boat travels ahead

rudder straight

When enough turn
has been made, the
rudder is brought
back to the center.
The boat straightens
out and travels ahead
on its new course.

Under the stern

Here, the propeller and rudder of a cargo ship are
being cleaned of barnacles in dry dock. In almost
all ships and boats, the rudder is fixed behind the
propeller under the stern. The rudder is turned
by machinery in the stern that is controled from
the bridge. The propeller pushes water past the
rudder, which makes the ship easier to turn from
side to side at slow speed.

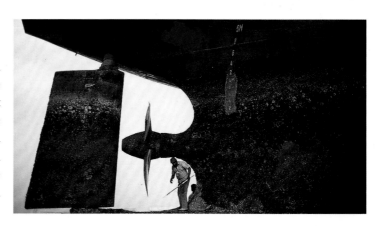

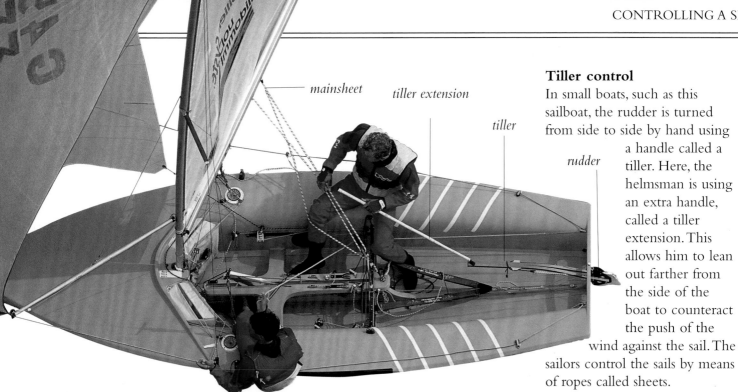

mainsheet   *tiller extension*

tiller

rudder

Tiller control

In small boats, such as this sailboat, the rudder is turned from side to side by hand using a handle called a tiller. Here, the helmsman is using an extra handle, called a tiller extension. This allows him to lean out farther from the side of the boat to counteract the push of the wind against the sail. The sailors control the sails by means of ropes called sheets.

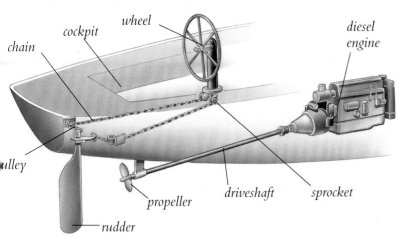

On the bridge

The bridge (also sometimes called the wheelhouse) is the control center of a ship. There are rudder and engine controls and navigation equipment, such as a compass and radar. The bridge is high up on the ship to give good, all-round visibility.

Steering wheel

On larger yachts a tiller would be too cumbersome to use. Instead, the rudder is operated by a large wheel linked to the rudder by a system of pulleys. The helmsman steers the yacht from the cockpit.

chain   *cockpit*   *wheel*   *diesel engine*

pulley   *propeller*   *driveshaft*   *sprocket*

rudder

Connecting up the wheel and the propeller

In this large cruising yacht, the rudder is moved by wires linked to the wheel in the cockpit. The wheel drives a sprocket, which moves a chain. Wires attached to the chain move the rudder via a set of pulleys. The yacht is also equipped with a diesel engine that is connected to a single propeller via a driveshaft. A soundproof engine room insulates the hull from noise and vibration made by the engine.

POWER AND STEERING

THE PROJECT below will show you how to build a simple boat driven by a propeller and controlled by a rudder. The propeller is powered by the energy stored in a wound-up elastic band. The two blades of the propeller are set at different angles and push the water backward as the propeller spins. In turn, this makes the boat move forward. When you have built your model, you could try making other designs of propeller (for example more blades set at different angles) and testing them to see which works best. After making the propeller you can add a rudder. The rudder can be moved to different positions to make your model boat turn to the left or right, but it will only work when the boat is moving along. Without the rudder, the boat does not go in a straight line very well. So, as well as making the boat turn from side to side, the rudder also helps your model (as it does a full-size boat) travel straight ahead.

Simple propeller
The simplest propeller has two blades that twist in opposite directions. This is the propeller of a small pleasure boat. Three- and four-bladed propellers are more powerful. The hole in the center is where the driveshaft from the engine fits into the propeller.

MAKE A POWERED BOAT

You will need: cork, bradawl, scissors, small plastic bottle, large plastic bottle, large paper clip, ruler, pliers, bead, long rubber bands, small pencil, thin garden cane.

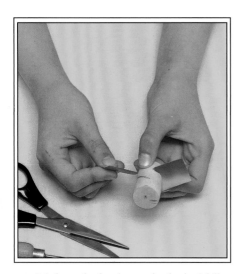

1 Make a hole through the middle of the cork using a bradawl. Cut a diagonal slot in either side of the cork. Push two strips of plastic cut from a small bottle into the slots.

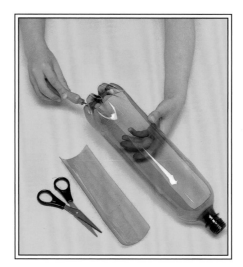

2 Cut an oblong strip from one side of the large plastic bottle. This slot is the top of your boat. With the bradawl, make a small hole at the back of your bottle in the bottom.

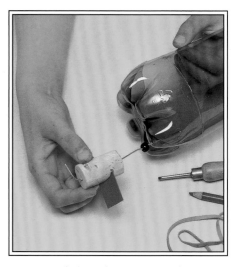

3 Straighten a large paper clip (you may need pliers). Bend the last ½in of wire at right angles. Push the wire through the cork and thread it through the bead and small hole.

P R O J E C T

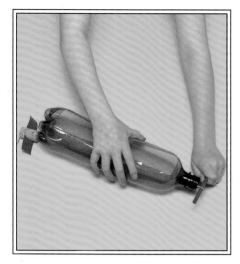

the model will go in circles

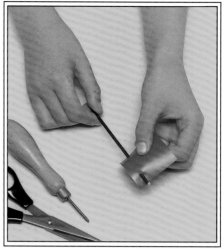

4 Bend over the end of the wire inside the bottle. Hook a rubber band over the wire and stretch it up through the neck of the bottle. Secure in place with a pencil.

5 To wind up the band, turn the pencil as you hold onto the propeller. Keep holding the propeller until you put the boat into the water and release it. What happens?

6 Now make a rudder for your boat. Cut a piece of plastic about 1½ sq. in and pierce two holes near one edge. Push thin cane through the two holes.

Straight and turning
This is the finished model of the boat. To test the controls, start with the rudder centred to make the boat go straight. How tight a circle can you make your boat turn in?

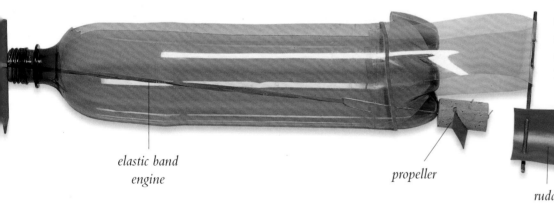

elastic band engine

propeller

rudder

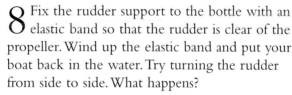

8 Fix the rudder support to the bottle with an elastic band so that the rudder is clear of the propeller. Wind up the elastic band and put your boat back in the water. Try turning the rudder from side to side. What happens?

7 Use the strip of plastic cut from the large bottle to support your rudder. Pierce two holes about ¾in apart in the center of the strip and push the cane through them.

CARGO SHIPS

Carrying cargo has always been the main job of ships. Even today, in the age of air travel, it is still the cheapest way of transporting goods. In fact, more that 95 percent of goods are transported around the world in the holds of cargo ships. A cargo ship is basically a long, box-shaped vessel, providing the maximum amount of room inside for cargo. The first cargo ships carried their cargoes in barrels or jars in the hold. Modern ships have been developed to carry specific cargoes, such as oil and cars. There are still many general cargo ships, including container ships. Different types of cargo ship have also been developed for use in rivers, in coastal waters and for long-distance ocean travel. Ocean-going ships are huge and expensive to build, so they are designed to spend as little time as possible in port.

Canal-sized

The Panama Canal in Central America provides an important short-cut for ships traveling between the Atlantic and Pacific oceans. Many cargo ships are built to dimensions called panamax – the largest size that can fit through the canal.

Parts of a container ship

A container is a standard-sized steel box that can be filled with any sort of cargo. On a container ship, the prepacked containers are stacked in piles in the hold and on the deck. Some of the containers on deck may be refrigerated. The ship is driven by a giant diesel engine.

River barge

A slow, wide barge carries cargo along the river Rhine in Germany. The river reaches from the North Sea deep into the industrial heartland of Germany. Coal, grain and timber are often carried by barges like this one.

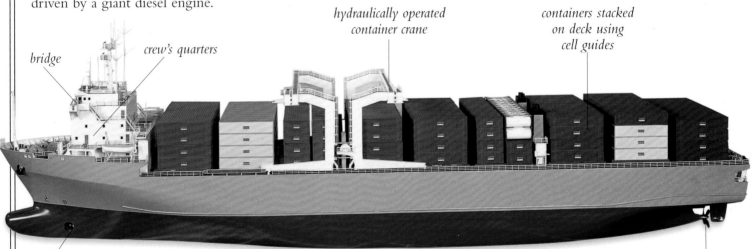

hydraulically operated container crane

containers stacked on deck using cell guides

bridge

crew's quarters

bow thruster

single main propeller

Unloading containers

In port, giant cranes transfer the containers from the ship. The standard-size containers are lowered onto specialized trucks, which carry them to huge dock-side parking lots where they are stacked in rows. The containers are then loaded onto trucks or railway cars and taken to their final destination.

FACT BOX

• The oil tanker *Jahre Viking* is the world's largest ship. It has a deadweight of 564,763 tons and is 1,500ft long.

• The world's largest container ship can carry 6,000, 20ft-long containers.

• A lighter aboard ship (LASH) carries river barges stacked like containers on its deck. A reefer ship carries vegetables in its refrigerated holds.

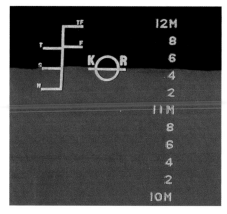

Not too deep

Load lines (also called Plimsoll lines) show how low a ship is safely allowed to float in the water when it is fully loaded. The load lines on the left of the picture are for different types of water. TF means tropical fresh, F is fresh water, T is tropical salt water, S is salt water in summer and W is salt water in winter. The scale on the right shows the distance to the keel of the ship in meters.

Return to sail

A few cargo ships have experimental computer-controled sails. The rigid sails are used to save fuel. When set, they move automatically. They are rotated by electric motors guided by computer. Sails like this are very efficient at achieving the best angle to the wind.

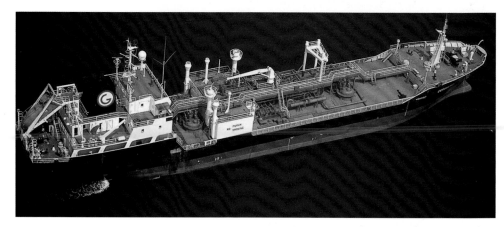

Specialized carriers

This ship is specially designed to carry just one sort of cargo – liquefied petroleum gas (LPG), such as methane or butane. The gas must be cooled to a very low temperature to keep it liquid. The pipes on the deck control the gas.

SHIP STABILITY

Many SHIPS look top heavy, so how do they manage to stay upright and not capsize? These projects will help you find out what makes a ship stable. The shape of the hull's cross-section is important – some hull shapes are more stable than others. When a ship tips over, the hull on that side sinks into the water. On the other side it rises up out of the water. The water creates more upthrust on the side that sinks in, pushing the ship upright again. The more one side of the hull sinks in, the bigger the push and the more stable the hull. The position of the cargo in the hull is important, too. Heavy cargo high up on deck makes the ship top heavy and more likely to tip over. Heavy cargo or equipment low down in the hull makes the ship more stable. Cargo that can move is dangerous, because it could slip to one side of the ship, making it more likely that the ship will tip over. The first project looks at the stability of a multi-hulled boat called a catamaran.

Pile it high
Containers are piled high on the deck of a container ship. The containers are loaded evenly to prevent the ship becoming unstable.

Two hulls
The two hulls of a catamaran are joined together by a strong bridge. This double-hulled shape makes the boat very stable.

MAKE A CATAMARAN

You will need: *small plastic bottle, scissors, thin garden cane, rubber bands, some small wooden blocks or other cargo.*

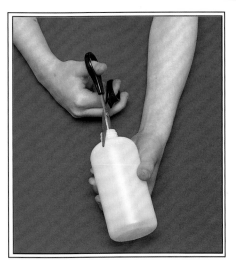

1 Remove the top from a small plastic bottle and carefully cut the bottle in half lengthwise. This will leave you with two identical shapes to form the catamaran hulls.

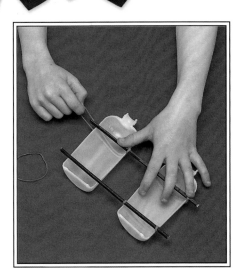

2 Place the two halves of the bottle side by side. Lay two medium-length pieces of garden cane on top. Securely fasten the canes to the bottle halves using rubber bands.

3 Put your completed catamaran into a tank or bowl of water. Load the hulls with cargo such as wooden blocks. Can you make your boat capsize?

PROJECT

LOADING CARGO

You will need: *plastic bottle and square tub of about the same size, scissors, wooden blocks, non-hardening modeling material.*

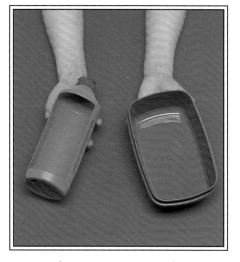

1 For this project you need one container with a round hull shape and another about the same size with a square hull shape. Cut a strip from the round container to make a hold.

2 Put both containers in a tank or bowl of water. Gradually load one side of each hull with wooden blocks. Which hull capsizes first? Which hull is more stable?

3 Load the square hull evenly with wooden blocks. You should be able to get a lot more in. Press down on one side of the hull. Can you feel the hull trying to right itself?

Unstable round hull
When a round hull tips to one side, there is little change to the amount of hull underwater. This makes the shape unstable.

Stable square hull
When a square hull tips to one side, there is a great change in the amount of hull underwater on that side. This makes it stable.

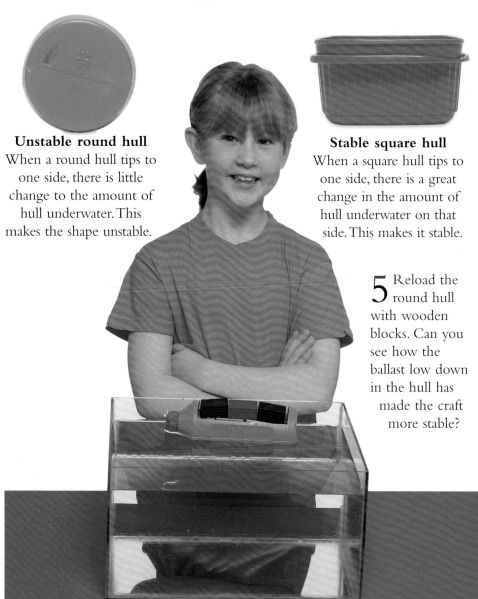

5 Reload the round hull with wooden blocks. Can you see how the ballast low down in the hull has made the craft more stable?

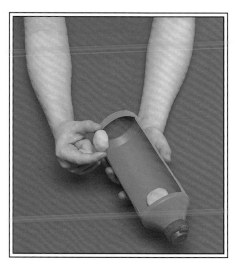

4 To stabilize the round hull, press some lumps of modeling material onto the bottom of the rounded hull. This adds weight called ballast to the bottom of the hull.

FERRIES

FERRIES ARE ships and boats designed to carry passengers, cars, busses, trucks and sometimes even trains across water. There are several different types of ferry. Each one is designed for a different type of crossing, such as small, raft-like ferries for short river crossings of a few minutes, or larger cruise-liner ferries for long sea crossings of several days. Most vehicle-carrying ferries have wide doors and ramps at the bow and stern. These allow cars and lorries to drive on and off the ship quickly. They are known as a roll-on, roll-off (or ro-ro) ferry. In a typical large ferry, the lower decks are like a multi-story car park. The passengers travel on the upper decks, where there are lounges, restaurants and shops. Ferries like this work day and night, all year round. Some ferries, such as catamarans, hydrofoils and hovercraft, are designed for short sea and lake crossings and are much faster.

Cable-drawn ferry
This ferry travels along a chain stretched between the two river banks. Its engine pulls on the chain instead of working a propeller.

FACT BOX
• Large superferries have three huge decks to carry up to 850 cars, trucks and busses. There is room for up to 1,250 passengers in the cabins above.

• Train ferries carry railway cars. They have rail tracks on deck that the cars roll onto at the docks.

• The world's fastest car ferry is called the *Finnjet* and it operates on the Baltic Sea. It is capable of more than 30 knots (35mph).

Loading and unloading
Cars drive along a ramp to reach the car deck of a small ro-ro ferry. The ferry's bow slots into a special dock for the loading process. The ferry will be unloaded through doors at the stern. Larger ferries have separate ramps for loading cars and trucks.

Superferry
The huge ferries that travel on long sea routes are called superferries. They can carry hundreds of cars and lorries and thousands of passengers. There are cabins for passengers to sleep in on overnight sailings and shops, restaurants and cinemas to keep people entertained.

Speedy cat

Catamarans like the SeaCat are some of the fastest vehicle-carrying ferries. Having two hulls instead of one and super-powerful, gas turbine engines makes this ferry much faster than a traditional passenger ferry.

Flying in water

A hydrofoil is the fastest type of ferry. Under its hull there are wing-like foils. These lift the hull clear of the water as it speeds along. Lifting the hull out of the water reduces water resistance (drag), allowing the hydrofoil to travel much faster.

curved upper surface

lift

flow of water

flat lower surface

low speed

high speed

How a hydrofoil works

Water flows faster over the foil's curved upper surface than it does over the flat lower surface, so creating lift. Foils only work when traveling at high speed. At low speed the boat's hull sits in the water.

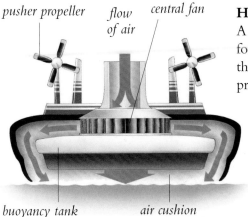

pusher propeller   *flow of air*   *central fan*

buoyancy tank   *air cushion*

How a hovercraft works

A central fan draws in air and forces it between the hull and the skirt. Two large pusher propellers drive the craft along.

Hovering on air

A hovercraft skims across water supported on a cushion of air. The air is held in place by a rubber skirt. A hovercraft can also travel on flat ground, so it can leave the water to load and unload. Buoyancy tanks stop the hovercraft from sinking if the air cushion fails.

FISHING BOATS

THERE ARE millions of fishing boats in the world. Most of them are small traditional boats sailed by a single person or a small crew. Others are larger commercial fishing boats. The very largest, called factory ships, are able to stay at sea for up to a month. Fishing was one of the earliest uses of boats and dozens of different styles of fishing boat have been developed all over the world. Some fish are caught with hooks and lines or traps, such as pots, left in the sea and attached to the seabed by an anchor. Most fishing, however, is done with nets that trap shoals of fish. Different types of net are used to catch different species of fish. Commercial fishing boats have special equipment for handling the nets and storing the fish they have caught. Many also have sonar equipment for tracking shoals of fish under the water. In the 1970s many countries' fishing industries collapsed due to overfishing. International regulations now limit the number and size of fish caught in order to preserve fish stocks.

Fishing fleets
Coastal towns and villages all over the world have their own fishing fleets based in small harbors. This one is on the island of Skye in Scotland. Most people in the town are involved in the fishing industry. Laws to reduce catches and conserve fish stocks have hit many small ports.

Inshore fishing boat
This is a typical wooden fishing boat used for fishing in inshore (coastal) waters. It is used up to 65 miles from port and catches surface-living fish such as herring, mackerel and anchovies.

Deep-sea trawler
Ships designed for fishing hundreds of miles off shore have high bows for breaking through waves. Trawlers like this catch fish such as cod, hake and flounder.

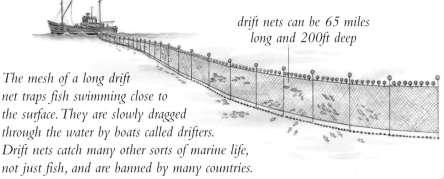

drift nets can be 65 miles long and 200ft deep

The mesh of a long drift net traps fish swimming close to the surface. They are slowly dragged through the water by boats called drifters. Drift nets catch many other sorts of marine life, not just fish, and are banned by many countries.

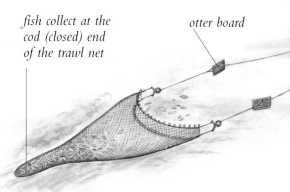

fish collect at the cod (closed) end of the trawl net

otter board

Bringing in the catch

A net bursting with cod and other fish is hauled on board. Fishing nets are pulled in after they have been in the sea for a few hours. A mechanical hoist lifts the full net out of the water. The net's closed end is released and its catch emptied out on deck.

Processing the catch

A catch is sorted as soon as it is on board. The fish may be cleaned and gutted before being frozen. Larger trawlers have equipment on board to process the fish – cutting off heads and tails and removing the bones.

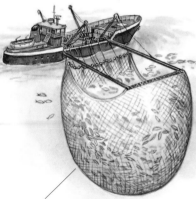

A dip net is used to scoop up fish over the side of the boat.

dip net

A stern trawler drags a large trawl net behind it. Ships like this were developed to catch huge shoals of cod living at depths below 50ft.

FACT BOX

• The largest vessels are whaling ships. These are used to catch whales and process the meat. Whales have been hunted almost to extinction, so whaling is now banned by most countries.

• Seagulls often follow fishing vessels. Superstitious sailors believe that three seagulls flying together overhead are a sign of death.

• Older fishing vessels are often called sidewinders. This is because the net is hauled in over the side.

Traditional fishing

Off the coast of Tanzania, East Africa, many fishermen use outrigger sailboats and dhows. Small fishing boats like these have not changed for many centuries. Nets, lines and spears are used to bring in the catch. Small-scale fishing like this does not deplete fish stocks as large commercial vessels can.

floats keep the top of the net on the surface

A shoal near the surface of the sea is quickly encircled by a purse seine net. The net is closed by gathering together the bottom edges like a purse.

Fishing boats and nets

The type of net a boat carries depends on the fish it is going to catch. Some boats fish for species that live near the surface of the sea, while others trawl the waters deeper down. Floats and weights are attached to the net to keep it in shape under the water. For example, otter boards are used to force open the mouth of a trawl. There are regulations restricting the size of the holes in the net so that young fish can escape.

ANCHORS

Ship's anchor
This type of anchor is called a stockless anchor and is used on most metal ships. The points of the anchor dig into the seabed, securing the ship.

A N ANCHOR is a device for stopping a ship or boat drifting in the wind or current. It is used when the engines are turned off or the sails taken down. The anchor is attached to the ship by a strong chain and its particular shape makes it catch firm in the seabed. There are several reasons for using an anchor. The most common is for stopping close to shore when there is no harbor or the ship is too big for the harbor (such as an oil tanker). In an emergency, such as an engine failure in bad weather, an anchor can stop a ship drifting onto the shore and being wrecked. Different designs of anchor are suitable for different sizes of ships and for different types of seabed, such as sandy or rocky. The projects on these pages will show you how to make two different types of anchor that are used in very different conditions.

MAKE A ROCK ANCHOR

You will need: *large paper clip, pliers, ruler, short pencil, rubber bands, thin bamboo stake, scissors, string, tray of pebbles (about 4in in size).*

Catching the rocks
Your model is similar to an anchor used on a traditional fishing boat. The spikes catch hold of the crevices on a rock-strewn seabed.

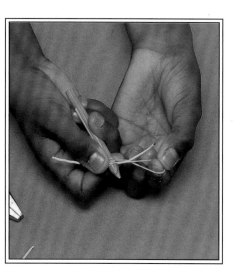

1 Unbend a large paper clip using pliers. Cut about 4in of wire off and bend it slightly. Attach the wire to a short pencil with a rubber band wound tightly around the join.

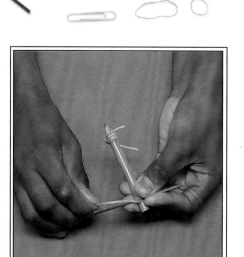

2 Cut a piece of bamboo stake also about 4in long. Attach this to the other end of the pencil, but at right angles to the wire. Use a rubber band to secure the stake.

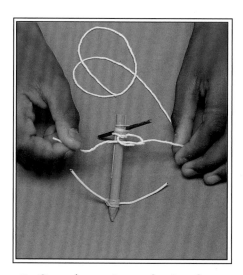

3 Cut a long piece of string for an anchor chain. Tie one end of it to the pencil, below the stake. Fill a tray with pebbles to test out your anchor (see opposite).

MAKE A SAND ANCHOR

You will need: *large paper clips, pliers, sticky tape, plastic straw, scissors, sheet of plastic, coins, string, tray of sand.*

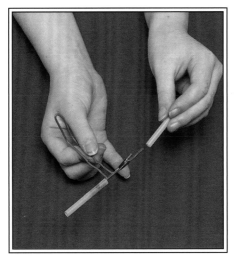

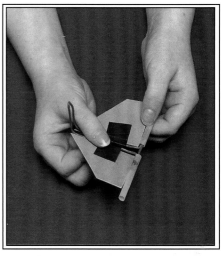

1 Bend a paper clip into a T-shape with a foot. Use pliers to cut another piece of wire to fit across the top of the T. Attach together with tape and two lengths of plastic straw.

2 Cut two blades from a sheet of plastic. Make sure that they will fit inside your T-shape. Tape the blades securely to the upright of the T and the two straws.

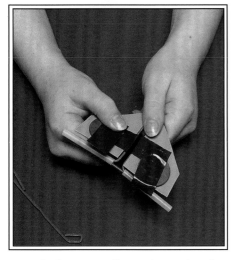

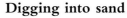

blade

3 Find two medium-size coins the same size. Tape one to each blade. The coins add weight to make it dig into the sand better.

Digging into sand

This is a model of a Danforth anchor. The wide, flat blades dig deep into either a muddy or a sandy seabed.

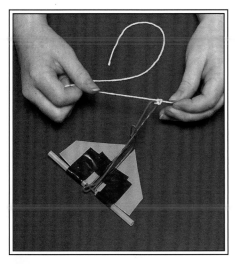

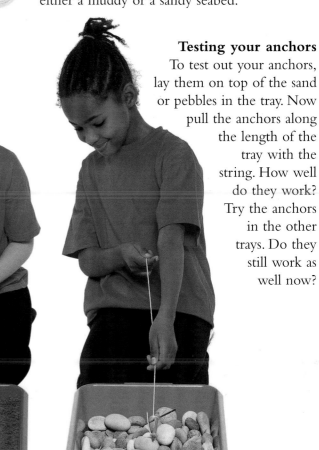

Testing your anchors

To test out your anchors, lay them on top of the sand or pebbles in the tray. Now pull the anchors along the length of the tray with the string. How well do they work? Try the anchors in the other trays. Do they still work as well now?

4 Shape another paper clip to make a straight arm with a hook at each end. Hook one end to the anchor and rest the arm in the upright foot. Tie a length of string to the other end. Use a tray of sand to test your anchor.

SAILING

S AILS CATCH the power of the wind to propel the boat or ship along. Today, sail power is mainly used by leisure craft, for racing and cruising. In some parts of the world, sail power is still common for fishing boats. Sails were originally made of strong cloth called canvas, but are now usually made of synthetic fabrics. Sails are supported by masts and ropes or wires called rigging. Ropes used to trim (adjust) sails are called sheets. Large yachts have different sets of sails for different wind conditions, including small storm sails. There are many different arrangements of masts, sails and rigging. Most modern sailboats and yachts have two triangular sails called a mainsail and jib supported by a single mast. The keel on a yacht and the centerboard on a sailboat stop the boat drifting sideways in the wind. A heavy keel also makes a yacht more stable.

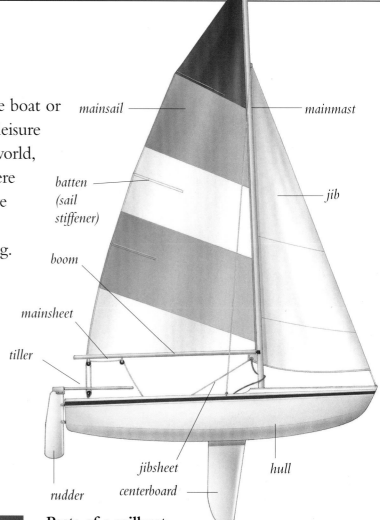

mainsail — mainmast

batten (sail stiffener)

jib

boom

mainsheet

tiller

jibsheet

hull

rudder centerboard

Parts of a sailboat
The main parts of a typical sailboat are shown above. A sailboat like this would usually have a crew of two people – a helmsman who operates the tiller and the mainsail and a crew who works the jib and centerboard. The jib is a small triangular sail in front of the mainmast. Sailboats also use spinnakers (three-cornered sails used in racing) for extra speed.

Racing sailboat
In very windy conditions, the helmsman and crew lean out over the side of the boat. They do this to keep the boat balanced and upright. The crew uses a harness called a trapeze attached to a wire running to the top of the mast. They lean out to the windward side of the boat.

Racing yacht
Large racing yachts have enormous sails and need a large crew to change them quickly. Sails are raised and lowered using winding wheels called winches. Yachts like this are designed to be sailed across oceans.

Cruising yacht

A cruising yacht has comfortable cabins, a galley and head. It has smaller sails than a racing yacht and is easier to sail. This type of yacht, rigged with one mast, is known as a sloop. It has two jib sails so it is called cutter rigged.

Fastest of all

A trimaran has a main hull and two outriggers. The outriggers make the yacht very stable, which means it can use enormous sails for its size. Although multihulled vessels have been in use for centuries, offshore racing trimarans have only been developed since the 1960s. Since then, they have set records for the fastest transatlantic crossing.

Old designs

These big, two-masted yachts are called schooners. A schooner has a foremast ahead of the mainmast. Here, their sails are gaff rigged (supporting poles at an angle to the masts).

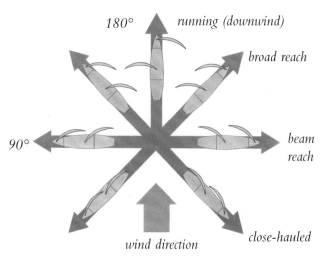

180°   running (downwind)

broad reach

90°   beam reach

close-hauled

wind direction

Points of sailing

A boat can use the wind to sail in every direction, except straight into the wind. The crew adjust the sails to go in different directions called the points of sailing. To head upwind a boat must follow a zigzag course. This is called tacking. If a boat turns when the wind is behind it, it is known as jibing. Running (sailing downwind) is not the fastest direction. Reaching (sailing across the wind) is faster.

FACT BOX

• The first person to sail solo around the world was Joshua Slocum from America. The voyage took three years and Slocum could not swim.

• The record time for sailing around the world is 74 days, 22 hours and 17 minutes. It was set in 1994 by the catamaran *Enza*.

• In the galley (kitchen) of a yacht, the stove is mounted on pivots. This keeps it level when the boat heels over in the wind.

SAILS FOR POWER

THE PROJECT on these pages will show you how to make a model of a simple sailboat. Once you have made your model, use it to find out how a sailing boat works and how sailors use the wind. To sail in the direction the sailor wants to go, he or she must look at the direction that the wind is blowing from and adjust the position of the sails to make the most use of the wind. A boat can sail in every direction except straight into the wind. When a boat faces directly into the wind, its sails flap uselessly and the boat is in the no-go zone. To sail toward a place where the wind is blowing from, the sailors must sail a zigzag course. This means first sailing across the wind one way, then sailing across it the other. This is called tacking. Making the most of the wind is the art of sailing and it takes lots of practice. Sailors have to learn to control many different parts of the boat at the same time.

Finished boat
Once you have finished your boat, you could try adding a centerboard. Does it make any difference to the boat's handling?

MAKE A SAILBOAT

You will need: pencil, ruler, cardboard, scissors, sticky tape, plastic sheet, stapler, bradawl, non-hardening modeling material, thin garden canes, colored paper, plastic straws, small plastic bottle, string, paper clip.

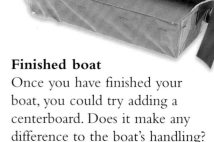

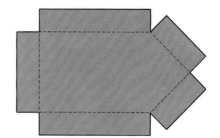

Template
Use this template to make your model. The dimensions are 10in by 4in, with sides about 1½in deep.

1 Cut out your hull shape from thick cardboard, using the template above as a guide. Score along the broken lines with the scissors. Use sticky tape to attach the sides together.

2 Lay the hull on a plastic sheet. Cut around it leaving a 2in gap around it to overlap the sides. Fold the plastic over the sides of the hull and staple it in place.

3 Pierce a hole in a strip of cardboard a little wider than the hull. Staple in place. Put modeling material under the hole. Push a 12in cane through the hole into the material.

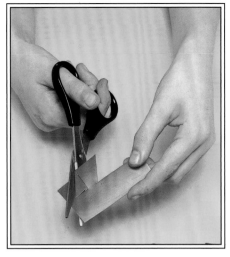

4 Cut a sail from paper. Attach a straw along the side and a cane along the bottom with sticky tape. Slip the straw over the mast.

5 Cut an L-shape (about 3in long, 1½in wide at bottom and ¾in wide at top) from the small plastic bottle. Cut the base of the L in half to make two tabs, as shown.

6 Fold back the L-shape's two tabs in opposite directions and staple them to the stern (back) of the boat. This is the boat's rudder.

Finding out about the points of sailing

When you first try your boat out, try setting the sails in these different positions. Alter the position of the sail by using the string taped to the boom (cane). Follow the arrows shown here to see which way the wind should be blowing from in each case. Why not try blowing from other directions to see if this makes a difference to your boat?

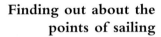

direction of wind

8 To try out how your sailboat works, make a breeze by waving a large sheet of paper near to the boat. Adjust the string to move the sail into the right position.

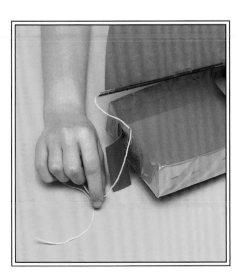

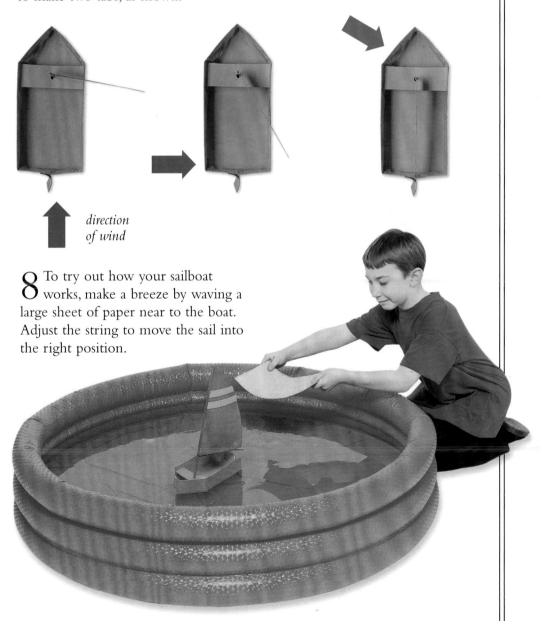

7 Cut a piece of string about 8in long. Tape one end to the back of the boom (the cane) and feed the other end through a paper clip attached to the back of the boat.

WARSHIPS

Operations room
At the heart of a warship is the operations room. From here the crew monitor what other ships and aircraft are doing and make decisions about what actions to take.

THE FIRST true warships were the many-oared galleys of ancient Greece and Rome. By the 1400s, heavily armed galleons with many cannons were developed. In the early 1900s, steam-driven, iron battleships were the forerunners of modern warships. Today's warships carry a huge amount of special equipment. They have weapons for attacking other ships and submarines, weapons for defending themselves against air attack, and electronic equipment for tracking ships and aircraft and controling their weapons. The largest warships are aircraft carriers, which act as air bases at sea. Smaller warships, such as frigates and destroyers, are designed for speed and have powerful gas turbine engines. The smallest ships are minesweepers and patrol boats. A country's navy defends its waters, transports and supports fighting troops and helps in emergencies around the world. A navy needs many ships to keep its warships supplied with fuel, food and ammunition.

Frigate
A frigate is a small, fast-moving ship used to escort convoys of larger ships. It carries anti-submarine and anti-aircraft weapons. Small frigates are sometimes called corvettes.

FACT BOX
• Aircraft carriers are the largest warships. They have displacements of more than 90,000 tons and crews of 5,000 sailors and air crew.

• During World War I (1914–18) huge battleships with enormous guns fought at sea. Hulls were protected by 14in-thick armor.

• The world's largest submarines are Russian Typhoon class. They have displacements of 26,500 tons and are 550ft long.

Destroyer
A destroyer is generally larger than a frigate and is an all-purpose warship. This guided-missile destroyer has several radar dishes for weapons control as well as navigation. It also has a helicopter deck at the stern.

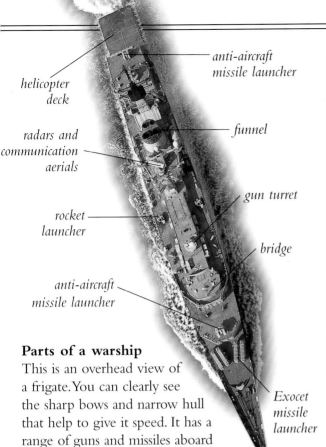

helicopter deck

anti-aircraft missile launcher

funnel

radars and communication aerials

gun turret

rocket launcher

bridge

anti-aircraft missile launcher

Exocet missile launcher

Parts of a warship

This is an overhead view of a frigate. You can clearly see the sharp bows and narrow hull that help to give it speed. It has a range of guns and missiles aboard ship as well as armed helicopters.

Naval guns

Modern naval guns, such as this 114mm single gun, are aimed automatically. A fire-control radar keeps track of the target and moves the gun from side to side and up and down. Missiles are also used to bring down enemy aircraft. Some have on-board sensors that home in on their target.

Support ships

This ship is a specialized support ship used in landing troops. In the stern is a dock for landing craft to be loaded. The landing craft ferry troops and equipment to the shore.

Airfield at sea

An aircraft carrier's deck is a runway where aircraft take off and land. The runway is short so a steam catapult is used to help launch the aircraft at take-off. Underneath the deck is a hangar where aircraft are stored and serviced. The aircrafts' wings fold up to save storage space below deck.

Inflatables

Special forces, such as commandos, use small, fast inflatable craft for transferring from ship to shore. This boat can be used above the water or underwater as a diving craft. It can even be submerged and hidden on the seabed until it is needed. You can see the electrically powered propeller for underwater use.

inflatable dinghy (small boat) is powered by two outboard motors

SUBMARINES

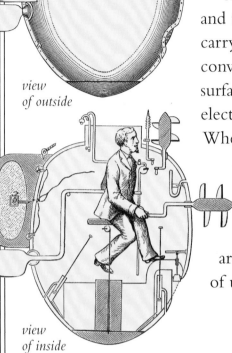

view of outside

view of inside

A SUBMARINE is a vessel that can travel submerged under the water as well as on the water's surface. Most submarines are naval ships. There are two main types – patrol submarines, which search for and try to sink enemy shipping, and ballistic missile submarines, which carry nuclear missiles. Naval submarines use two different types of power – conventional and nuclear. When a conventional submarine is on the surface its diesel engine makes electricity. The electricity is used to run the electric motors that work the propeller and also to recharge the batteries. When the submarine is submerged, the diesel engine is turned off and the electric motor is powered by the batteries. In a nuclear submarine, the power comes from a nuclear reactor. The main weapon of a patrol submarine is the torpedo – a sort of underwater missile. Another type of underwater vessel is the submersible. Submersibles are small diving craft used for ocean research, exploration and the repair of undersea pipes and cables.

The *Turtle*

American engineer David Bushnell built the first working submarine in 1775. It was called the *Turtle* and made of wood. It was moved by two screw-shaped, hand-operated propellers.

Nuclear submarine

A nuclear submarine, such as this Trident, can stay submerged for months on end. Its reactor can run for this long without refuelling.

An air-conditioning plant recycles the air on board to make fresh air.

U-boat

The potential of the submarine as a weapon was realised during World War II (1939–45). The German U-boats (*Unterseeboot*) had greatly increased range and speed. They sank thousands of Allied ships with their torpedoes.

Parts of a submarine

A modern submarine, such as this nuclear ballistic missile submarine, is nearly as long as a soccer field – around 300ft. It has a crew of around 140 who work in shifts. Like other ships, it has an engine, propeller and rudder at the stern. Heat from the nuclear reactor generates steam. This drives the turbines that turn the submarine's propeller. Like all submarines, its hull is strong, but very few submarines can go below 1,600ft. Buoyancy tanks fill with water to submerge the submarine. To resurface, compressed air pushes the water out of the tanks. Small movable wings, called hydroplanes, control the submarine's direction.

Towers and periscopes

The conning tower stands clear of the water when a submarine surfaces. Communication masts and periscopes top the tower. Periscopes are a device that allows the crew to see above water when the submarine is submerged. There are usually two periscopes – a large one for general observation and a smaller one for attack.

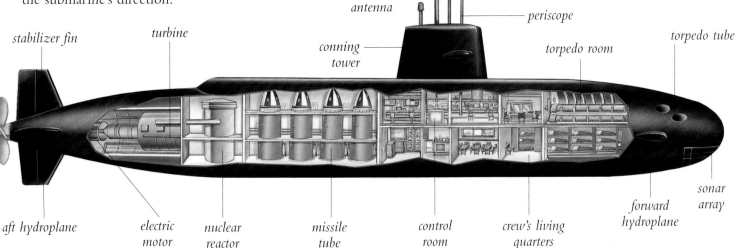

communication antenna

periscope

conning tower

torpedo room

torpedo tube

stabilizer fin

turbine

aft hydroplane

electric motor

nuclear reactor

missile tube

control room

crew's living quarters

forward hydroplane

sonar array

Mini-submersible

Small submersibles, carrying one or two people, are used to work at depths that would be too dangerous for a free-swimming diver. They are equipped with cameras, floodlights and robot arms. Highly accurate navigation systems allow the crew to find their way in the pitch black of the seabed. A mini-submersible runs on batteries and can stay under only for a short time – less than a day.

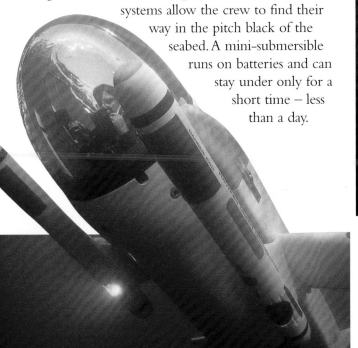

Research submersible

Teams of people dive to the ocean floor in submersibles. They have extremely strong hulls for diving very deep, up to about 5 miles. Submersibles dive and return to a support ship waiting on the surface. Special, deep-diving vessels called bathyscaphes can dive even farther – up to 7 miles.

DIVING AND SURFACING

A SUBMARINE dives by making itself heavier so that it sinks. It surfaces again by making itself lighter. To do this, it uses large tanks called buoyancy tanks. When the submarine is on the surface, the buoyancy tanks are full of air. To make the submarine dive, the tanks are flooded with seawater, making the submarine heavy enough to sink. To make the submarine surface again, compressed air is pumped into the tanks, forcing the water out. This makes the submarine lighter and it floats to the surface. In this project, you can make a model submarine that can dive and surface using buoyancy tanks. When it is underwater, a full-scale submarine moves up and down using hydroplanes. These are like tiny wings and work like rudders as the submarine moves along. Submarines need very strong hulls to prevent them from being crushed by the huge pressure under the water. As submarines dive down, the weight of the water pressing down on them becomes greater and greater. The tremendous pressure from the water builds up quickly.

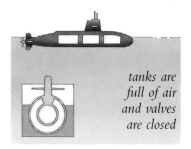

tanks are full of air and valves are closed

valves open and tanks fill with water

tanks full, submarine submerged

air is forced in, so water is forced out

MAKE A SUBMARINE

You will need: *large plastic bottle, sand, plastic funnel, two small plastic bottles, bradawl, scissors, ruler, two plastic drinking straws, rubber bands, non-hardening modeling material, two small bulldog clips.*

Diving and surfacing
Water is let into buoyancy tanks by opening valves to let the air out. Water is expelled by pumping in air stored in tanks of compressed air.

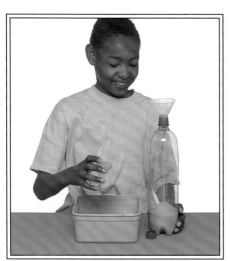

1 Fill the large plastic bottle with sand using a funnel. Fill it until it just sinks in a tank of water. Test out the bottle (cap firmly screwed on) to find the right amount of sand.

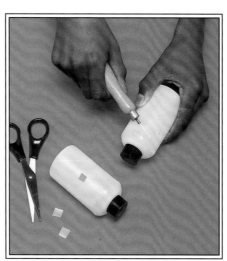

2 Make a large hole (about ½in across) in one side of two small plastic bottles. On the other side make a small hole, big enough for a plastic straw to fit into.

3 Attach the two small bottles to either side of the large bottle using rubber bands. Twist the small bottles so that the small hole on each one points upward.

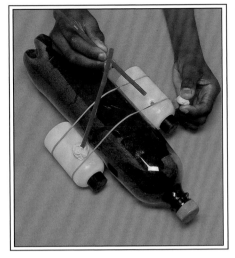

4 Push a plastic drinking straw into each small hole so that a bit pokes through. Seal the base of the straws with modelling material to make a watertight join.

5 Put a small bulldog clip about halfway down each straw. The clips need to be strong enough to squash the straw and stop air being forced out by the water.

6 Put your model submarine in a tank of water. With the clips on it should float. Remove the clips and water will flood the buoyancy tanks. The submarine will sink.

Final adjustments
This is the finished model submarine. You might find your model sinks bow first, or stern first. If this is the case, level it by shaking the sand evenly inside the bottle.

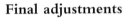

8 When your model submarine has resurfaced, keep blowing slowly into the tanks. Replace each bulldog clip and your model submarine will remain floating on the surface.

7 To make the submarine surface again, blow slowly into both straws at once. The air will force the water out of the buoyancy tanks and the submarine will rise to the surface.

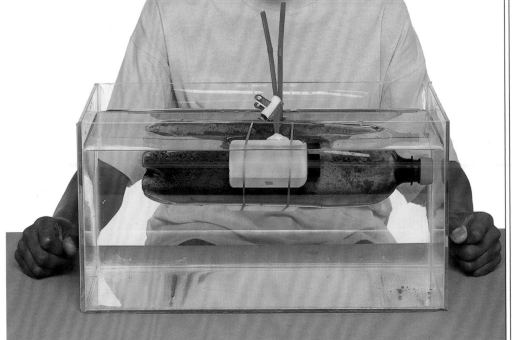

PLEASURE CRAFT

THERE ARE many boats and ships designed for relaxation and sport. Boats offer a huge range of activities, from hiring a rowing boat to cruising the oceans in a luxury yacht. Many people enjoy cruising and touring holidays afloat. Some holidaymakers operate the boat themselves, while others take the opportunity to relax with a crew to do the sailing. The ocean liners that regularly sailed across the world's seas have long gone, but their place has been taken by cruise liners. These ships are like floating hotels and are specifically designed for people on vacation. A cruise ship usually calls at a number of different ports. Some enthusiasts even sail right around the world. Watersports such as rowing, canoeing, sailing and windsurfing are very popular. Spectacular tricks and stunts can be executed on windsurfers, surfboards and body boards. Canoes and kayaks offer the excitement of shooting down whitewater rapids. Other people enjoy racing in sailboats, yachts, rowing boats and powerboats.

Wind and waves
In strong winds a windsurfer can perform amazing flying leaps using a funboard. The surfboard is steered by a sail. Experienced surfers take part in competitions, such as course racing and wave performance.

White-water racing
A kayak has a closed cockpit so that no water can get into the hull, even in very rough water. This makes it excellent for whitewater racing. There are two types of racing. In wildwater racing, canoeists are timed over a course of obstacles such as rocks and rapids. In slalom, canoeists negotiate a course of gates.

Touring canoe
The canoe is an open boat, as opposed to the closed cockpit of a kayak. The canoeist sits or kneels and can use either single or double-bladed paddles. Canadian canoes are used for slalom races over a set course. Open canoes are a good way of seeing the natural world, because they move quietly through the water, not disturbing the peace.

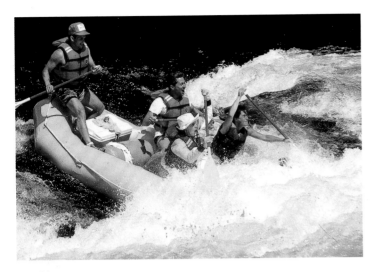

Rafting

Traveling down the turbulent waters of a mountain river in an inflatable raft is a popular adventure sport. Rafters use single-bladed paddles. Everybody wears a lifejacket because there is a danger of falling out of the raft.

Sailing cruiser

Many people enjoy days out and longer holidays on sailing cruisers. This yacht, the *Wind Spirit*, is a cross between a sailing yacht and a cruise liner.

Luxury cruiser

A few people are lucky enough to be able to afford a large luxury motor yacht, or cruiser, like this. These yachts are equipped with every sort of luxury as well as the latest in satellite navigation equipment and cruise control.

Powerboat racing

A ride in a powerboat is incredibly fast, but very bumpy. Their hulls are specially shaped to skim across the surface. There are two types of powerboat racing – inshore and offshore. Boats are put into different classes, depending on their size and engine. Fast Formula 1 powerboats race all over the world.

Cruise liner

Many people spend their vacations on cruise liners. The liners travel around scenic parts of the world, stopping at interesting ports. A large cruise liner is part resort and part luxury hotel. It may be equipped with swimming pool, whirlpool, sundecks, tennis courts, gym, theatre and even a golf course.

SERVICE BOATS

SERVICE VESSELS do special jobs in rivers or at sea to help other boats and ships. The most common service boat is the tug. The tug's main job is to move other ships, sometimes to tow them into harbor, other times because their engines have failed. The largest tugs, called salvage tugs, can tow even huge cargo ships and also help in emergency situations. Tugs have high bows to break through large waves, a high bridge to give a good view, a large deck to carry cargo and on-board winches. They also have extremely powerful engines and are highly maneuvrable. A selection of service vessels is shown here. There are many more, however, such as cable-laying ships, oil drilling vessels and light ships. Lifeboats are also service boats.

Towing to sea

These tugs are towing part of an oil rig. They will tow it all the way from where is was built to its station at sea. Each tug has a strong towing hook where two steel ropes are attached.

Dredger

A dredger digs silt (mud and particles carried by water) from the bottom of rivers and canals. It does this to stop them from becoming too shallow. A bucket dredger is shown below. It uses a long line of buckets to scoop silt into a barge.

Research ship

An ocean research ship is a floating science laboratory. This ship has a bathymetry system for surveying the seabed. It also has on-board computer systems and equipment for lowering instruments and submersibles into the sea. It can carry 18 marine and technical staff on voyages of over 40 days. The engines have been specially modified to reduce engine noise, which might affect sensitive recordings. Research vessels like this help biologists to explore life on the seabed. They also help oceanographers (scientists who study the oceans) to examine undersea mountains and trenches.

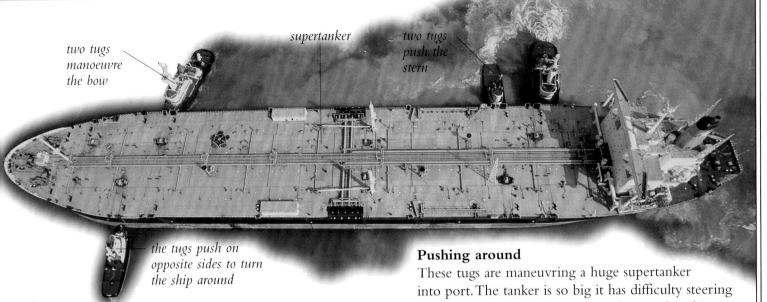

two tugs manoeuvre the bow

supertanker

two tugs push the stern

the tugs push on opposite sides to turn the ship around

Pushing around

These tugs are maneuvring a huge supertanker into port. The tanker is so big it has difficulty steering in enclosed waters. Tugs using towlines and pushing with their bows can turn the ship around. They gently nudge it into its berth or to an offshore mooring buoy.

Fire fighting

Every major port has a fireboat on stand-by all the time. It sprays foam or water, which is sucked from the sea by powerful pumps. The water is fired from guns on the upper deck onto burning ships or port buildings. Foam is used to smother oil and chemical fires from tankers.

Floating crane

A salvage barge is like a floating crane. It is used to recover sunken or capsized vessels. Huge cranes like this can lift large cargo ships from the seabed.

Breaking the ice

An icebreaker has a very strong hull. It is designed to ride up on the ice so that the ship's weight breaks through the thick ice. Most icebreakers have propellers in the bow to draw the smashed ice back behind the ship. Some also have special tanks on board to allow the ship to heel over if necessary to free it from the surrounding ice. Icebreakers are used to keep shipping lanes in northern waters open during winter. They are used in countries such as Canada, Denmark, Russia, Sweden and the United States.

NAVIGATION AND SIGNALING

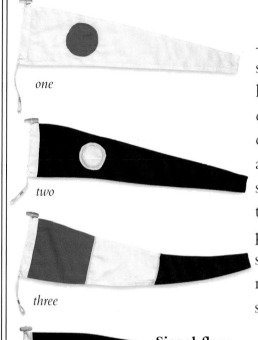

one

two

three

A<small>T SEA</small>, navigation includes many different jobs. It involves planning a safe route, checking the ship's position regularly to see how it is progressing, avoiding collisions with other vessels, and keeping an eye on the weather. The basic tools of navigation are a chart (map) of the sea and a magnetic compass. The chart shows coastlines, the depth of the water, landmarks on shore, hazards such as wrecks, the strength of tides and so on. Modern navigating tools, such as satellite-controlled Global Positioning System (GPS), mean that boats and ships with the correct equipment always know their position. Lighthouses and buoys help with navigation by indicating safe shipping channels and hazards. Signals are a way of sending messages to the shore or another vessel without using radio. Ways of signaling include signal flags and lamps.

Signal flags
An international system of signal flags has been used for centuries. Each flag stands for a number, a letter or a complete message. A flag's basic meaning can be changed by hoisting it on a different mast or in a certain combination with other flags. A selection of flags, with their meanings, is shown here.

C (yes)

N (no)

O (man overboard)

G (I require a pilot)

A light at sea
A lighthouse warns of dangerous islands, rocks and headlands. It sends out a bright beam of light that sweeps round in a circle. At sea, it appears as a flashing light. Anchored light ships are also used to mark treacherous spots.

Signal lamp
Morse code (a code of long and short pulses) is another way of sending messages. An Aldis lamp has a trigger that the operator uses to turn the light on and off.

Aldis lamp

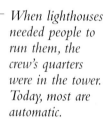

lantern

When lighthouses needed people to run them, the crew's quarters were in the tower. Today, most are automatic.

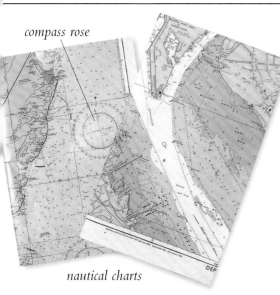

compass rose

dividers

Navigation tools

The simple equipment here can be used to plot a course on a chart. Plotting a course involves drawing a series of lines on the chart that the ship will follow. The pilot also checks the boat's position from landmarks. Shown on the chart is the compass rose used for taking bearings (directions).

magnetic compass

nautical charts

Breton plotter

parallel ruler

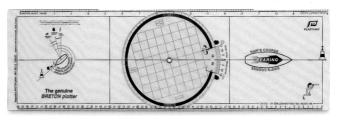

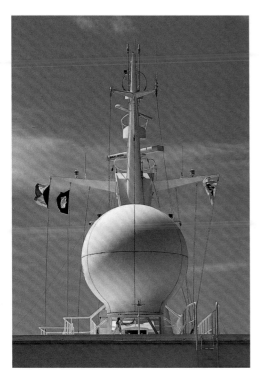

A red port buoy marks the left side of a channel.

A green starboard buoy marks the right side of a channel.

Yellow and black cardinal buoys mark hazards or points of interest.

Navigation buoys

The shape and color of a buoy give it its meaning. Most buoys are red or green and indicate the sides of a safe channel. All buoys have flashing lights as well.

Electronic navigation

The navigation equipment on a modern ship includes radar, sonar and satellite receivers. Radar shows the position of the coast and other ships. Sonar shows the depth of water under the ship. Satellite GPS gives the ship's exact position to within a few feet.

Computers in navigation

At the chart table of this yacht are several computers. One receives images directly from a weather satellite. Another displays the ship's position on an electronic chart.

SHIPPING DISASTERS

Running aground
Once a ship has run aground it is hard to refloat. If it runs aground on rocks it may even be punctured. Eventually a wreck like this will break up in the waves.

THE SEAS and oceans can be very dangerous places. Every year, hundreds of ships are lost and many of their crews drown. The worst hazard is the weather. Strong winds blowing across a wide expanse of water create huge waves as tall as a house. The waves can swamp a small boat or cause a ship to capsize. Long, high waves can break the back of a ship if they lift its bow and stern, leaving its center unsupported. Another main cause of accidents is human error. Mistakes in communication or navigation cause collisions between vessels, perhaps sinking one of them. Ships also run aground due to errors in navigation. Other accidents are caused by engine failures, fires or explosions. These can have very serious consequences if a ship is carrying a dangerous cargo that may cause long-lasting damage to the environment.

Fire on board
Despite being surrounded by water, fire is one of the worst hazards at sea. This ship is lucky that there is a fire boat in range. Usually the crew have to fight the fire themselves.

FACT BOX
• At sea, distances are measured in nautical miles. One nautical mile equals 6,075ft. Speed is measured in knots. One knot equals one nautical mile per hour.

• Depth was once measured in fathoms. One fathom was 6ft.

• The biggest collision at sea was between two oil tankers. Their combined deadweight was 660,000 tons. Around 300,000 tons of oil were spilled into the Caribbean Sea.

Tanker disaster
The oil tanker *MV Braer* ran aground in the Shetland Islands, Scotland, in 1993. The hull was punctured and 80,000 tons of oil leaked into the sea, creating a huge oil slick. Spills like this result in major ecological damage.

Deadly oil
Seabirds caught in an oil slick are most at risk. They try to clean their feathers and swallow the harmful oil. If birds are caught in time, they can be cleaned with detergents.

Beach clean up
If an oil slick reaches the shore, it coats the rocks with oily sludge. Clearing up a large spill with suction pumps takes months and is very expensive. The coastline takes years to recover.

Capsize
Once a boat has capsized it can be difficult to right it again. The crew may survive by holding on to the hull or sitting on top of it. Even the largest ships can capsize if they are hit by a very large, rogue wave.

The sinking of the *Titanic*
The most famous shipping disaster of all was the sinking of the ocean liner *Titanic* on April 15, 1912. With the loss of 1,517 lives, it remains one of the worst peacetime disasters. This painting of the event is exaggerated – the ship's hull was punctured by ice under the water. The disaster was made worse because there were not enough lifeboats.

IN AN EMERGENCY

Lifeboat stations
In an emergency, passengers on this cruise liner would get in the lifeboats shown here. The lifeboats would be lowered down the side of the ship, into the sea.

WHEN AN ACCIDENT does happen, the crew immediately begin to follow an emergency procedure. If they have a radio, they will send a May Day call to the emergency services. Other vessels in the area will go to help, a lifeboat may be launched, or a helicopter sent to search. To help rescuers locate their stricken vessel, flares are fired and emergency horns sounded. Larger boats and ships have an automatic radio beacon that sends out a distress call when it falls into the sea. The emergency services can home in on the beacon. If the crew have to abandon ship, they put on life jackets, perhaps survival suits, and launch lifeboats or life rafts. All but the smallest vessels have fire-fighting equipment on board. A cruise liner will have a computerized warning and sprinkler system.

FACT BOX
• Ships on which there is a risk of explosion, such as drilling and gas-carrying ships, have lifeboats next to the crew compartments. These drop into the sea for quick evacuation.

• If a submarine cannot surface, its crew escape in buoyant personal escape suits. These act as life rafts on the surface.

• The crew of an offshore lifeboat wear helmets and are harnessed to their seats to stop them flying about as waves crash into the boat.

Inshore lifeboats
Small lifeboats, such as this Australian surfboat, help to rescue people near the coast. Swimmers, surfers and sailboat users are rescued quickly by boats like this. It is specially designed to ride over the high surf.

Lifeboat launch
Offshore lifeboats can be swiftly launched down a slipway. When the emergency call comes through, the crew jump into the boat, start the engine and release a holding wire. The boat hits the water at speed. This is a much faster way to launch a boat than setting off from a harbor.

Life rafts

Inflatable life rafts are stored in a container on the deck of a ship or yacht. When the container is thrown into the sea, the raft inflates automatically. It is designed to maintain body heat and not capsize. Inside the raft are medical and food supplies.

Lifeboat at sea

Offshore lifeboats are designed to operate in the worst weather at sea. They have very powerful engines for reaching an emergency quickly. Lifeboats are self-righting and quickly come upright if a wave knocks them flat.

Helicopter rescue

A helicopter winchman is lowered onto a lifeboat. He carries a cradle to pick up a casualty from the boat. Air-sea rescue helicopters take part in searches, winch crew from stricken ships and carry casualties quickly to hospitals on shore.

foghorn

flares

The Coast Guard

Some countries have coastal patrol boats. This Canadian patrol boat is operated by the Coast Guard service. It acts as a police boat as well as a lifeboat.

Flares and horns

Sailors in trouble fire flares and sound foghorns to show up their position. Flares are like large fireworks. Some simply burn brightly. Others fire a burning light into the sky. The foghorn uses compressed air to make an ear-piercing noise.

KEEPING AFLOAT

MAKE A SELF-RIGHTING BOAT

You will need: pencil, ruler, polystyrene tile, scissors, non-hardening modeling material, rubber bands, small plastic tub.

A CREW'S first reaction in a collision or grounding is to try to keep their ship afloat if possible. For a start, all ships have bilge pumps. These are used to pump water out of the bottom of the boat's hull and into the sea. Small boats, such as sailboats and canoes, have bags of air or blocks of polystyrene inside to keep them afloat. Most lifeboats are self-righting, which means that they bob back upright if they capsize. Lifeboats are built of tough, lightweight materials such as plastic and foam. They are completely watertight – even their air inlets have seals to keep out the water. Their heavy engines are set low down, while the hull and high-up cabins are full of air. This arrangement ensures that the lifeboat flips upright without needing help. You can find out how to make a simple self-righting boat in the first project.

The hull of a large ship below the waterline is divided into watertight sections by strong metal walls called bulkheads. The doors in the bulkheads are also watertight when they are closed. These are designed so that if one section floods, the water cannot fill the whole hull. Even if a ship is sinking, bulkheads stop it from capsizing due to water rushing to one side. In the second project you can test out how a hull with bulkheads works much better than one without bulkheads.

1 Cut a boat-shape 6in by 4in from polystyrene. Attach a golf-ball size lump of modeling material to one side with an rubber band.

2 Put your boat into a tank or bowl of water. Have the modeling material, which represents the crew and equipment, on top. If you capsize the boat it will stay capsized.

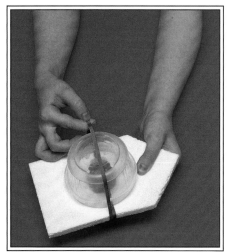

3 Add another lump of modeling material underneath the boat to represent heavy engines or ballast. Add an upturned plastic tub on top to represent a watertight cabin.

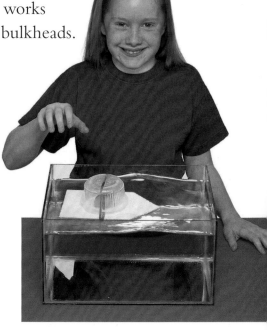

4 Now try to capsize it again and it will flip back upright. This is because air trapped underwater by the tub and a heavy weight on top forces the boat upright again.

INSTALLING BULKHEADS

You will need: *plastic container and lid, bradawl, marbles, scissors, non-hardening modeling material, wooden blocks.*

1 Pierce a hole in one corner of a plastic container using a bradawl. This represents the punctured hull of a cargo ship.

2 Add some marbles (cargo) and lower the container into a tank of water. It will fill up with water and slowly sink.

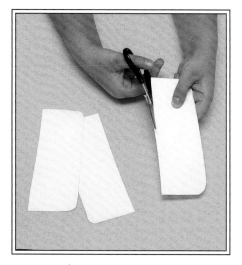

3 Cut three rectangles from the lid of the container. Make sure they fit across the tub. Round off the bottom corners if you need to.

4 Position the plastic walls inside the container so that they divide it into four compartments. Press modeling material around the edges to make a watertight seal.

5 Put some cargo in each section of the hull and put the whole thing back into the water. This time the container will stay afloat because only one section floods. The bulkheads prevent the water filling the whole hull.

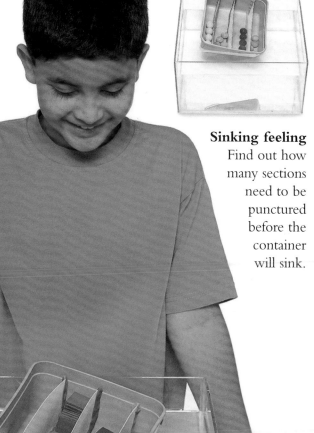

Sinking feeling
Find out how many sections need to be punctured before the container will sink.

IN PORT

SHIPS AND BOATS move cargo and people from place to place, so they need ports where they can load and unload. Every port has areas called docks where ships tie up along the wharves. The docks are often inside an area of water called a harbor, which is protected from the sea by a massive stone wall or natural cliffs. On the dock are huge cranes for unloading the ships and warehouses for storing cargo. In the port area there may be ship repair yards, parts shops and customs offices. Until recently, large numbers of people were employed as longshoremen and many major coastal towns and cities have grown up around ports. But the increased use of containers has dramatically reduced the number of workers. Huge merchant ships now dock at specially built ports or terminals, which are designed for handling cargoes, such as containers, oil and gas.

Tying up
Berthing ropes hooked over bollards are used to tie ships to the quays. Wharves may also be known as quays.

Container port
An aerial view shows part of Hong Kong's vast container terminal. Special loading cranes, called straddle carriers, are used to carry the containers.

The pilot
The entrance to a harbor is often narrow and busy. It may also have treacherous shallow areas such as sandbars outside it. A pilot is a person who knows the harbor well. He or she always takes control of large ships to guide them as they enter and leave the port.

Marina

A marina is a small harbor area where leisure craft such as motorboats and sailing yachts tie up. Marinas are usually separate from the normal harbor. They are also common on coasts where there are few natural harbors for small boats to shelter in. Each bay, called a berth, in a marina has water and electricity supplies.

High and dry

Repair and maintenance facilities in port may include a dry dock. This submarine is being repaired in dry dock. The submarine entered the dock when it was flooded with water. The gates were then closed and the water pumped out. Scaffolding is erected to keep the submarine upright.

Unloading in port

A dockside crane unloads a Japanese ship in the port of Vladivostock, Russia. The crane can be moved along the dockside on railway tracks. This ship's decks, as well as its hold, are piled with freight packed in boxes called tea chests.

Old harbors

The old harbor at Sydney, Australia, is a popular tourist attraction. Many old docks are too small for modern merchant ships. After years of neglect, their harbors are being renovated to provide leisure facilities.

TRAINS

The ancient Greeks recognized the value of railed tracks along which wheeled vehicles could run smoothly. But it was not until the early 1800s that rails were combined with steam power to launch one of the greatest transportation revolutions in history. The social and economic impact of trains was enormous. Goods that had been too heavy, or that degraded too quickly to travel long distances, could now be transported quickly and efficiently. Raw materials and foodstuffs reached parts of countries that had previously been out of range. Ordinary people were given a new degree of freedom to travel as never experienced before. This insight into the railroad story explores trains inside and out, explains how different types of engine work, takes a look at stations from around the world and the people who keep them running, and takes a glimpse into the future.

CONSULTANT
Michael Harris

RUNNING ON RAILS

THROUGHOUT HISTORY, people have looked for ways to move themselves and their possessions faster and more efficiently. Wheels were invented about 5,500 years ago. As wheels are round, they turn well on smooth surfaces and reduce the rubbing, slowing force called friction. However, it soon became clear that wheels do not work well on rough, soft or muddy ground.

To solve this problem, tracks of wood or stone were cut into or laid onto the ground to provide a smooth surface on which wheels could turn. This kept friction to a minimum, so that vehicles could move more easily and shift heavier loads.

The ancient Greeks made the first railed tracks in about 400BC by cutting grooved rails into rock. They hauled ships overland by setting them on wheeled cars that ran along the tracks. Iron rails came into use in Europe by the mid-1700s. They were laid, mainly in mines, to transport cars loaded with coal or metal ores. Steam-powered locomotives were developed in the early 1800s. Before then, cars in mines were pulled by horses or by the miners themselves, which was slow and only possible for short distances.

Pulling power
A horse pulls a freight car along rails. Modern railroads developed from ones first laid in European mines in the mid-1500s. Heavy loads, such as coal and metal ore, were carried in cars with wheels that ran along wooden planks. The cars were guided by a peg under the car, which slotted into a gap between the planks. Horses and sometimes even human laborers were used to haul the cars long before steam locomotives were invented.

Riding rails
It is just possible to make out the grooves where iron rails were laid at the Penydarran Ironworks in South Wales in the early 1800s. The world's first steam-powered train ran along these rails on February 13, 1804. The locomotive was designed by British engineer Richard Trevithick and hauled cars loaded with 11 tons of iron and 70 passengers at a speed of 5mph.

1769–1810	1811–1830	1831–1860	1861–1880
1769 FRENCHMAN NICHOLAS CUGNOT builds the first steam-powered vehicle. **1804** BRITISH ENGINEER RICHARD TREVITHICK tests the first steam locomotive for the Penydarran Ironworks in Wales. **1808** TREVITHICK builds a circular railroad in London, Britain, and exhibits the *Catch Me Who Can* locomotive.	**1825** THE STOCKTON AND DARLINGTON Railway opens in Britain – the first public railroad to use steam-powered locomotives. **1827** THE BALTIMORE AND OHIO RAILROAD is chartered to run from Baltimore to the River Ohio .in the United States. **1829** ROBERT AND GEORGE STEPHENSON'S *Rocket* wins the Rainhill Trials. It becomes the locomotive used for the Liverpool and Manchester Railway. 	**1833** GEORGE STEPHENSON devises the steam brake cylinder to operate brake blocks on the driving wheels of steam locomotives.  **1840s** SEMAPHORE SIGNALING is introduced. First tickets for train journeys are issued.	**1863** LONDON UNDERGROUND'S Metropolitan Line opens and is the world's first underground passenger railroad. **1864** AMERICAN GEORGE PULLMAN builds the first sleeping car, the *Pioneer*. **1868** PULLMAN BUILDS the first dining car. **1869** THE CENTRAL PACIFIC and Union Pacific railroads meet at Promontory Summit, linking the east and west coasts of the USA. **1872** AMERICAN GEORGE WESTINGHOUSE patents an automatic air-braking system.

Trackless trains

The world's longest trackless train runs at Lake County Museum in Columbia, South Carolina, in the United States. Trackless trains are common in theme parks. They carry passengers in carts or wagons running on rubber-tired wheels. The trains are pulled by a tractor that is made to look like a railroad locomotive.

Puffing Billy

The locomotive in this painting was nicknamed *Puffing Billy* because it was one of the earliest to have a smokestack. It was designed by British mine engineer William Hedley and built in 1813. The first steam engines were built in the early 1700s. They were used to pump water from mineshafts, not to power vehicles. *Puffing Billy* can be seen today in the Science Museum in London, Britain. It is the world's oldest surviving steam locomotive.

Modern rail networks

Today, nearly all countries in the world have their own railroad network. Thousands of miles of track crisscross the continents. Steam power has now given way to newer inventions. Most modern trains are hauled by locomotives powered by diesel engines, by electricity drawn from overhead cables, or from an electrified third rail on the track.

1881–1900	1901–1950	1951–1980	1981–present
1883 THE LUXURIOUS *ORIENT-EXPRESS* first runs on June 5 from Paris, France, to Bucharest in Romania.	**1901** THE FIRST COMMERCIAL monorail opens in Wuppertal, northwestern Germany.	**1955** THE WORLD'S MOST POWERFUL single-unit diesel-electric locomotives, the Deltics, first run between London and Liverpool.	**1981** TGV (*TRAIN À GRANDE VITESSE*) first runs between Paris and Lyon in France.
1893 THE NEW YORK CENTRAL AND HUDSON River Railroad claims that its steam locomotive *No. 999* travels faster than 100mph.	**1904** THE NEW YORK CITY SUBWAY opens.	**1957** TRANS-EUROP EXPRESS (TEE) fleet of trains operates an international rail service across western Europe.	
	1938 *MALLARD* SETS the world speed record for a steam-powered locomotive (126mph).		
1895 BALTIMORE AND OHIO *No. 1* is the first electric locomotive to run on the mainline Baltimore and Ohio Railroad.	**1940s** UNION PACIFIC BIG BOYS are built by the American Locomotive Company.	**1964** THE BULLET TRAIN first runs on the Tokaido Shinkansen between Tokyo and Osaka in Japan.	**1994** CHANNEL TUNNEL completed, linking rail networks in Britain and the Continent.
1900 THE PARIS *METRO* opens.		**1980** THE FIRST MAGLEV service opens at Birmingham Airport in Britain.	**1996** MAGLEV TRAIN ON THE Yamanashi test line in Japan reaches a staggering 350mph.

RAILROAD TRACK

A FULLY LADEN freight or passenger train is heavy, so the track it runs on has to be tough. Today, rails are made from steel, which is a much stronger material than the cast iron used for the first railroads. The shape of the rail also helps to make it tough. If you sliced through a rail from top to bottom you would see it has an "I"-shaped cross section. The broad, flat bottom narrows into the "waist" of the I and widens again into a curved head. Most countries use a rail shaped like this.

Tracks are made up of lengths of rail, which are laid on wooden or concrete crossbeams called ties. Train wheels are a set distance apart, so rails must be a set distance apart, too. The distance between rails is called the gauge. In Britain, the gauge was fixed at 4ft 8½in in the mid-1800s. Before then, the width of trains and gauges varied from one rail network to the next. So a train from one rail network could not run over the lines of another rail network.

Hard labor

Laying rail track is backbreaking work. Up until the mid-1900s, it was always done by hand. The ground is leveled first. Then crushed rock is laid to form a solid base before the ties are put into position. The rails rest on metal baseplates to hold them firm. The baseplates are secured to the ties either by spikes (big nails), track bolts or large metal spring-clips. Today, machines are used to lay track in most countries, although some countries still use manual labor.

MAKING TRACKS

You will need: *two sheets of stiff card measuring 10¼ x 4¼in, pencil, ruler, scissors, glue and glue brush, silver and brown paint, paintbrush, water pot, one sheet of foam board measuring 8 x 5in, one sheet of paper (11 x 8½in), masking tape, one sheet of thin card measuring 4 x 2in.*

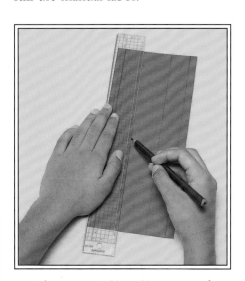

1 Place one 10¼ x 4¼in piece of card lengthwise. Draw a line ½in in from each of the outside edges. Draw two more lines, each 1⅜ in from the outside edges. This is side A.

2 Turn the card over (side B) and place it lengthwise. Measure and draw lines 1⅛in and 1¾in in from each edge. Repeat steps 1 and 2 with the second piece of 10½ x 4¼cm card.

3 Hold the ruler firmly against one of the lines you have drawn. Use the tip of a pair of scissors to score along the line. Repeat for all lines on both sides of both pieces of card.

PROJECT

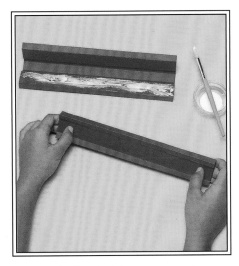

4 Place the cards A side up. For each one in turn, fold firmly along the two pairs of outer lines. Fold up from the scored side. Turn the card over. Repeat for inner lines.

5 With the A side up, press the folds into the I-shape of the rail. Open out again. Glue the B side of the ⅜in-wide middle section as shown. Repeat for the second rail.

6 Give your two rails a metallic look by painting the upper (A) sides silver. Leave the paint to dry, then apply a second coat. Leave the second coat to dry.

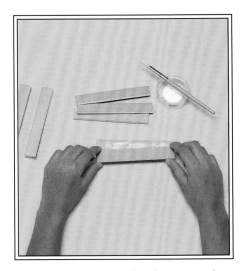

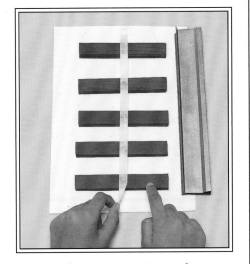

7 Use a pencil and ruler to mark out ten 5 x ¾in strips on the foam board. Cut them out. Glue two strips together to make five thick railroad ties. Leave them to dry.

8 Paint the ties brown on their tops and sides to make them look like wood. Leave them to dry, then apply a second coat of paint. Leave the second coat to dry, too.

9 Lay the ties on a piece of paper, 1⅜in apart. Run a strip of masking tape down the middle to hold them in place.

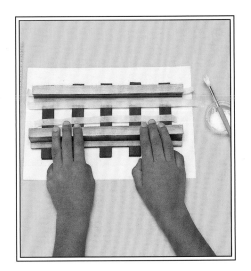

10 Glue the base of one rail and press it into place along the line of ties. The outside edge of the rail should be ⅝in in from the edge of the tie. Glue the other track into position in the same way. Secure the rails in place with masking tape until the glue is dry. Then gently remove all the masking tape.

11 Make at least two sets of rails. These will be able to carry the *Toy Train* and *Brake Van* described in later projects. To join the rails together, roll up the 4 x 2in length of thin card. Insert one end into the top of the I-shape in one rail. Gently push the second rail on to the other end.

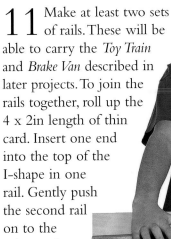

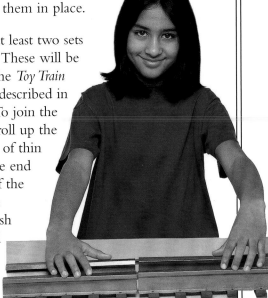

STEAMING AHEAD

Horses, oxen or people provided the pulling power for cars on rails and roads for thousands of years. In the 1800s, inventors came up with an alternative. They worked out how to use steam power for pulling wheeled vehicles. In 1825, the world's first public steam railway, the 25-mile-long Stockton and Darlington line, opened in England. On its opening day, the train hauled both freight and passenger cars. Later, it was used mainly for carrying coal. Five years later, the Liverpool and Manchester line opened with its new, steam-driven passenger trains. The company had run a competition called the Rainhill Trials to find the best locomotive for its railway. Both horse-drawn and steam locomotives took part. The steam-driven *Rocket* won.

The success of the *Rocket* convinced investors to back the development of steam-powered locomotives. The brains behind the *Rocket* and the Stockton and Darlington and Liverpool and Manchester railways were George Stephenson and his son Robert. In 1823, they set up the world's first locomotive factory. Other British engineers began to experiment with steam power, and locomotives were made for use in Britain and around the world.

Race to success
The *Rocket,* designed and built by George and Robert Stephenson, convinced people that steam power was better than horse power. At the Rainhill Trials in 1829, the *Rocket* traveled 70 miles at an average speed of 15mph.

Slow train to China
This Chinese locomotive is a KD class, which followed an American design. The Chinese did not make their own locomotives until they began to set up their own factories in the 1950s. Before then, locomotives had been imported from countries such as the United States, Britain, and Japan. Some Chinese trains are still steam-driven today, although diesel and electric ones are rapidly replacing them.

firebox

cab

hot gases pass through to boiler

regulator valve

engine

boiler tubes surrounded by water

steam passes through pipes into cylinders

smokestack

smokebox

steam valve

piston inside cylinder

driving wheels

coupling rod

connecting rod

leading truck

Steam traction

A steam engine converts the energy released from combustion into kinetic energy or movement. First, fuel (most often coal) is burned in a firebox to produce hot gases. The gases pass through boiler tubes that run the length of the water-filled boiler. The hot, gas-filled tubes heat the surrounding water and turn it into steam. This steam passes into cylinders, each of which contains a close-fitting piston. The steam pushes the piston along. The steam then escapes via a valve (one-way opening), and the piston can move back again. Rods connect the piston to the wheels. As the piston moves back and forth, it moves the rods, which, in turn, make the wheels go around.

FACT BOX
• Steam locomotives need about 26gal of water for every mile they travel. It takes 26–55lb of coal – equivalent to seven or eight times the weight of the water – to turn the water into steam.

Big wheels
The Stirling Single locomotive had only one pair of large driving wheels (third in from the left). The driving wheels are driven directly by the piston and connecting rod from the cylinder. Most steam locomotives had two or more pairs of driving wheels linked by coupling rods. The Single, designed by British engineer Patrick Stirling in the 1870s, reached speeds of 80mph.

The Big Boys
In the 1940s, American engineers were designing huge steam locomotives such as this Union Pacific Challenger. At more than 130ft, the Union Pacific's Big Boys were the world's longest-ever steam locomotives – more than five times the length of the Stephensons' *Rocket*. They could haul long passenger or freight trains speedily across the United States's vast landscape.

BEARING THE LOAD

Staying power

The coupling rod that connects the driving wheel to the other wheels is the lowest of the three rods in this picture. The connecting rod just above links the driving wheel with the cylinder. To stop train wheels from slipping sideways and falling off the rails, there is a rim called the flange on the inside of each wheel. This is a little different from the wheels you will make in this project, which have two flanges so that they sit snugly on the model rails from the *Making Tracks* project.

THE VEHICLE and machinery carried by a modern locomotive's underframe and wheels may weigh up to 110 tons. As bigger and more powerful locomotives were built, more wheels were added to carry the extra weight. Early steam locomotives such as the Stephensons' *Rocket* had only two pairs of wheels. Most steam locomotives had two, three, or four pairs of driving wheels, all of which turn in response to power from the cylinders. The cylinders house the pistons, whose movement pushes the driving wheels around via a connecting rod.

The other wheels are connected to the driving wheel by a coupling rod, so that they turn at the same time. The pair of wheels in front of the driving wheels are called the leading truck. The ones behind are the trailing wheels. Locomotives are defined by the total number of wheels they have. For example, a 4-4-0 type locomotive has four leading, four driving, and no trailing wheels.

MAKE AN UNDERFRAME

You will need: sheet of stiff card (22 x 17in), pencil, ruler, pair of compasses, scissors, glue and glue brush, masking tape, four 4in lengths of ³⁄₁₆in diameter dowel, four pieces of 2 x 2in thin card, silver and black paint, paintbrush, water pot, four map pins.

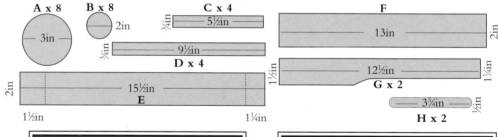

1 Draw and cut out the templates from the stiff card. Use a pair of compasses to draw the wheel templates A and B.

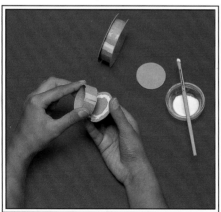

2 Roll the rim templates C and D into rings. Glue and tape to hold. Glue each small wheel circle onto either side of a small ring as shown. Repeat for big wheels. Leave to dry.

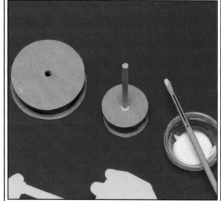

3 Use a pencil to enlarge the compass hole on one side of each wheel. Glue one end of each piece of dowel. Push the dowels into the holes of two big and two small wheels.

4 Roll the 2 x 2in card into sleeves to fit loosely over each piece of dowel. Tape to hold. Make wheel pairs by fixing the remaining wheels on to the dowel as described in step 3.

5 When the glue is dry, paint all four pairs of wheels silver. You do not need to paint the dowel axles. Paint two coats, letting the first dry before you apply the second.

6 Use a ruler and pencil to mark eight equal segments on the outside of each wheel. Paint a small circle over the compass hole, and the center of each segment black.

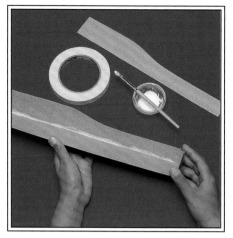

7 Fold along the dotted lines on E. Glue all three straight edges of template G and stick to template E. Repeat this for the other side. Secure all joins with masking tape.

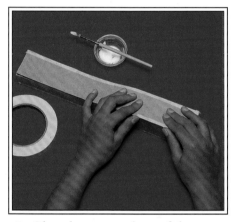

8 Glue the open edges of the underframe. Fit template F on top and hold until firm. Tape over the joins. Give the underframe two coats of black paint. Leave to dry.

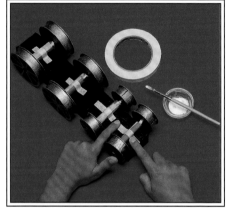

9 Glue the card sleeves on to the base of the underframe. Small wheel axles go 1³⁄₁₆ and 2¾in from the front, big wheels 1⅜in and 5in from the back. Tape to secure.

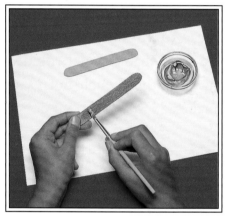

10 Give the coupling rods (H) two coats of silver paint. Let the paint dry between coats.

11 Press a map pin through each end of the coupling rods, about ³⁄₁₆in from edge. Carefully press the pin into each big wheel about ⅝in beneath the center.

12 The wheels on this underframe are arranged for a 4-4-0 type locomotive. You will be able to run the underframe along the model tracks you made in the *Making Tracks* project. The wheels will fit on the rails just like those of a real train. In real locomotives, however, the wheels are mounted on swiveling units called trucks. When the train comes to a curve in the track, the trucks move to allow the train to follow the curve. Each truck has four to six wheels.

MAPPING THE RAILROADS

Trains cannot easily climb mountains or cope with sharp corners. Planning and mapping the route of a railroad is not simply a matter of drawing a straight line between two destinations. New routes have to be worked out carefully, so that difficult terrain is avoided and time and money will not be wasted on tunnel- or bridge-building. Geographically accurate maps are made before work starts to show every bend of the planned track and the height of the land it will run through. Once construction starts, separate teams of workers may be building sections of track in different parts of the country. The maps are essential to make sure they are all following the same route and will join up when the separate parts meet.

Passengers do not need such detailed maps. They just need to find out which train to catch to get to the place they want to go. They do not need to know each curve or bridge along the way, just the names of the stations. Passenger maps provide a simplified version of the railroad routes, or sometimes a diagram.

Railroads in the Wild West
You can see how the railroads often followed a similar route to the wagon trails, passing through mountain passes or river valleys. After the first east-to-west-coast railroad was completed (the Central Pacific Railroad joined the Union Pacific Railroad in 1869), people could cross the continent in just ten days.

Early American railroad
A train runs along the Mohawk and Hudson Railroad, New York State, in the United States. This railroad line opened in 1831 and was built to replace part of the 40-mile route of the Erie Canal. This section of the canal had several locks, which caused delays to the barges. The journey took half the time it had taken by canal.

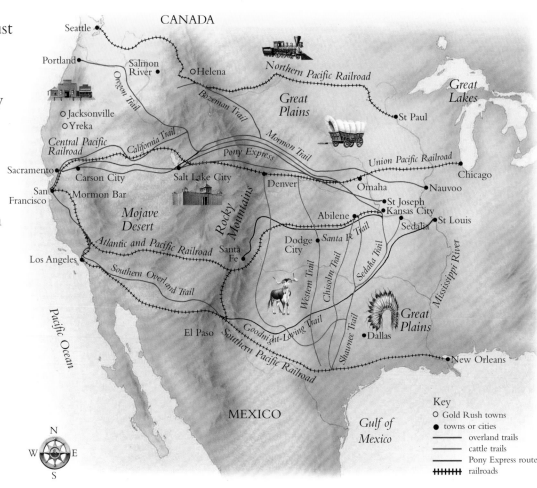

Neat networking

India's massive railroad network was one of the best planned in Asia thanks in large part to the British influence in the region. The Great Indian Peninsular Railway (GIPR) company was the first to open a line, a 25-mile stretch between Bombay and Thana in April 1853. India is a vast country, and railroad engineers had to plan routes for thousands of miles of track. They also had to find ways of taking railroads across every kind of difficult terrain, from boggy marshes to arid deserts, high mountains and deep ravines.

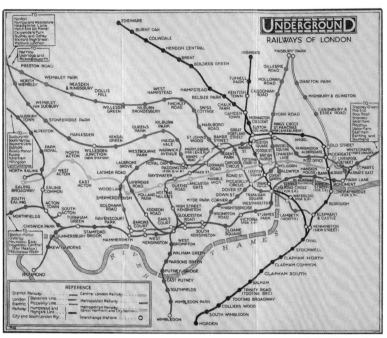

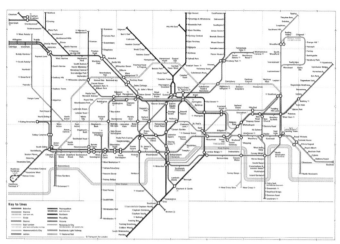

Designing ideas

Apart from the color-coded routes, the 1927 map of the London Underground (at left) looks very different from the one of today (shown above). Early route maps were hard to follow because they tried to show the real geographical route of lines. More abstract, diagrammatical maps were the brainwave of British engineering draughtsman Henry C. Beck. His 1933 redesign of the London Underground map was inspired by electrical circuit diagrams. It makes no attempt to show the real geographical route and is not drawn to scale.

Surveying railroad lines

Today, computer programs are used to plan and design new railroad routes. Data collected from on-the-ground surveying equipment (shown here), or the latest high-tech global positioning systems, is fed into a computer. The information is analyzed to insure that the new rail route is feasible. The most direct route is not always the cheapest. Surveyors must consider factors such as difficult terrain, environmental benefits, and existing rail networks when planning new routes.

LOAD-BEARING TUNNEL

Keystone is key

Before a tunnel is built, engineers have to make sure the rock and soil are easy to cut through but firm enough not to collapse. A framework is used to build brick arches. The bricks are laid around both sides of the framework up toward the center. When the central keystone is in place, the arch will support itself and the framework can be removed.

TUNNELS OFTEN have to bear the weight of millions of tons of rocks and earth – or even water – above them. One way of preventing the tunnel collapsing is to make a continuous brick arch run along the length of the tunnel. Wedge-shaped keystones at the peak of the arch lock the whole structure together and support the arch and everything else above it. An arched roof is much stronger than a flat roof, because any weight above the tunnel is passed down through the sides of the arch and out toward the ground.

Between 1872 and 1882, a 9⅓-mile-long railway tunnel was driven through Europe's highest mountains, the Alps, to link Switzerland to northern Italy. The St. Gotthard tunnel was the greatest achievement in tunnel engineering of the time. Today, a long, train-like machine is used to build tunnels such as the Channel Tunnel. A big drill carves out the hole, sending the spoil backward on a conveyor belt. Behind it, robotic cranes lift precast concrete sections of the tunnel into place.

SUPPORTING ARCH

You will need: two wooden building blocks or house bricks, two pieces of thick card (width roughly the same as the length of the blocks or bricks), a few heavy pebbles.

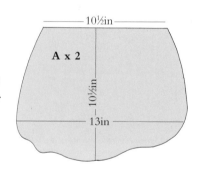

1 Place one of the pieces of card on top of the building blocks. Place pebbles on top as shown above. You will see that the tunnel roof sags under the weight.

2 Curve a second piece of card under the flat roof as shown. The roof supports the weight of the pebbles because the arch supports the flat section, making it stronger.

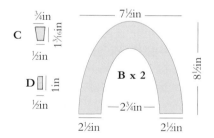

KEYSTONE

You will need: masking tape, piece of thick card measuring 18 x 10½in, two sheets of thick card measuring 14¼ x 12in, ruler, pencil, scissors, piece of thin card measuring 17¼ x 16in, newspaper, cup of flour, ½ cup of water, acrylic paints, paintbrush, water pot, piece of thin card (11 x 8½in), glue and glue brush.

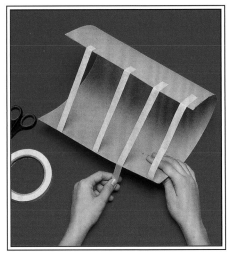

1 Tear off about four long strips of masking tape. Curve the 18 x 10½in rectangle of card lengthwise. Use the tape to hold the curve in place as shown above.

2 Copy the two templates A on to two 14½ x 12in pieces of thick card. Cut out the shapes. Attach each one to the sides of the tunnel and secure with tape as shown above.

3 Fold the 17¼ x 16in thin card in half. Copy the arch template B on to the card. Cut out to make two tunnel entrances. Stick these to the tunnel with masking tape as shown.

4 Scrunch newspaper into balls and tape to the tunnel and landscape. Mix the flour and water to make a thick paste. Dip newspaper strips in the paste. Layer them over the tunnel.

5 Leave to dry. When completely dry and hard, remove the tape and paint the tunnel and landscape green. Apply three coats, letting each one dry before you apply the next.

6 Paint the 11 x 8½in thin card to look like bricks. Draw and cut out templates C and D. Draw around C to make two keystones and D to make lots of bricks. Carefully cut the shapes out.

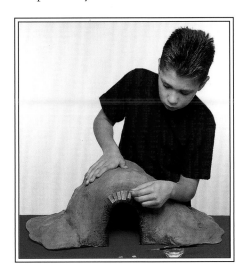

7 When the paint is dry, glue the keystones at the very top of each tunnel entrance. Then glue bricks around the arch either side of the keystone as shown. In a real tunnel, there would have been lots of central keystones running along the length of the tunnel.

8 Add finishing touches to your model using brown and green paints. Scrunch up newspaper into balls and dip them in the paste to make fake bushes. Leave them to dry and then paint them with brown and green paints. Do at least two or three coats. Leave them to dry between coats.

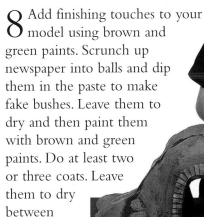

STATION STOP

ONCE PASSENGER trains began running in the 1830s, people needed special buildings where they could buy tickets and shelter from the weather while they waited to board. No one had ever designed or built train stations before. The owners of the new railroad companies wanted to make as much money as possible, so they had big, impressive mainline stations built to attract customers. Long platforms were essential for trains with many cars, so that passengers could get on and off trains safely. There also had to be waiting rooms and restaurants, as well as offices where station staff worked.

London's Euston Station was the first to have separate platforms for arrivals and departures. This train station was also among the earliest to have a metal and glass roof over the platforms. Euston was opened in 1838. From then on, most big train stations had glass and metal roofs. They were relatively cheap and easy to build, and they also let in a lot of daylight, which helped to save money on artificial lighting. In those days, lighting was provided by expensive gas lamps.

Housed in style
An early steam train puffs out of the first circular roundhouses, built in 1847 in London. Even the roundhouses where steam locomotives were housed for maintenance or repair were well designed. In the middle of these circular sheds was a turntable with short sections of track arranged around it, rather like the spokes of a wheel. Locomotives were parked on each section of track and released when they were needed for a journey.

Decorative ironwork
The iron pillars of stations in the 1900s were cast into a fantastic variety of shapes and then beautifully painted. At this time, cast iron was one of the latest building materials. Cast-iron pillars and arches were fairly cheap and quick to erect, as well as being a strong framework for station walls and roofs.

Temples of fashion
Bristol Temple Meads Station, Britain, looked like this in the 1800s. Engineers and architects tried to make their train stations stylish as well as be functional. During the 1800s, it was fashionable to copy the great building styles of the past. Bristol Temple Meads Station imitated the magnificent Gothic cathedrals and churches of medieval times. Small country stations, on the other hand, often looked like cottages or suburban villas.

Classical train station

The main station building of Washington Union Station in the United States is typical of train stations built in the early 1900s. It has a lofty vaulted ceiling and interiors made of paneled wood. It was opened in 1907 and was built by the Washington Terminal Company, which was specially formed by railroad companies serving the city.

German hub

Busy Cologne *Hauptbahnhof* (main train station) is at the center of Germany's vast rail network in the northwest of the country. The old steel-and-glass train shed was damaged during World War II (1939–45) but was later rebuilt. The front of the station has today been completely rebuilt with a more modern frontage.

Simple fare

Unlike the train stations that serve cities, country train stations are often very basic, such as this one at Pargothan, India. There are no platforms, and passengers climb into the trains from the track.

Single span

Atocha is the terminal of Spain's *Alta Velocita Española* (AVE) high-speed rail link between the capital, Madrid, and Seville in southern Spain. It was built in the early 1890s, and it serves all routes to the south, east and southeast of Madrid. It is Spain's largest train station and is famous for its single-span arched roof.

FACT BOX
• The world's largest train station is Beijing West Railway Station in China. It covers 133 acres and is bigger than the world's smallest country, the Vatican City in Rome, Italy.

• The world's highest train station is at Condor in Bolivia, South America. It is at 15,702ft above sea level, 1,010ft higher than the Matterhorn Mountain in the Alps.

• The world's busiest train station is Clapham Junction in south London, Britain. More than 2,000 trains pass through the station every 24 hours.

SHRINKING WORLD

Ticket to ride
Cheap, speedy trains meant that for the first time ordinary people, rather than the wealthy, could travel for pleasure. Train companies began offering day-excursion trips in the early 1830s. Outings to the seaside were particularly popular.

BEFORE THE coming of the railroads, the fastest way to travel was on horseback. Even though the swiftest racehorse can gallop at more than 37mph, it cannot keep this speed up for longer than a few minutes. Trains, on the other hand, can travel at high speed for hours on end. They can also transport hundreds of people at a time, or tens of carloads of freight, across vast distances. As more and more railroad lines began snaking across the countryside, life speeded up and the world seemed to grow smaller. People and goods could reach places they had never been to before.

During the 1800s, railroad technology spread from Britain all over the world. Tracks were laid between towns and cities at first. Later, railroads slowly grew to link countries and span continents. The world's first transcontinental railroad was completed in the United States in 1869. The expansion of the railroad system in the United States was rapid. Railroads were built through areas that had not yet been settled and played an important part in opening up many parts of the country.

Ceremonial spike
On May 10, 1869, a golden spike was hammered into the track when the world's first transcontinental railroad was completed, linking the east and west coasts of the United States. The railroad was built by two companies. The spike marked the meeting place of the two tracks at Promontory Summit in Utah.

FACT BOX
• With more than 149,000 miles of rail track, the United States has the world's longest network of railroads – just about enough to wrap around the Equator six times.

• It takes just over eight days to ride the entire length of the world's longest railroad, the Trans-Siberian line in Asia. This railroad, which opened in 1903, runs for 5,972 miles from Moscow to Vladivostok.

Desert runner
When surveyors planned the western section of Australia's transcontinental railroad, they plotted what is still the world's longest stretch of straight track. This 297-mile section lies within a vast, treeless desert called the Nullarbor Plain between Port Augusta and Kalgoorlie in southwestern Australia. The western section of this transcontinental railroad opened in 1917. The luxury Indian Pacific service was launched in 1969. Today, the 2,461-mile journey from Sydney to Perth takes just under three days.

Ruling by rail

A steam train passes over a bridge in India. During the 1800s, the British gradually introduced railroad networks to India and other countries in the British Empire. By speeding up the movement of government officials and the military, trains helped Britain keep control of its empire. Trade goods could be moved more quickly, too, which benefited British-owned companies. By 1939, India had more than 31,000 miles of track.

Keeping up with the times

The time in any place in the world is calculated from Greenwich Mean Time, which is the local time at 0 degrees longitude at Greenwich in London, England. Local time in other countries is calculated as either behind or in front of Greenwich Mean Time. Before the railroads, even cities within the same country kept their own local time, and accurate timetables were impossible. Timekeeping had to be standardized if people were to know when to catch their trains. British railroad companies standardized timekeeping using Greenwich Mean Time in 1847.

Coast-to-coast challenge

Pulled by diesel locomotives, passenger trains can today make the spectacular 2,890-mile journey across Canada in three days. When the Canadian Pacific transcontinental railroad was completed in 1887, the trip took steam trains about a week. The biggest challenge for the army of workers who built the railroad was taking the track through the Rocky Mountains – at Kicking Horse Pass, it climbs to 5,328ft.

A PASSION FOR TRAINS

I N 1830, a young British actress called Fanny Kemble wrote to a friend about her railroad journey pulled by a "brave little she-dragon … the magical machine with its wonderful flying white breath and rhythmical unvarying pace."

Over the years, all sorts of people – young and old, male and female, rich and poor – have caught Fanny's enthusiasm for trains. Some people love traveling on them, enjoying the scenery flickering past the windows and chatting to the strangers they meet on the journey. Others are happiest when they are standing at the end of a platform, spotting trains and noting down locomotive numbers. Other train buffs spend their spare time building their own private museum of railroad history. They collect anything from old tickets, timetables, and luggage labels, to early signaling equipment, station clocks, and locomotive numberplates. Some people "collect" journeys and take pride in traveling on some of the world's most famous railroads.

Museum piece
You can still ride a real steam train today, although in most countries only where short stretches of line have been preserved. Many classic locomotives of the past are on display in railroad museums. Visitors can usually get close enough to touch, and sometimes they are allowed to climb up inside the engineer's cab. You should never get this close when spotting working trains, however. Always stand well back on the platform, and never climb down onto the track.

Railroad mania
The walls of this train buff's room are decorated with prizes collected during years of hunting through junk shops and rummage sales, and attending specialist auctions. Lamps and many other pieces of railroad and station equipment came onto the market in Britain during the 1960s, when the government closed down hundreds of country railroad stations and branch lines.

Collecting signals

During the late 1900s, many old semaphore signals such as the ones in this picture were made redundant. They were replaced with color-light signals controlled from towers. Much of the old signaling was purchased by Britain's heritage railroads, but a few train buffs bought signals for their gardens. The ones in this picture are Great Western Railroad design signals, dating from the 1940s.

Museum pieces

The Baltimore and Ohio Museum was set up in the city of Baltimore, Maryland, by the Baltimore and Ohio Railroad in 1953. The main exhibits are displayed in a full-circle roundhouse in what used to be the railroad's shops. The exhibits feature a full range of locomotives from the last 180 years. They include a replica of the first American steam locomotive and a recently retired diesel passenger locomotive.

Tickets, please

Railroad tickets and timetables are all collectable items for those who are interested in trains and train journeys. A trainspotter's handbook and a set of railroad timetables are essential equipment for the serious train buff. In many countries, specialist bookshops sell handbooks that list all the working locomotives of the day.

WARNING BOX
- At stations, always stand well back from the platform edge.
- On bridges, never climb up walls or fences to get a better view – move somewhere else.
- Railroad lines sometimes have fences on either side of the track to keep people a safe distance from passing trains. Stand behind the fence – never climb over it.
- Modern trains are fast and make very little noise. If you disregard these simple rules, you will be risking your life.

Number crunching

Locomotives have number plates in much the same way that cars have license plates. The number plate is usually on the front of the engine, as can be seen on the front of this locomotive from the Czech Republic. In many countries, train buffs aim to collect the number of every working locomotive, but with so many locomotives in operation, it is a very time-consuming hobby.

TRAINS IN MINIATURE

ODEL TRAINS are just about as old as steam locomotives. The first ones were not for children, though. They were made for the locomotive manufacturers of the early 1800s to show how the newly invented, full-sized machines worked.

Although most toy trains are miniature versions of the real thing, they come in different scales or sizes. Most are built in O scale, which is $\frac{1}{48th}$ the size of the real train. The smallest are Z scale, which is $\frac{1}{220th}$ the size of a real train. Z-scale locomotives are small enough to fit inside a matchbox! It is extremely difficult to make accurate models to this small a scale, so Z-scale train sets are usually the hardest to find in stores and the most expensive to buy.

All the exterior working parts of the original are shown on the best model locomotives, from the smokestack on top of the engine to the coupling and connecting rods.

Smile, please
In the early 1900s, a few lucky children owned their own toy train. Some early toy trains had clockwork motors or tiny steam engines. Others were "carpet-runners." These were simply pushed or pulled along the floor.

Top-class toys
One British manufacturer of model trains was Bassett-Lowke, the maker of this fine model of *Princess Elizabeth*. Another manufacturer was Hornby, whose trains first went on sale in the 1920s. Hornby grew into Britain's most popular model. Lionel is probably the leading manufacturer of miniature trains in the United States. All these companies produce many different models of real-life trains.

A model world
In the 1920s, toymakers began producing small-scale tabletop model railroads. Train stations and track took up less space than older, larger-scale models had needed. Many of these models were electric-powered and made from cast metal and tin plate by the German firm Bing. Today, these models are very valuable.

The German connection

Model trains are being made at the Fleischmann Train Factory, Nuremberg, Germany. Fleischmann produces highly detailed models of the full range of modern European trains. Like earlier model-railroad manufacturers, Fleischmann does not only make the trains. Collectors and model-railroad buffs can also buy everything that goes to make up a railroad, including signals and towers, lights and level crossings, roundhouses, bridges, and tunnels. There are even train stations and platforms with miniature newspaper stands, station staff, and passengers.

Model behavior

In the earliest train sets, miniature locomotives hauled cars on a never-ending journey around a circular track. Gradually, toymakers began selling more complex layouts, with several sets of track linked by points. Trains could switch from one track to another, just as in real railroads.

Ticket to ride

Model trains come in all sizes, including those that are large enough for children and adults to ride on. These miniature trains have all the working parts and features of their full-sized parents, including a tiny firebox which the engineer stokes with coal to keep the train chuffing along. In the United States in the late 1890s, small-gauge lines were appearing at showgrounds and in amusement parks. By the 1920s, longer miniature railroads were being built in Britain and Germany. Today, many theme parks feature a miniature railroad.

MODEL LOCOMOTIVES

A precision toy

As manufacturing techniques improved, so toy trains became increasingly sophisticated. Today, accurate, working, scale models have all the features of full-size working trains.

TOY TRAINS started to go on sale during the mid-1800s. Early toy trains were made of brightly painted wood, and often had a wooden track to run along. Soon, metal trains went on sale, many of them made from tin plate (thin sheets of iron or steel coated with tin). Some of these metal toy trains had windup clockwork motors. Clockwork toy trains were first sold in the United States during the 1880s. The most sophisticated model trains were steam-powered, with tiny engines fired by methylated-spirit burners. Later model trains were powered by electric motors.

Railroad companies often devised special color schemes, called liveries, for their locomotives and cars. Steam locomotives had brass and copper decoration, and some also carried the company's special logo or badge. Many toy trains are also painted in the livery of a real railroad company. The shape of the locomotive you can make in this project has a cab typical of the real locomotives made in the 1910s.

TOY TRAIN

You will need: *10¼ x 10¼in card, masking tape, scissors, ruler, pencil, 4 x 4in card, glue and glue brush, card for templates, paints, paintbrush, water pot, underframe from earlier project, two thumbtacks, 4½ x ½in red card, split pin.*

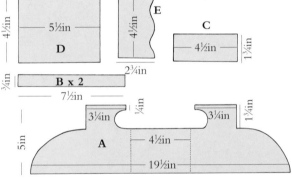

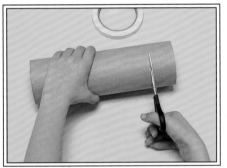

1 Roll the 10¼ x 10¼in card into an 3⅛in diameter tube. Secure it with masking tape. Cut a 2½in slit, 2in from one end of the tube.

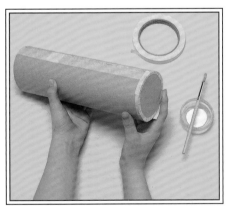

2 Hold the tube upright on the 4 x 4in piece of card. Draw around it. Cut this circle out. Glue the circle to the tube end farthest away from the slit. Tape to secure.

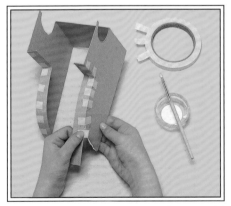

3 Copy and cut out templates. Fold template A along the dotted lines. Fold templates B across, 1¾in from one end. Glue both strips to the cab as shown and secure with tape.

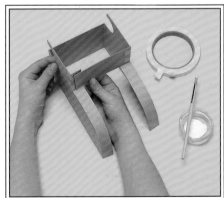

4 When the glue is dry, gently peel off the masking tape. Now glue on template C as shown above. Hold it in place with masking tape until the glue dries.

PROJECT

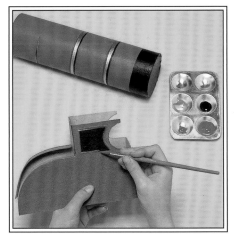

5 Apply two coats of green paint to the outside of the locomotive. Let the first coat dry before applying the second. Then paint the black parts. Add the red and gold last.

6 Glue around the bottom edge of the cab front C. Put a little glue over the slit in the tube. Fit the front of the cab into the slit. Leave the locomotive to one side to dry.

7 Give roof template D two coats of black paint. Let the paint dry between coats. Glue the top edges of the cab, and place the black roof on top. Leave until dry and firm.

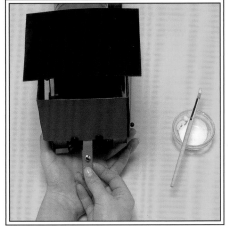

8 Glue the bottom of the cylindrical part of the train to the underframe you made in the *Underframe* project. Press thumbtacks into back of cab and underframe.

9 Glue both sides of one end of the red strip. Slot this between the underframe and the cab, between the thumbtacks. When firm, fold the strip and insert the split pin.

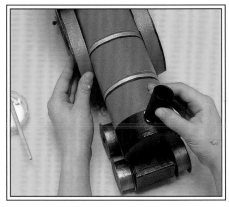

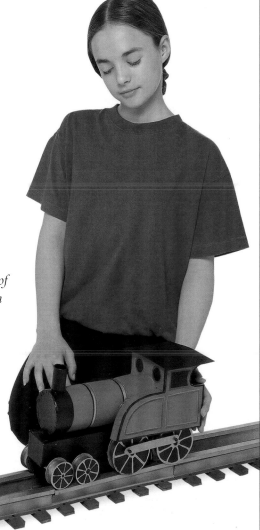

10 Paint one side of template E black. When dry, roll into a tube, and secure with masking tape. Glue wavy edge and secure to front of locomotive as shown above.

Just like a real locomotive, the basic color of your model train has been enhanced with red, black, and gold decoration. The locomotive is now ready to run on the railroad line you made in the Making Tracks *project. The engineer and fireman would have shared the cab of the locomotive. The engineer controlled the speed of the train, following the signals and track speed restrictions. The fireman insured a good supply of steam by stoking the fire and filling the boiler with water.*

SIGNALS AND SIGNALING

THE EARLIEST railroads were single tracks that ran directly between one place and another. Later, more tracks were laid and branched off these main lines. Trains were able to cross from one line to another on movable sections of track called switches.

To avoid crashes, a system of signals was needed to show engineers if the track ahead was clear. The first signalers stood beside the track and waved flags during daylight or lamps at night. From 1841, human signalers were replaced by signals called semaphores on posts with wooden arms.

By 1889, three basics of rail safety were established by law in Britain – block, brake, and lock. Block involved stopping one train until the one in front had passed by. Brakes are an obvious safety feature on passenger trains. Lock meant that switches and signals had to be interlocked, so that a lever in the tower could not be pulled without changing both the switch and the signal.

Hand signals
The first people to be responsible for train safety in Britain were the railway police. The policemen used flags and lamps to direct the movements of trains. In the absence of flags, signals were given by hand. One arm outstretched horizontally meant "line clear," one arm raised meant "caution" and both arms raised meant "danger, stop."

Lighting up the night
Electric signals were not used until the 1920s, when color-light signals were introduced. Color-light signals look like road traffic lights. A green light means the track is clear, red shows danger, and yellow means caution. Color-light signals, such as these in France, are accompanied by displays showing the number of the signal, speed restrictions, and other information for engineers.

Mechanical signals
A policeman operates a Great Western Railway disk and crossbar signal. The disk and crossbar were at right angles and rotated so the engineer could either see the full face of the disk, meaning "go," or the crossbar, meaning "stop."

Signal improvements

This hand-operated signal frame features details dating from the 1850s, when a signaling system called interlocking was introduced. Signals and switches were interlocked (linked) so that a single lever moved a signal and the set of switches it protected at the same time. Tower levers were moved by hand to set signals and switches in those days. In many countries today, signals are set automatically by computers that are housed in a central signaling control room.

Safety first

Semaphore signals such as these made a major difference to railroad safety when they were introduced during the 1840s. At first, railroad companies throughout the world used semaphore signals with oil lamps behind colored glass to show if the track was clear at night (green light) or at danger (red light). From the 1920s, many countries upgraded their systems by introducing electric color-light signals.

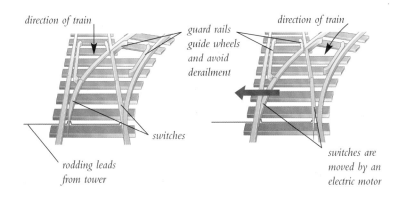

direction of train

direction of train

guard rails guide wheels and avoid derailment

switches

rodding leads from tower

switches are moved by an electric motor

Switches and humpyard

Trains are "switched" from one track to another using switches. Part of the track, called the blade, moves so that the wheels are guided smoothly from one route onto the other. The blade moves as a result of a signaler pulling a lever in the tower. The blade and lever are connected by a system of metal rods, and the lever cannot be pulled unless the signal is clear. From the late 1800s, railroad companies built humpyards. These made it easier to shunt freight cars together to make a freight train. As the cars went over a hump in the yard, they uncoupled. When they went down the hump, they could be switched into different sidings using a set of switches.

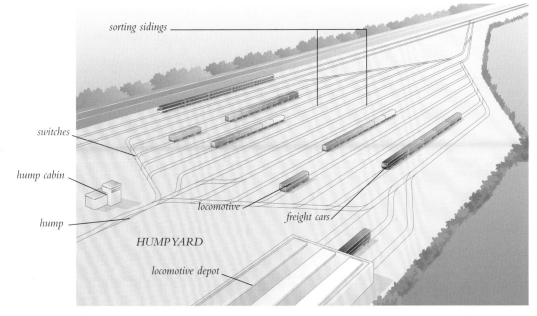

sorting sidings

switches

hump cabin

hump

locomotive

freight cars

HUMPYARD

locomotive depot

SAFETY FIRST

ACCIDENTS ARE a tragic feature of railroad travel today, but trains remain the safest form of land transport in most countries. Modern technology is largely responsible for the improvements in rail safety. In Britain, trains are fitted with an Automatic Warning System (AWS). If the signal indicates that the track ahead is clear, electric magnets between the rails send a message to equipment under the train. This causes a bell to sound in the engineer's cab. If the signal is not clear, the magnet stays "dead," and a horn sounds in the cab. If the engineer does not react, the brakes come on automatically. An improved system, called Train Protection and Warning System (TPWS), uses existing AWS but also provides an automatic stop at a red signal and a speed trap in advance of the signal.

A more advanced system is Automatic Train Protection (ATP). The train picks up electronic messages from the track, and they tell the engineer to slow down or stop. If he or she fails to respond, there is a warning and the brakes come on. ATP also slows or stops the train if it exceeds the speed limit.

On collision course
Head-on crashes were more common in the early days of the railroads, even though there were far fewer trains. On some routes, there was only a single-track line. A train heading toward a station was in danger of meeting another train leaving it. In most countries today, trains are timetabled so that no two are on the same line at the same time. This situation can only arise if a train passes a stop signal at a set of switches.

Japanese crash
A crane lifts a derailed train along the Hanshin Railway near Shinzaike Station. The accident was caused by an earthquake that devastated the city of Kobe on the Japanese island of Honshu in 1995. Several stations and several miles of elevated railroad lines were destroyed on the three main lines that run from Kobe to Osaka.

Control center

From the 1960s, signaling over large areas has been controlled from centralized towers. The towers have a control panel that displays all the routes, signals, and switches that the tower controls. Signalers set up safe routes for trains in the area by operating switches and buttons. Signals work automatically, and the switches change using electronic controls. This insures trains cannot get onto routes where there is an oncoming train. In the most modern signaling centers, the routes appear on computer monitors. The signaler uses a cursor to set up routes instead of using buttons and switches.

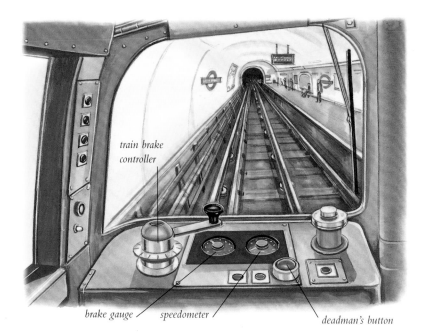

train brake controller

brake gauge   speedometer   deadman's button

In the driving seat

The control desk of a London Underground, or "Tube," train has a number of standard safety features. The train brake controller is a manual control to slow the train. The deadman's button must be pressed down continually by the motorman while the train is moving. If the motorman collapses, the button comes up and the train stops.

Onboard safety

In the event of an emergency, passengers will always find standard safety devices, such as fire extinguishers and first-aid kits, on board a train.

Buffer zone

Buffers stop trains at the end of a line. They are made of metal or wood and metal and are fixed to the track. They are strong enough to absorb much of the energy of a colliding train. Signals control a train's speed so that even if a train collides with the bufferstops, it is usually traveling slowly.

CABOOSE

EW EARLY steam locomotives had brakes. If the engineer needed to stop quickly, he had to throw the engine into reverse. By the early 1860s, braking systems for steam locomotives had been invented. Some passenger cars also had their own handbrakes that were operated by the conductors. A caboose was added to the back of trains, too, but its brakes were operated by a brakeman riding inside.

The problem was that the engineer had no control over the rest of the train. When he wanted to stop, he had to blow the engine whistle to warn each of the conductors to apply their brakes.

The brakes on a locomotive and its cars or freight cars needed to be linked. This was made possible by the invention of an air-braking system in 1869. When the engineer applies the brakes, compressed air travels along pipes linking all parts of the train and presses brake shoes. Air brakes are now used on nearly all the world's railroads.

Coupling up

A locomotive is joined up to a car by a connection called a coupler. At first, chains or rigid bars were used to join cars. Later, a rigid hook at the end of one vehicle connected to chains on the front of the next. From the late 1800s, couplers made from steel castings and springs were used, but uncoupling was done by hand. Today, passenger trains couple and uncouple automatically.

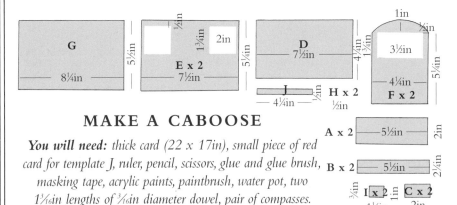

MAKE A CABOOSE

You will need: *thick card (22 x 17in), small piece of red card for template J, ruler, pencil, scissors, glue and glue brush, masking tape, acrylic paints, paintbrush, water pot, two 1³⁄₁₆in lengths of ³⁄₁₆in diameter dowel, pair of compasses.*

1 Copy the templates on to card and cut them out. Glue templates A, B and C together to make the underframe as shown. Tape over the joins to secure them.

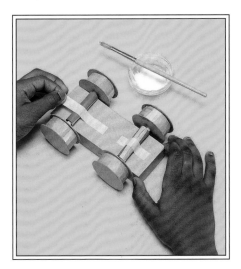

2 Make and paint two pairs of small wheels (diameter 2in) following steps 1 to 5 in the *Underframe* project. Glue and tape the wheel pairs to the underframe.

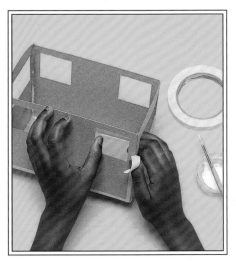

3 Glue the bottom edges of the caboose sides (E) to the caboose base (D). Then glue on the caboose ends (F). Secure the joins with masking tape until the glue is dry.

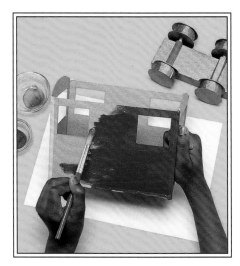

4 Paint the caboose brown with black details and the wheels and underframe black and silver. Apply two coats of paint, letting each one dry between coats.

5 Paint one side of template G black. Let the paint dry before applying a second coat. Glue the top edges of the caboose. Bend the roof to fit on the top of the caboose.

6 Apply glue to the top surface of the underframe. Stick the caboose centrally on top. Press together until the glue holds firm. Leave to dry completely.

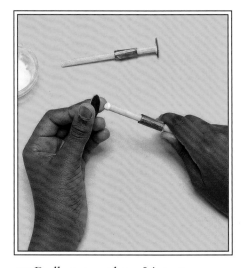

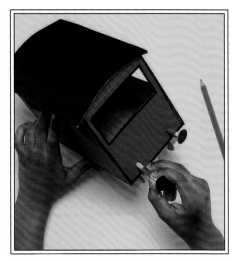

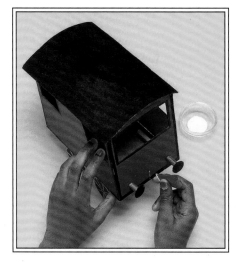

7 Roll up templates I into two ¾in tubes to fit loosely over the dowel. Tape to hold and paint them silver. Paint the buffer templates H black and stick on each dowel.

8 Use compasses to pierce two holes 1in from each side of the caboose and ⅝in up. Enlarge with a pencil. Glue the end of each dowel buffer. Slot it into the hole. Leave to dry.

9 Cut a slot between the buffers. Fold red card template J in half. Glue each end to form a loop. Push the closed end into the slot. Hold it in place until the glue dries.

The caboose will also run on the tracks you made in the Making Tracks *project. You can also join the red-card coupler to join the caboose to the model locomotive you made in the* Toy Train *project. On old-style railroads, the caboose was at the back of the train so that the conductor could make sure that all the carriages stayed coupled. The caboose had one of two brake systems. One had hand-operated brakes that worked on the tread of the caboose's wheels. The other had a valve that allowed the brakeman to apply air brakes to all vehicles in the train.*

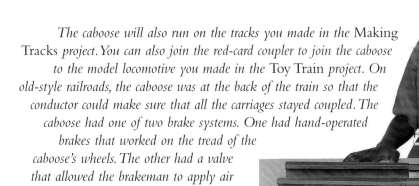

HAULING FREIGHT

Most of the traffic on the world's railroads is made up of freight trains that transport goods such as coal and iron ore from mines and cloth and other manufactured goods from factories. The earliest freight trains were slow because they did not have effective braking systems. Technical developments now mean that freight trains can run much faster than before.

Freight trains made a vast difference to everyday life as the rail networks expanded and brought the country nearer to the city. For the first time, fresh food could be delivered quickly from country farms to city markets. People could also afford to heat their homes. The price of coal for household fires came down because moving coal by train was cheaper and faster than by horse-drawn carts or canal.

In the mid-1900s, motor vehicles and airplanes offered an alternative way of transporting freight. However, concerns about congestion and the environment mean that freight trains continue to be the cheapest, quickest, and most environmentally friendly way of hauling a large volume of freight overland.

Four-legged freight service
The world's first public railroad opened in 1803 – for horse-drawn freight cars. The Surrey Iron Railway ran for a little more than 8 miles between Wandsworth and Croydon near London. It went past a number of mills and factories. The factory owners paid a toll to use the railroad and supplied their own horses and cars.

Rolling stock
Freight cars were ramshackle affairs when the first steam trains began running during the 1820s and 1830s. They had metal wheels but, unlike locomotives, they were mainly built from wood. Their design was based on the horse-drawn carts or coal cars they were replacing. Waterproof tarpaulins were tied over goods to protect them from the weather.

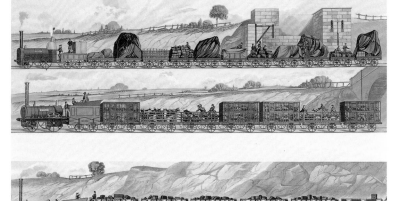

Slow but steady
In the early 1800s, the first steam locomotives hauled coal cars called chaldrons from collieries to ships on nearby rivers. The locomotives were not very powerful. They could pull only a few cars at a time. Going any faster would have been dangerous because neither the locomotives nor the cars had much in the way of brakes!

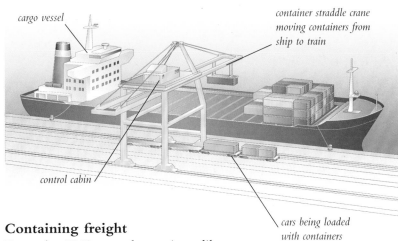

cargo vessel

container straddle crane moving containers from ship to train

control cabin

cars being loaded with containers

Mail by rail

Railroads first carried mail in the 1830s. A special mail car was introduced in Britain in 1838. Post Office workers on board sorted the mail for delivery while the train was moving. Modern versions of these traveling mail rooms still operate today.

Containing freight

From the 1960s, metal containers like giant boxes have transported goods by sea, rail, and road. They are a way of combining different methods of transporting goods in the most effective way possible. The containers are simply lifted from one vehicle to another using large cranes called straddle cranes. The trains usually have specially designed flatcars onto which the containers are locked into position. The containers remain sealed, apart from when they are inspected by customs officials.

Bulk transportation

Today, freight trains mainly transport heavy, bulky loads such as coal, iron ore, grain, or building materials. Smaller, lighter goods are usually sent by road or air. Railroad companies pioneered the idea of specially designed vehicles for different types of freight – tankers for liquids such as milk or chemicals, for example, and hoppers that tip sideways for unloading gravel or coal.

FACT BOX

• Today, freight trains haul bulky loads, such as coal, oil, and minerals, in purpose-built cars.

• As many as 10,000 freight trains crisscross the United States every day.

• Some of the world's freight trains have 200 cars and can be up to 2½ miles long.

• Modern diesel and electric freight trains can haul heavy loads at speeds of up to 75 miles.

Chinese circle

From the mid-1900s, Chinese electric locomotives such as this hauled ore hoppers. The trains carried iron ore to be smelted in blast furnaces on an 50 mile circular line. The locomotives were based on a Swiss design. They had a sloping front so that the driver could see easily from the cab.

GOING UNDERGROUND

RAILROAD NETWORKS made it easier for people to travel from the country to cities and towns to shop or work. During the 1800s, the streets within cities became extremely crowded with people and traffic. One way of coping with the problem of moving around the cities was to tunnel underground.

The world's first passenger subway system opened in 1863. It was the Metropolitan Line between Paddington Station and Farringdon Street in London, Britain. Steam locomotives hauled the passenger cars, and smoke in the tunnels was a big problem. The locomotives were fitted with structures called condensers that were supposed to absorb the smoke, but they did not work properly. Passengers on the trains traveled through a fog-like darkness. Those waiting at the stations choked on the smoke drifting out from the tunnels.

The answer was to use electric trains, and the first underground electric railroad opened in London in 1890. Today, nearly every major city in the world has its own subway system.

Cut-and-cover construction
The first underground passenger railroads were built using a new method called cut-and-cover construction. A large trench – usually 33ft wide by 16ft deep – was cut into the earth along the railroad's proposed route. Then the trench was lined with brickwork and it was roofed over. After that, the streets were re-laid on top of the tunnel.

Tunnel maze
This cross section of the underground system in central London in 1864 shows the proposed route of the new Charing Cross line beneath the existing Metropolitan Line. Deep-level subways were not built until 1890, when developments such as ways of digging deeper tunnels, electric locomotives, better elevators, and escalators became a reality.

Underground shelters
Londoners came up with another use for their city's warren of underground railroad tunnels during World War II (1939–45). They used them as deep shelters from night-time bombing raids. The electric lines were switched off, and people slept wherever they could find enough room to lie down. Canteens were set up on many platforms. More than 130,000 gallons of tea and cocoa were served every night.

Keeping up with the times

The Washington DC Metro in the United States was opened in 1976. It is one of the world's newest and most up-to-date subway systems. The trains have no motormen and the entire network is controlled automatically by a computerized central control system. Passengers traveling in the air-conditioned cars have a smooth, fast ride due to the latest techniques in train and track construction. The airy, 200-yard-long train stations are much more spacious than those built in the early 1900s.

FACT BOX

• The world's busiest subway is in New York City and has 468 train stations. The first section opened in 1904.

• The London Underground is the world's longest subway system. It has nearly 250 miles of track.

• The world's second electric subway system was the 2½-mile-long line in Budapest, Hungary. It opened in 1896.

Overground undergrounds

Work started on the first 6-mile-long section of the Paris *Metro* in 1898 and took over two years to complete. The engineers who designed early underground subways, such as the Paris *Metro*, often found it quicker and easier to take sections above ground, particularly when crossing rivers. The station entrances were designed by French architect Hector Guimard in the then-fashionable Art Nouveau style. They made the Paris *Metro* one of the most distinctive and stylish subway systems in the world.

Mechanical earthworm

The cutting head of a Tunnel-Boring Machine (TBM), which was used to bore the Channel Tunnel between England and France. The 26ft-wide cutting head is covered with diamond-studded teeth. As the TBM rotates, the teeth rip through the earth. The waste material, or spoil, falls onto a conveyor belt and is transported to the surface. The cutting head grips against the sides of the tunnel and inches farther forward under the pressure of huge rams. As the tunnel is cut, cranes line the tunnel with curved concrete segments that arrive on conveyors at the top and bottom of the TBM.

RIDING HIGH

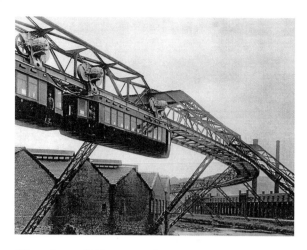

Wonder of Wuppertal
The oldest working monorail in the world is located in Wuppertal, Germany. Almost 20 million passengers have traveled along the 8-mile-long route since it opened in 1901. It is suspended about 33ft above the ground. The wheels run along the top of the rail.

IN SOME of the world's cities, the solution to overcrowded streets was to build railway networks above ground level. The earliest kind of overhead trains ran on a twin-rail track. The track was raised above the ground on arching, viaduct-like supports. These "elevated railways" were built in several American and European cities from the mid-1800s onward.

Today, some overhead trains run along a single rail called a monorail. Some are suspended systems in which the train hangs beneath the rail. Others are straddle systems in which the train sits over the rail.

Twin-rail systems called Light Rapid Transit (LRT) are now more common than monorails. They are described as "light" because they carry fewer people and therefore need lighter-weight vehicles and track than mainline, or "heavy," railways. In many cities, LRT cars are like a cross between a streetcar and a train. They run on rails through town and city streets, as well as through underground tunnels and along elevated tracks.

Flying train
Inventor George Bennie's experimental monorail was one of the strangest ever built. The streamlined machine was named the Railplane. It had airplane propellers front and back to thrust it along. It first "flew" in July 1930, along a 44-yard-long test line over a railroad track near Glasgow in Scotland.

Climb every mountain
The Paris funicular climbs to the city's highest point, the top of Montmartre. Funiculars were invented during the 1800s and are used to move cars up and down hillsides or steep slopes. Usually, there are two parallel tracks. Each one has a passenger-carrying car attached. In the early days, each car carried a large water tank that was filled with water at the top of the slope and emptied at the bottom. The extra weight of the car going down pulled the lighter car up. Later funiculars have winding drums powered by electricity to haul a cable up and down.

Tomorrow's world

During the 1950s, American film producer Walt Disney wanted to have a monorail for his futuristic Tomorrowland attraction when he built his first Disneyland theme park in California. The monorail opened in 1959 and was an immediate success with visitors. Disney was trying to promote monorails as the transportation system of the future, but his railroad had just the opposite effect. For many years, monorails were seen as little more than amusement-park rides.

FACT BOX
• New Yorkers nicknamed their elevated railroad the "El." It opened in 1867. By 1900, more than 300 steam locomotives and 1,000 passenger cars were operating on its 36-mile-long network.

Not everyone's darling

The monorail system in Sydney, Australia, links the heart of the city to a tourist development in nearby Darling Harbour. It has proved to be popular since it opened in 1988, carrying about 30,000 people a day along its 2-mile-long route. Many people who lived in Sydney were concerned that the elevated route would be an eyesore, particularly in older parts of the city. Protesters tried hard to block the monorail's construction. Today, it has become part of everyday life for many people who live in Sydney.

London's LRT

The Docklands Light Railway in London opened in 1987. It was Britain's first Light Rapid Transit (LRT) to have driverless vehicles controlled by a computerized control system. However, it was not Britain's first LRT. That prize went to Newcastle's Tyne and Wear Metro, which began running in 1980. LRTs provide a frequent service, with unstaffed stations and automatic ticket machines. Many cities throughout the world have chosen to install them in preference to monorails because they are cheaper to run.

MONORAIL

$\mathbf{M}$ONORAILS DATE back to the 1820s. As with early trains, these early monorails were pulled by horses and carried heavy materials such as building bricks, rather than passengers. About 60 years later, engineers designed steam locomotives that hauled cars along A-shaped frameworks. However, neither the trains nor the cars were very stable. Loads had to be carefully balanced on either side of the A-frame to stop them tipping off.

Today's monorails are completely stable, with several sets of rubber wheels to give a smooth ride. They are powered by electricity, and many are driverless. Like fully automatic LRTs, driverless monorail trains are controlled by computers that tell them when to stop, start, speed up or slow down.

Monorails are not widely used today because they are more expensive to run than two-track railroads. The special monorail track costs more to build and is more of an eyesore than two-track lines. The cars cannot be switched from one track to another, and it is expensive to change or extend a monorail line.

Staying on track
Vertical sets of running wheels carry the weight of this modern monorail and keep it on top of the huge rail. Other horizontal sets of wheels, called guides and stabilizers, run along the sides of the rail. They keep the train on course and stop it from tipping when it goes around bends.

MODEL MONORAIL

You will need: sheet of protective paper, 28¼in length of wood (1½in wide and 1½in deep), acrylic paints, paintbrush, water pot, 26½in length of plastic curtain rail (with screws, end fittings and four plastic runners), saw, screwdriver, sheet of red card, pencil, ruler, scissors, double-sided scotch tape, 7in length of 1in-thick foam board, glue and glue brush, black felt-tip pen.

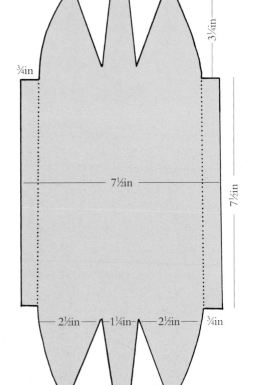

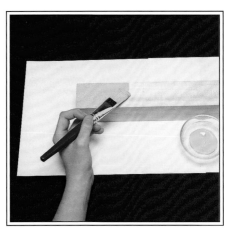

1 Cover the work surface with paper to protect it. Then paint the block of wood yellow. Let the first coat dry thoroughly before applying a second coat of paint.

2 Ask an adult to saw the curtain rail to size if necessary. Place the track centrally on the wood and screw it into place. Screw in the end fittings at one end of the rail.

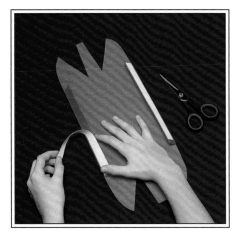

3 Copy the template onto the red card and cut it out. Score along the dotted lines and fold inward. Stick double-sided scotch tape along the outside of each folded section.

4 Remove the backing from the tape. Stick one side of the foam onto it. Fold the card over and press the other piece of double-sided tape to the opposite side of the foam.

5 Overlap the pointed ends at the back and front of the train and glue. Then glue the inside end of the top flaps, back and front. Fold them over and press firmly to secure.

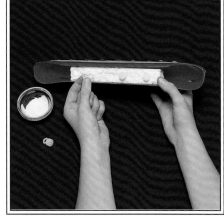

6 Pencil in windows along both sides of the train. Fill them in with a black felt-tip pen. Paint decorative black and yellow stripes along the bottom of the windows.

7 Put a dab of glue on the "eye" end of each plastic runner. Hold the train, foam bottom toward you. Push each runner in turn into the foam at roughly equal intervals.

8 Stand the track on a flat surface. At the end of the track without an end stop, feed each plastic runner into the track. Run the train back and forth along the track.

The train you have made in this project is called a "straddle" system monorail. Monorail trains running on the straddle system rest on a single rail and are balanced and guided by side panels on either side of the train.

WORKING ON THE RAILROADS

A S THE railroads grew ever larger, so did the number of people employed to keep them running safely and on time. In Britain, for example, about 47,000 people worked for the railroad companies by the late 1840s. Today, about 95,000 people are employed on the British railroads – seven times less than during World War I (1914–18). One reason is that some jobs that were once done by people, such as selling tickets, are now done by machines. Automation has not been widespread, however. Most railroads around the world have little money to buy computers and control systems.

Stationmasters and train conductors are just some of the people who talk to passengers and deal with their needs. Most railroad employees work behind the scenes, however, and rarely meet passengers. Managers plan how many trains should run on a particular line, how often, and how fast. Engineering teams check and keep the tracks, signals, and other equipment in safe working order.

Standing on the footplate
Two men worked in the cab. They stood on the footplate because there were no seats. The engineer was in charge. He managed the engine controls and the main brakes and kept a sharp look out for signals and anything blocking the track. The fireman stoked the fire and insured the boiler contained enough water.

Laying track
Track workers check a section of track that has been newly laid with stone ballast, ties, and rail. Rails should be checked regularly for cracks and deterioration. The ground beneath the rail can also subside and twist the rails.

Building trains
Workers in a factory are assembling an aluminum-bodied diesel train. Modern trains are built of either steel or aluminum sections welded together into a strong single unit. Separate units such as the driving cab, air-conditioning engine, and restrooms are fixed on the car later.

In the driving seat

Compared to the older steam engines, life is fairly comfortable in the cabs of modern locomotives. For a start, the engineer can sit down. They are also protected from the weather inside fully enclosed cabs, and they do not have to stick their heads outside to see the track ahead. Today's engineers still manage the controls and brakes, and watch out for signals and obstacles on the track. They also have a lot of help from computerized railroad systems.

FACT BOX

• There are more than 2,500 stations on Britain's mainline railroads. Twenty of them are major terminals in London and other large cities.

• New York City's subway has more than 460 stations, London's Tube has 300, and Moscow's Metro about 150.

• Five people work on each World Heritage steam-powered locomotive on the Darjeeling–Himalaya Railway in India. As well as the driver, one man breaks the coal for the fireman. Two ride out front and sand the rails to stop the engine slipping on the steep slopes.

Insect debris

The windows of this train are being cleaned by hand, since this is the most effective way to remove the accumulation of flying insects on the cab windows. The bodies of most trains are cleaned in automatic washing plants using revolving brushes, high-pressure water jets, and powerful cleaning agents that meet high environmental standards. In most cases, trains are cleaned every 24 hours when they come back to their home depot for examination and routine servicing.

Chefs on board

Armies of chefs and kitchen staff play an important role in making sure passengers do not go hungry during the journey. Most cooked food is prepared onboard the train using microwave ovens and electric burners. Almost all long-distance trains have dining and lounge cars, where passengers can take refreshments during their journeys. Even smaller trains often have buffet cars or mobile buffet carts.

TRAVELING IN STYLE

First-class comforts
By the late 1800s, first-class passengers such as these elegantly dressed ladies enjoyed every comfort on their journey. There were soft, padded benches and armchairs and cloth-covered tea tables. The design of luxury railroad cars was based on that of top-class hotels. Windows had thick, plush curtains and fittings were made of polished wood and shiny brass.

IT WAS some time before traveling on a passenger train was as comfortable as waiting in one of the splendid stations. Before the 1850s, there were few luxuries and no restrooms, even on long journeys. The overall comfort of the journey depended on how much money you had paid for your ticket. First-class cars were – and still are – the most expensive and the most comfortable way to travel. Then came second class, third class, and sometimes even fourth class.

The pioneer of comfortable rail travel was a US businessman called George Pullman. In 1859, after a particularly unpleasant train journey, he designed a coach in which "people could sleep and eat with more ease and comfort." Pullman launched his sleeping car in 1864, and was soon exporting luxury sleeping and dining cars around the world.

Royal seal of approval
This luxurious railroad car was made specially for Britain's Queen Victoria, who reigned from 1837 until her death in 1901. It had padded walls, thick carpets, expensive paintings on the walls, and the finest decoration. Many European kings and queens had their own cars built so that they could travel in royal style. Queen Victoria's royal car included a sleeping compartment, and it is thought she enjoyed sleeping in it more than at her palaces.

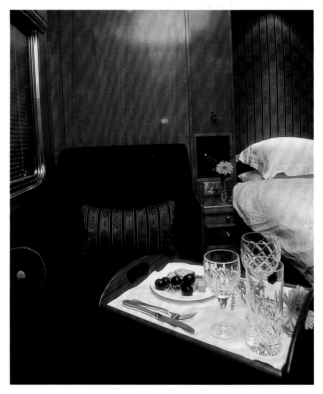

The Blue Train
South Africa's Blue Trains run between Cape Town and Pretoria in South Africa and are regarded as the most luxurious trains in the world. Passengers benefit from a 24-hour butler and laundry service and two lounge cars, and all the suites are equipped with televisions and telephones.

Lap of luxury

The *Orient-Express* first graced the railroads of Europe in 1883. It formed a scheduled link between Paris, France, and Bucharest in Romania. The scheduled service stopped running in May 1977, and it was replaced by a new "tourist-only" *Orient-Express* in May 1982. Passengers can once again enjoy the comfortable sleeping cars with velvet curtains, plush seats, and five-course French cuisine in a Pullman dining car like the one shown above.

A rocky ride

The Canadian has a domed glass roof so that it offers spectacular views during the 2,776-mile journey from Toronto, in central Canada, to Vancouver, on the west coast. The journey lasts for three days and takes in the rolling prairies of Saskatchewan, Edmonton, and Alberta. It then begins the gradual ascent through the foothills of the Rocky Mountains.

Lounging about

Long-distance trains on the Indian Pacific line from Sydney, on the Pacific Ocean, to Perth, on the Indian Ocean, are well equipped for the 65-hour journey across Australia. Indeed, they are described as being "luxury hotels on wheels." Passengers can relax and enjoy the entertainment provided in the comfortable surroundings of the train's lounge cars. These trains also have cafeterias, smart dining cars, club cars, and two classes of accommodation. Passengers can eat, drink, and sleep in comfort. The trains are even equipped with a honeymoon suite and a sick bay.

HIGH-SPEED TRAINS

THE RECORD-HOLDERS of today are the high-speed electric trains that whisk passengers between major city centers at 155–185mph. These high-speed trains are the railroad's answer to the competition from airplanes and freeways that grew up after World War II (1939–45). High-speed trains can travel at well over the legal limits for road traffic. Although they cannot travel as fast as planes, they save passengers time by taking them to city centers. In some cases, high-speed trains even beat the flying time between major cities such as London and Paris.

The world's first high-speed intercity passenger service was launched in Japan on October 1, 1964. It linked the capital, Tokyo, with the major industrial city of Osaka in the south. The average speed of these trains – 137mph – broke all the records for a passenger train service. The service was officially named the *Tokaido Shinkansen* (new high-speed railroad), but the trains soon became known as Bullet Trains to describe their speed and the bullet-shaped noses of the locomotives.

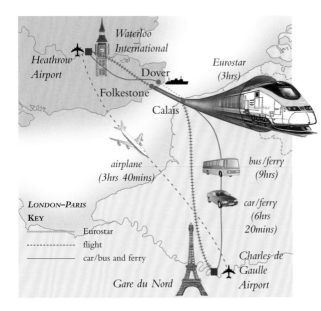

Market leader
The Eurostar has become the quickest way to travel between the city centers London, Britain, and Paris, France. It cuts out time-consuming airport check-in and transfer periods. Ferry crossings dramatically increase the journey times by car and by bus.

Rocket on rails
The latest high-speed JR500 trains to operate on Japan's *Tokaido Shinkansen* are as streamlined as a jet plane. Today, they can haul their 16 passenger carriages at 185mph. The average speed of the trains in 1960 was 135mph.

Stacking the odds

On some high-speed trains, such as this French TGV, passengers ride in double-decker cars. The initials "TGV" are short for *Train à Grande Vitesse* (high-speed train). The operational speed of these French trains is 185mph. TGVs also hold the current world speed record for a wheeled train. On May 18, 1990, a TGV Atlantique reached an amazing 320mph.

Swedish tilter

The Swedish X2000 tilting electric trains have an average speed of 95mph and a top speed of 125mph. Tilting trains lean into curves to allow them to travel around bends at faster speeds than non-tilting trains.

Melting the ICE

Germany's ICE (InterCity Express) high-speed trains reached speeds of more than 250mph during tests, before they entered service in 1992. Their maximum operating speed is about 175mph. Like other high-speed trains, they are streamlined to reduce the slowing effects of drag.

Spanish speeders

Spain's elegant high-speed trains are called AVEs (*Alta Velocidad España,* or high speed of Spain). Their average operational speed is about 135mph. They entered service on Spain's first high-speed railroad, between Madrid and Seville, in 1992. The AVEs' design was based on the French TGVs. AVEs are made in France with some Spanish parts. Like all high-speed trains, AVEs take their power from overhead electricity lines.

INVESTING IN THE FUTURE

To accelerate to speeds of up to 185–215mph, trains need to run on specially constructed tracks, with as few curves and slopes as possible. The tracks have to be wider apart than was usual in the past. A speeding train stirs the wind into eddies, which can buffet a passing train and jolt its passengers. The ride is also smoother and faster if continuously welded rails are used. If they have their own, dedicated lines, high-speed trains do not have to fit in with the timetables of ordinary, less speedy trains that would slow them down.

Throughout the world, railroad companies are investing billions of dollars in building new lines or upgrading old track to carry their high-speed trains. In a few countries, people believe the future of land travel lies with an entirely different kind of train. Called maglevs, these trains "fly" less than an inch above the track, raised and propelled by magnetism.

Star performers
The Eurostar trains operate between England and Continental Europe. They can accelerate to 185mph only when they reach the specially built, high-speed railroad lines in France. The speed of the trains through southern England is limited because they run on normal track. Work on a new, British, high-speed line, the Channel Tunnel Rail Link between London St. Pancras and Folkestone, is underway. It is expected to be completed in 2007 at a cost of more than $8 billion.

Scandinavian shuttle
These sleek, three-car, stainless-steel electric trains began running late in 1999 on a new railroad built to link the center of Oslo, the capital of Norway, with the new Gardermoen Airport, 30 miles to the north of the city. The maximum speed of these trains is 130mph, which enables them to cover the journey in just over 19 minutes. The line includes Norway's longest railroad tunnel at just under 8½ miles.

Virgin express
Britain's Virgin Trains is investing a lot of money in new high-speed electric trains for its West Coast route between London and Glasgow. Work on upgrading old track to carry the trains is also underway. If all goes to plan, journey times between the two cities will be reduced from just over five hours in 1999 to just under four hours in 2005.

High-speed magnetism

Japanese maglev (short for magnetic levitation) trains have reached the astonishing speed of 343mph on this specially constructed Yamanashi test line. This outstrips the world's fastest wheeled train, the TGV, by 24mph. Maglevs are so speedy because they float above their track. They do not have wheels and they do not touch the rails. Rails solved the problem of the slowing force of friction between wheels and roads. Maglevs are the answer to reducing friction between wheels and rails.

Spanish AVE

Based on the design of the French TGV, the average operational speed of these trains is around 135mph.

French TGV

A slightly modified TGV unit set the current world speed record for a train in a trial in 1990, reaching 320mph.

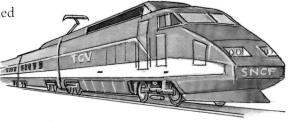

British Pendolino

A new generation of British high-speed tilting trains, designed to reach speeds of 135mph.

German ICE

A former world speed record holder in 1988, reaching 250mph. These trains entered into service in 1991.

Italian Pendolino

These trains run at speeds of around 155mph on the existing network in Italy, tilting as they travel around curves.

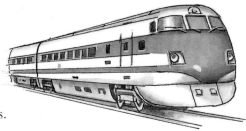

high-speed lines – existing or under construction

planned high-speed lines

Oslo · Stockholm

Glasgow · Edinburgh Göteborg

Belfast

Dublin Liverpool Copenhagen

Cork Manchester

Cardiff Hamburg

Bristol London Berlin

Hanover

Bonn Leipzig

Rennes Paris Prague

Nantes Strasbourg

Orléans Munich Vienna

Bratislava

Bordeaux Lyon Zagreb

Bilbao Turin Milan Ljubljana

Porto San Toulouse Genoa

Sebastián Marseille La Spézia

Nice

Madrid Rome

Lisbon Barcelona

Huelva Naples

Cádiz Alicante Brindisi

Málaga Palermo

On the move in Europe

Many European railroads are planning to develop high-speed rail networks over the next few years. One of the fastest routes will be the high-speed link between Madrid and Barcelona in Spain. The line will have some of the world's fastest passenger trains in service, running at speeds of up to 215mph. By 2007, Spain will have 4,500 miles of high-speed rail networks with a fleet of over 280 trains.

By 2004 in France, tilting trains will cut around 30 minutes off the journey time between Paris and Toulouse. Some of the fastest short-distance trains are running in Norway between Oslo and Gardermoen Airport. They travel at up to 130mph and cover 30 miles in just 19 minutes.

FLOATING TRAINS

Maglev (magnetically levitated) trains need their own specially constructed tracks, called guideways, to move along. The trains are raised and propelled by powerful electromagnets. The special thing about magnets is that "unlike" poles (north and south) attract each other or pull together, while "like" poles (north and north, or south and south) repel or push apart. To make an electromagnet, an electric current flows through a wire or other conductor. When the direction of the current is changed, the magnetic poles switch, too.

A maglev train rises when one set of electromagnets beneath it repels another set in the guideway. The maglev is propelled by other electromagnets changing magnetic fields (switching poles). A set of electromagnets in the guideway ahead attracts electromagnets beneath the train, pulling it forward. As the train passes, the electromagnetic fields are switched. The maglev is repelled and pushed onward to the next set of magnets on the guideway.

The main advantage of maglevs over normal wheeled trains is that they are faster because they are not slowed by friction. In tests in Germany in 1993, a maglev train reached speeds of 280mph. Maglevs are also quieter and use less energy than wheeled trains.

Maglevs get moving
The technology behind maglevs was developed in the 1960s. The world's first service opened at Birmingham City Airport in Britain in the mid-1980s. Japan and Germany now lead the field in developing the technology. When the German Transrapid maglevs start running between Berlin and Hamburg in 2005, they will provide the world's first high-speed intercity maglev service.

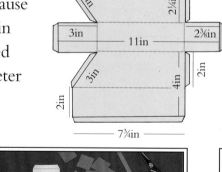

MODEL MAGLEV
You will need: yellow card, pencil, ruler, scissors, red card, green card, glue and glue brush, blue card, double-sided scotch tape, 12 x 4in wooden board, bradawl, two 3⅛in lengths thin dowel, wood glue, green and red paint, paintbrush, water pot, four magnets with holes drilled in their centers.

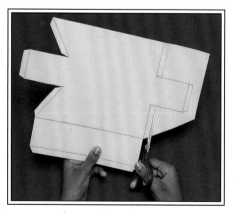

1 Copy the template on to a thin piece of yellow card. The tabs around the side of the template should be ⅛in wide. Carefully cut around the outline.

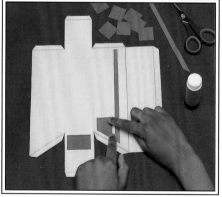

2 Cut two strips of red card and glue them to each side of the template as shown. Cut the green card into window shapes and glue them to the front and sides.

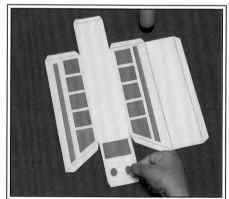

3 Continue to glue the windows to each side of the train to make two even rows. Cut two small blue card circles for headlights. Glue them to the front of the train as shown.

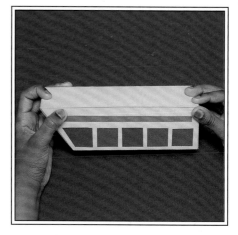

4 Leave the train template until the glue is completely dry. Then carefully use a pair of scissors and a ruler to score along the dotted lines for the tabs and the folds of the train.

5 Bend along the scored lines to form the basic shape of the train as shown above. Then cut small strips of double-sided scotch tape and stick them along each tab.

6 Stick the front and back sections of the train to the tabs on one side of the train. Repeat for the other side. Then stick the base section of the train to the opposite side.

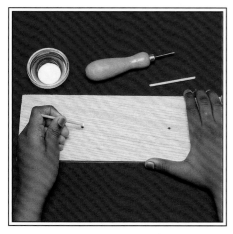

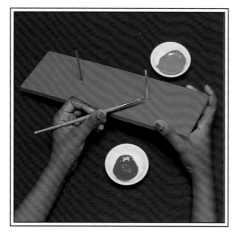

7 Use a bradawl to pierce two holes in the wooden base, 3½in in from each end. Enlarge with a pencil. Put wood glue on the end of each piece of dowel and push one into each hole.

8 When the glue is dry give the base a coat of green paint. Paint two coats, letting the first dry before you apply the second. Then paint the dowel uprights a bright red.

9 Press the two magnets together so that they repel. These sides are the same poles – north or south. Use double-sided tape to fix the magnets to the base with like poles facing up.

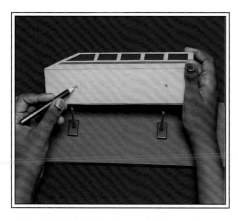

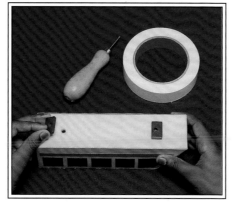

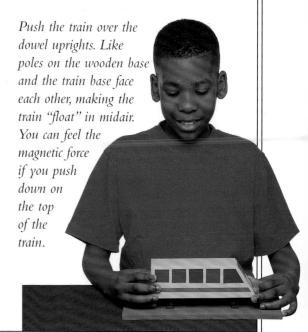

Push the train over the dowel uprights. Like poles on the wooden base and the train base face each other, making the train "float" in midair. You can feel the magnetic force if you push down on the top of the train.

10 Hold the base of the train up to the dowel uprights. Mark two points in the center of the base the same distance as between the uprights. Pierce through the marks.

11 Push magnets over the dowel uprights to repel those on the base. Take them off and tape them over the holes in the train base so that these like poles face upward.

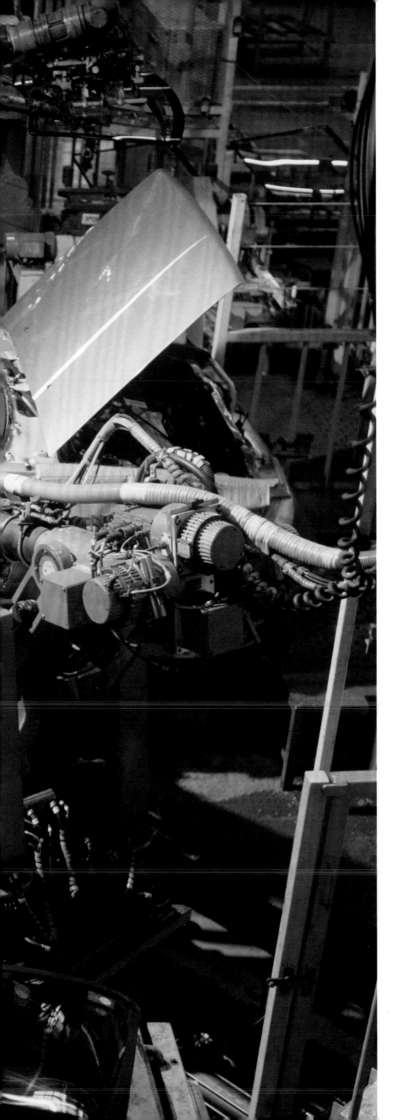

CARS

Millions of individuals and families in the world own a car. Compared with trains, boats and planes, motor cars are an affordable means of independent, door-to-door travel. They touch the everyday lives of ordinary people – even those who do not own one – in the way they have transformed both city and countryside. This journey through automobile history will make traveling by car more interesting. You will not only understand how a car works, but also learn about the improvements that have been made through the decades, see the changing fashions in design, and go behind the scenes of a Formula One event.

AUTHOR
Peter Harrison
CONSULTANT
Peter Cahill

THE JOURNEY BEGINS

CARS MAKE people mobile in a way that would have been impossible only a century ago. Then, a journey by road of just 30 miles could have taken an entire day. Nowadays, we can travel this distance in half an hour. The ability to go where you want, when you want, quickly, makes traveling much easier. Millions of people all over the world use cars to travel to work or to go shopping, to go on vacation and to visit friends and relations.

Horse-drawn carriages and carts and walking were the main forms of road transportation for thousands of years before cars. Many roads were badly made. Because cars moved under their own power, and encouraged better road building, they allowed people to travel much more.

Hold on tight
Very early cars such as this Velo, made in Germany in 1893 by Karl Benz, had no covering bodywork. When Benz's daughter Clara went driving, she sat high above the road with very little to hang onto if the car hit a bump in the road.

By the numbers
The tachometer (rev. counter), speedometer and clock from a Rolls–Royce Silver Ghost have solid brass fittings and glass covers. They were assembled by hand. The instruments on early cars were often made by skilled craftworkers. The Silver Ghost was made continuously from 1906 until 1925.

Bold as brass
A gleaming brass horn and lamp are proud examples of the detailed work that went into making the first cars. Early cars were made with materials that would be far too expensive for most people nowadays. Seats were upholstered with thickly padded leather, because the cars had poor suspension and bumped a lot. This prevented the drivers and passengers from being jolted up and down too much.

Old bruiser

This Bentley was built before 1931, when the company was taken over by Rolls–Royce. Bentley built powerful and sturdy sports cars, some weighing up to 3,730lb. They won many car races in the 1920s and 1930s, such as the Le Mans 24-hour race in France. Big cars such as these were built on heavy metal chassis (frames). They had wood-framed bodies covered in metal and leather, huge headlamps and large, wire-spoked wheels.

Egg on wheels

In the 1950s and 1960s, car makers began to make very small cars, such as this German BMW Isetta. Around 160,000 Isettas were produced between 1955 and 1962. Manufacturers developed small cars because they were cheaper to buy and to run, and used less parking space. The Isetta, like so many of the microcars, was powered by a small motorcycle engine.

Cool cruisin'

Cadillac was an American company known for its stylish designs. This Cadillac from the 1950s, with its large tail fins and shiny chrome, is a typical example. Many cars from the 1950s and 1960s, including this one, are known as classic cars. People like to collect them and restore them to their original condition.

Redhead

The Italian car maker Ferrari has a reputation for making very fast, very expensive cars. This 1985 Testarossa has a top speed of 180mph. Very few people can afford to own such a car. Even if they have the money, it takes great driving skill to get the best out of one.

Going nowhere?

The success of the car has its downside. Millions of people driving cars causes problems such as traffic jams and air pollution. Also, the building of new roads can spoil the countryside. These issues are being debated all over the world.

THE EARLIEST CARS

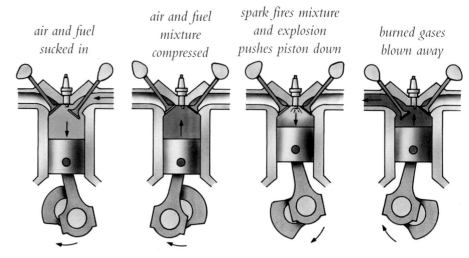

air and fuel sucked in

air and fuel mixture compressed

spark fires mixture and explosion pushes piston down

burned gases blown away

AMONG THE most important builders of early cars and car engines were the Germans Nikolaus Otto, Karl Benz and Gottlieb Daimler. In the late 1800s, they built the first internal combustion engines using sprockets and chains to connect the engine to the wheels. Car engines are called internal (inside) combustion (burning) engines because they burn a mixture of fuel and air inside a small chamber. People had long been trying to find ways to make engines for road transport. In 1770, the Frenchman Nicholas-Joseph Cugnot made a steam engine that drove a three-wheeled cart. It was too heavy to use, however, and only two were built. The achievement of Benz, Otto and Daimler was to make a small engine that could produce enough power for road vehicles. The earliest cars are known as veteran (built before 1905) and Edwardian (built between 1905 and 1919). They were not as reliable as modern vehicles, but were sometimes more finely built.

Suck, squeeze, bang, blow

A car's piston (like an upturned metal cup) moves in a rhythm of four steps called the Otto cycle, after Nikolaus Otto. First, it moves down to suck in fuel mixed with air. Then it pushes up and compresses (squeezes) the mixture. The spark plug ignites the fuel. The bang of the explosion pushes the piston down again. When the piston moves up again, it blows out the burned gases.

Trim trike

The three-wheeled Benz Motorwagen was first made in 1886. It was steered by a small hand lever on top of a tall steering column. Karl Benz began his career building carriages. He used this training when he built his first car in 1885. By 1888 Benz was employing 50 people to build his Motorwagens.

Follow my leader

Soon after the first cars were being driven on the roads, accidents started to happen. Until 1904, there was a law requiring a person carrying a red flag to walk in front of the car. This forced the car driver to go slowly. The flag was to warn people that a car was coming.

Remember this

Important military gentlemen pose for photos with their cars. They are not in the driving seats, however. They had chauffeurs to drive the cars for them. Car owners in the early 1900s liked to show their cars off. They often posed for photographs to keep for souvenirs.

Bad weather

Early cars were hard to control at times because their braking and steering systems were not very effective. When bad weather such as snow made the ground slippery the car could easily run off the road. Even in modern cars with efficient brakes, and good tires and steering, winter weather can make driving difficult.

Look out!

The car horns that early drivers sounded to warn pedestrians were very different from those in modern cars. When the driver squeezed the rubber bulb, air traveled through the tube and made a noise when it came out of the end.

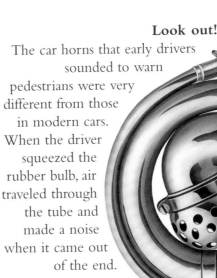

Nose-to-tail horses

This photograph from the late 1800s shows why we talk about nose-to-tail traffic jams. Before cars were invented, most road transportation was by horse-drawn carriage. City streets in those days could become just as jammed with vehicles as they do today.

All wrapped up

Drivers at the turn of the century wore thick goggles to protect their eyes, because their cars had no windshield nor, indeed, any protective bodywork. The roads were not smooth and stones and dust were flung up by the wheels. Cold winds felt even colder in a moving, open car, so thick caps and heavy driving clothes were worn to keep warm.

WHEELS IN MOTION

BEFORE A CAR MOVES, the engine must change the up-and-down movement of the pistons into the round-and-round movement of a shaft (rod) that turns the wheels. With the engine running, the driver presses down the clutch and pushes the gear stick into first gear in the gearbox. The engine turns a shaft called a crankshaft. The power from the turning crankshaft is then transmitted through the gearbox to the wheels on the road. The wheels on the road turn forward due to the combined movement. The wheels turn backward when the driver pushes the gear stick into reverse gear.

This project shows you how to make a simple machine that creates a similar motion, where one kind of movement that goes round and round can be turned into another kind of movement that goes up and down.

Wind up

The earliest cars did not have a starter motor. The driver had to put a starting handle into the front of the car. This connected the handle to the engine's crankshaft to turn it. Turning the handle was hard work and could break the driver's arm if not done correctly. Button-operated starters began to be used as early as 1912.

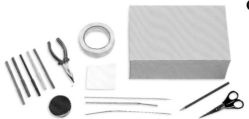

CHANGING MOTION

You will need: *shoebox, thin metal rod about ⅛in diameter, pliers, jam jar lid, masking tape, scissors, thick plastic straw, pencil, piece of stiff paper, at least four color felt-tipped pens, thin plastic straw.*

1 Place the shoebox narrow-side-down on a flat surface. With one hand push the metal rod through the center, making sure your other hand will not get jabbed by the rod.

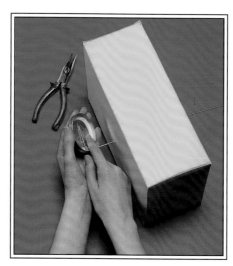

2 Bend the rod at right angles where it comes out of the box. Attach the jam jar lid to it with adhesive tape. Push the lid until it rests against the side of the box.

3 Carefully use the pliers to bend the piece of rod sticking out of the other side of the box. This will make a handle for the piston that will be able to turn easily.

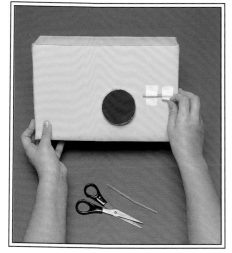

4 Cut a piece of thick plastic straw about 2in long and tape it to the side of the box close to the jam jar lid. Make sure that it just sticks up beyond the edge of the box.

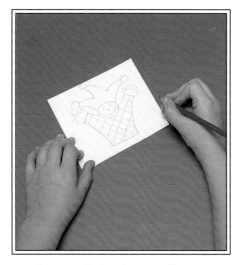

5 Draw a design in pencil on a piece of stiff paper. Copy the jester shown in this project or draw a simple clown. Choose something that looks good when it moves.

6 Using the felt-tipped pens, color the design until it looks the way you want it to. The more colorful the figure is, the nicer it will look on the top of the piston.

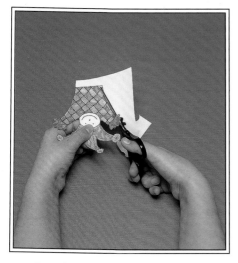

7 Carefully cut the finished drawing out of the paper. Make sure you have a clean-edged design. Try not to smudge the felt-tipped color with your fingers.

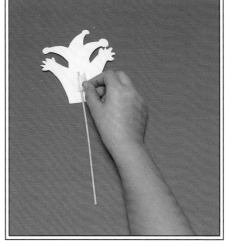

8 Use the adhesive tape to attach the thin plastic straw to the bottom of the drawing. About ¾in of straw should be attached.

9 Slide the straw attached to the drawing into the straw taped to the back of the box. It will come out of the other end. Push down so that the straw touches the edge of the jam jar lid.

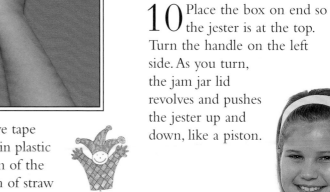

10 Place the box on end so the jester is at the top. Turn the handle on the left side. As you turn, the jam jar lid revolves and pushes the jester up and down, like a piston.

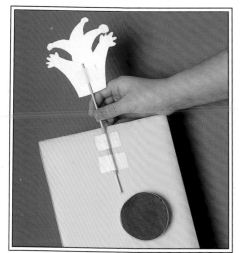

MASS PRODUCTION

ONCE WAYS had been found to power a small, wheeled road vehicle, more and more people wanted to own a car. Having one made getting around so much easier. However, early cars were built by hand, piece by piece, which took time. In 1903, the American inventor Henry Ford produced the Model A Ford, the first car designed to be built in large numbers. It gave him the idea to mass-produce all the separate parts of a car in the same place, then have his workers assemble many cars at the same time. This became known as the production-line method. By 1924, 10 million Ford cars had been built and sold. Today, almost all cars are built on production lines. Robots (automated machines) do much of the work. Some cars are still built by hand, but they can only be built very slowly. For example, the British sports-car maker Morgan made 11 cars a week in 1999. In comparison, the Ford Motor Company built about 138,000 cars a week in the same year.

Tin Lizzie
The Model T Ford was the world's first mass-produced (assembled on a production line) car. Millions were made and sold all over the world. Today, people collect examples of these cars, maintaining, restoring and repairing them, often to a gleaming state. It is unlikely that they would have been so well cared for by their original owners.

Herbert's big idea
The Austin Seven was one of the most popular cars ever. This version is a sporting two-seater. Between 1922 and 1938 there were many versions, including race cars and even vans. The Austin Motor Company was founded by Herbert Austin in 1903. The company allowed other car makers to build the Austin Seven in France, Japan, the United States and Germany.

Beetling about
In 1937, the German government founded a car company to build cheap cars. The car, designed by Dr Ferdinand Porsche, was called the Volkswagen, meaning "people's car," but it gained the nickname of the "Beetle" because of its unusual shape. Some people painted their Beetles for fun. By the 1960s, the car was popular worldwide. By 2000, over 21 million Volkswagons had been sold.

Next one, please

Modern cars are made with the help of machines in factories. Each machine does a different job. Some weld metal parts together, others attach parts and secure fastenings, others spray paint. The car's metal body parts come together on a moving track that runs past each machine. Making cars like this means they can be put together quickly and in vast numbers.

Big yellow taxi

For people without a car, such as tourists, taxis are a convenient way of getting around in towns and cities. Taxi drivers try to find the best short cuts for an easy journey. Hiring a taxicab also means that people don't have to find a place to park. The bright yellow "checker cabs" in New York, became a symbol for the city all over the world, because everyone recognized them.

FACT BOX

• Speedometers (dials showing a car's speed) were first used in cars in 1901.

• The American car maker Buick started life as a bath tub manufacturer.

• By 1936, more than 50 percent of all American families owned a car.

The people's servant

The Trabant was from East Germany. Many millions were built for ordinary people. Its name comes from a Hungarian word meaning "servant," and the Trabant served as a cheap, reliable car across Eastern Europe. This 601 model was first made in 1964.

Alec's big idea

Launched in 1959, the Morris Mini Minor was one of the most revolutionary cars of the last 50 years. It was cheap to buy and cheap to run, easy to drive and easy to park. Despite its small size, it could carry four people comfortably. The car's designer, Alec Issigonis, a British citizen of Greek parentage, also designed the Morris Minor, a small family car launched in 1948.

THE ENGINE

A CAR'S ENGINE is made up of metal parts. They are designed to work together smoothly and efficiently. In older cars, a valve called a carburetor feeds a mixture of air and fuel into the cylinder, where the mixture is burned to produce power. Newer cars often use an injection system, which measures and controls the amount of fuel into the engine more accurately. To keep the engine cool, water is pumped from the radiator and circulated around chambers in the cylinder block. The waste gases created by the burned fuel are carried away by the exhaust system. The engine sucks in the air and gasoline mixture and allows it to burn. To help the moving parts move against each other smoothly, they are lubricated with oil from the engine oil sump. A pump squirts the oil onto the parts.

A car's electrical power is driven by an alternator. The electrical current is stored in the battery. This provides the electricity for the spark that ignites the fuel mixture, for the car's electrical system, and for its heater, lights, radio, windshield wipers and instruments.

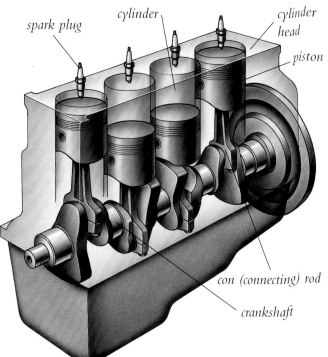

spark plug   cylinder   cylinder head   piston   con (connecting) rod   crankshaft

Working together

Most car engines have four cylinders. In each cylinder a piston moves up and down. Four rods, one from each piston, turn metal joints attached to the crankshaft. As the rods turn the joints, the crankshaft moves around and around. The movement is transmitted to the wheels, using the gearbox to control how fast the wheels turn relative to the engine.

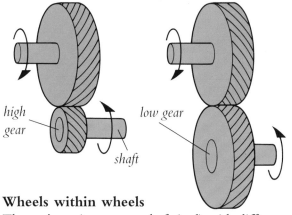

high gear   low gear   shaft

Wheels within wheels

The car's engine turns a shaft (rod) with different sized gears (toothed wheels) on it. High gears are used for more speed because when a big wheel turns a small one, it turns faster. The gear system is called the transmission, because it transmits (moves) the engine's power to the car's wheels. Many cars have five forward gears. The biggest is needed for slow speeds, and the smallest for high speeds. When the car goes round corners, its wheels move at different speeds. A set of gears called the differential allows the wheels to do this.

Turbo tornado

This 1997 Dodge engine can make a car go especially fast because it has a turbocharger that forces the fuel and air mixture faster and more efficiently into the engine cylinder head. Turbochargers are driven by waste exhaust gases drawn away from the exhaust system, which is a way of turning the waste gases to good use. Turbochargers are very effective at boosting engine power.

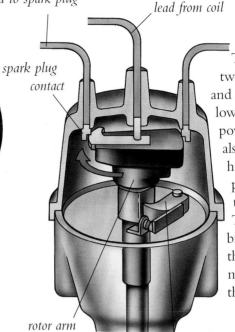

Power control
The distributor has two jobs. It connects and disconnects low-value electric power to the coil. It also supplies high-value electric power from the coil to each spark plug. This makes a spark big enough to ignite the air and fuel mixture at exactly the right time.

lead to spark plug

lead from coil

spark plug contact

rotor arm

contact breaker

What you see is what you get
This vintage racing Bentley displays its twin carburetors mounted on a supercharger (a mechanically driven device similar to a turbocharger) in front of the engine. The water pipes from the radiator to the engine, electric leads, plug leads and large open exhaust pipes can all be seen.

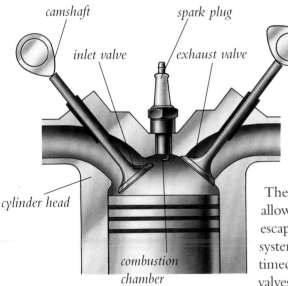

camshaft

spark plug

inlet valve

exhaust valve

cylinder head

combustion chamber

Double movement
The camshaft opens and closes the inlet and exhaust valves. The valves are fitted into the cylinder head, and open and close holes in the combustion chamber. The exhaust valve opens to allow burnt waste gases to escape into the car's exhaust system. The spark plug is timed to spark when both valves have closed both holes.

See and be seen
The lights used on early cars usually burned either oil or gas. Oil was carried in a small container in the bottom of the lamp. Gas was created by dissolving in water tablets of carbide (carbon mixed with metal) carried in a canister.

Blow them away
Mercedes-Benz fitted a supercharger to this 1936 540K to add power to the engine. The German company first used superchargers on their racing cars in 1927. This method of adding power had first been used on airplane engines in 1915.

IN THE RIGHT GEAR

GEARS ARE toothed wheels that interlock with each other to transfer movement. They have been used in machines of many kinds for over 2,000 years. In a car gearbox, the gears are arranged on shafts so that they interlock when the driver changes from one gear to the next. Cars have four, five or six forward gears according to the design, use and cost of the car. Several gears are needed because driving requires different combinations of speed and force at different times.

The largest gear wheel is low gear. It turns slower than the higher gears. It provides more force and less speed for when the car is moving from stop, or going uphill. In high gear, less force and more speed is provided. This gear wheel is the smallest and rotates the fastest. The project connects two gears to show the beautiful patterns that gears can make. Then you can make your own three-gear machine.

Uphill struggle
Pushing a car up a steep hill in a 1920s car rally put a lot of strain on the low gears in a car. On steep slopes, first and second gears are often the only ones that a driver can use. Fourth gear is for flat roads and fifth gear for cruising at high speeds.

DRAWING WITH GEARS

You will need: pair of compasses, 8½ x 11in sheet of white paper, black pen, scissors, 8½ x 11in sheet of thin cardboard, two strips of corrugated cardboard, sticky tape, three colored felt-tipped pens.

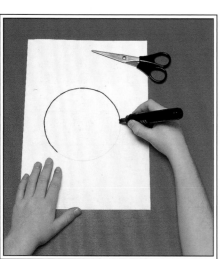

1 Using the pair of compasses, trace a 5½in diameter circle on the paper. Draw over it with the pen and cut it out. On the cardboard, trace, draw and cut out another circle with a diameter of 4½in.

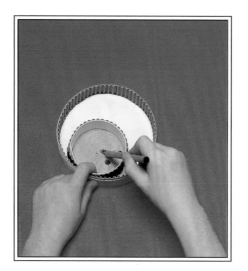

2 Tape corrugated cardboard around the circles, as shown. Make a hole in the small circle wide enough for the tip of a felt-tipped pen. Turn the small wheel inside the larger. Trace the path in felt-tipped pen.

3 Make a second hole in the small wheel. Turn the small gear inside the larger using another felt-tipped pen. Make a third hole in the small wheel and use a third color pen to create an exciting, geometric design.

THREE-GEAR MACHINE

You will need: *pair of compasses, 8½ x 11in sheet of cardboard, pen, scissors, three strips of corrugated cardboard, sticky tape, 8½ x 11in piece of fiberboard, glue, 2½in piece of ½in-diameter wooden dowel, three push pins.*

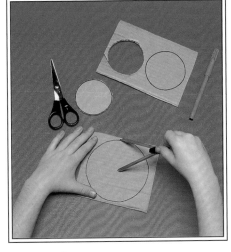

1 Use the compasses to trace one 5½in diameter and two 4½in diameter circles in the cardboard. Draw around the circle edges with the pen and cut the circles out.

2 Carefully wrap the strips of corrugated cardboard around the circles, using one strip per circle, corrugated side out. Tape each strip to the bottom of the circles.

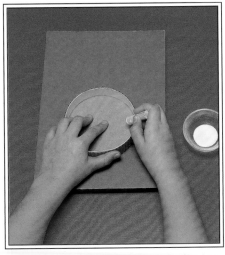

3 Place the largest gear wheel on the piece of fiberboard. Hold the gear down and glue the dowel onto the side of the gear base at the edge of the wheel. Set aside until it is dry.

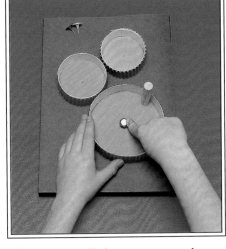

4 Position all three gears on the fiberboard, edges just touching each other. Pin each of them firmly to the fiberboard with a push pin but allow them to turn.

6 Now you have a three-gear machine where the energy from each gear is being transferred to the other, just like the gears in a car.

5 Gently turn the dowel on the largest gear. As that gear turns, the two others that are linked together by the corrugated cardboard will turn against it. See how they move in opposite directions to each other.

SAFE RIDE AND HANDLING

Most modern cars have four wheels. The wheels tend to be placed one at each corner, which helps to distribute the car's weight evenly on the road. An evenly balanced car rides and handles well and has good road grip and braking. Engine power usually drives either the front or rear wheels. However, with the growth in off-road driving for pleasure, all-wheel drive has become popular. Driving safely at speed in a straight line or round corners is a test of how well a car has been designed. Many cars now have power-assist steering to make steering easier. Tires are an important part of good road handling. The tread pattern and grooves are designed to make the tire grip the road efficiently, especially in wet, slippery conditions.

Big bopper
The French tire manufacturer Michelin has been making tires since 1888. The Michelin brand has been known for many years by the sign of a human figure that looks as though it is made out of tires.

Gripping stuff
Tire tread patters have raised pads, small grooves and water-draining channels to grip the road surface. There are different kinds of tires for cars, busses, trucks and tractors. Tire makers also make tires for different road conditions. Examples include winter tires and special run-flat tires that stay hard even when they are damaged.

Dig deep
Tractor tires are very deeply grooved. This allows them to grip hard in slippery mud. The width of the tires spreads the weight of the heavy vehicle over soft ground. The tires are high so that the tractor can ride easily over obstacles on the ground, such as big rocks.

Burn the rubber

Racing car tires are wide so that the car can go as fast as possible while maintaining grip and stability on the road. They are made in various very hard mixtures of rubber to cope with varying amounts of heat generated by racing in different conditions. Ordinary tires would melt.

Out for a spin

Until very light alloy wheels became available in the last 20 years, sports cars often had wire-spoke wheels. These combined strength with lightness, both important features in a sports car. When a sports car brakes or turns sharply, modern wire-spoke wheels are strong enough to take the strain.

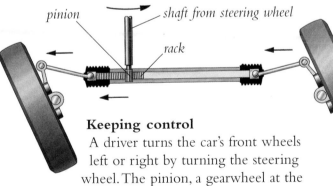

pinion   *shaft from steering wheel*

rack

Keeping control

A driver turns the car's front wheels left or right by turning the steering wheel. The pinion, a gearwheel at the bottom of the steering shaft, interlocks with a toothed rack. This is connected to the wheels via a system of joints and wheels. As the steering wheel turns, the movement of the pinion along the rack turns the road wheels.

King of the castle

Very large trucks that carry heavy loads use enormous tires to spread the weight. This flatbed truck has been fitted with earthmover tires for fun. Look how much bigger they are than the car the truck is rolling over.

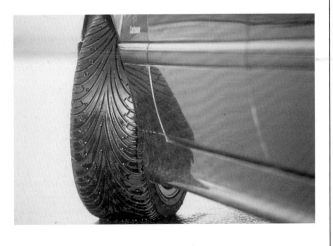

Firm in the wet

Traveling at speed on a wet road can be dangerous. Water can form a film that is able to lift a tire clear of the road surface for several seconds. To prevent this, tire makers mold drain channels into the tire's tread to push the water away from under the tire as it rotates.

SPEED CONTESTS

RACING CARS against one another to test their speed and endurance has gone on for over 100 years. The American car maker Henry Ford, for example, designed and built racing cars before he set up the Ford car factory in 1903. Many kinds of car race now take place, including stock car, rally, speedway and drag racing. The FIA (*Fédération Internationale de l'Automobile*) makes rules about issues such as the tracks, the design and power of the cars, and the safety of drivers and spectators.

The fastest and most powerful kind of track racing is Formula One, also known as Grand Prix racing. The cars can travel up to 200mph on straight sections of track. Because the races are so exciting, the best drivers are paid in the millions. Formula One winners, such as David Coulthard and Michael Schumacher, are international celebrities. Technological advances in production-line cars have often been developed and tested in Grand Prix cars.

Your move
When racing drivers complete a race and cross the finishing line, a race official waves a black and white flag known as the checkered flag. The black and white pattern of squares on the finishing flag looks like the pattern on a chessboard. It is known all over the world as the sign of motor racing.

Monster motors
Early Grand Prix cars, such as this 10.2 litre Fiat, had enormous engines. Grand Prix racing began in France in 1904 and slowly spread to other countries. The *Association Internationale des Automobiles Clubs Reconnus* (AIACR) set the rules for races until it was reformed as the FIA in 1946.

Round the bend
The Italian car maker Ferrari has been making racing cars since 1940. Here the German Michael Schumacher, driving the Ferrari F399, rounds a curve on the 3 mile Catalunya circuit at the 1999 Barcelona Grand Prix.

FACT BOX

• Between 1980 and 1982, the French driver Alain Prost won 51 Formula One races, the highest number so far achieved by any Grand Prix driver.

• Ayrton Senna won the Monaco Grand Prix a record six times between 1987 and 1993.

• The racetrack at Indianapolis was known as "the brickyard" because it was partly paved with bricks until 1961.

Take-off

The speeds at which rally cars travel mean they often fly over the tops of the hills on the course. The driver and navigator of this car in the 1999 Portuguese Rally are strapped into their seats to protect them from the tremendous thump that will come when the car's four wheels touch the ground in a second or two.

Take it to the limit

The heat generated by a Top Fuel drag racer's engine at the 1996 NHRA (*National Hot Rod Association*) Winternational makes the air vibrate around it. Drag races are short, like sprint races for athletes. The races take place over a straight course only 440 yards long, and the cars can reach speeds of 250mph. The flat spoilers on the front and rear of the cars are pushed down by the air rushing past, helping to keep the car on the road.

The chase

Tight bends are a test of driving skills for Formula One drivers. The cars brake hard from very high speeds as they approach the bend. Drivers try not to leave any gap that following cars could use for overtaking. As the drivers come out of the bend they accelerate as hard as is possible without skidding and going into a spin.

Making a splash

Rally car driving is extremely tough on the cars and on the drivers. Cars drive over deserts, mud-filled roads, rivers, snow and many other obstacles. The cars follow the same route, but start at different times. The course is divided into separate sections known as Special Stages. There is a time limit for each stage. The winner of the rally is the car that has the fastest overall time.

Race crash

The Brazilian Mauricio Gugelmin's car soars into the air at the 1985 French Grand Prix, crashing to the ground upside down. The driver survived and has since taken part in many Grand Prix races. Safety regulations have improved in recent years.

RACE TRACKS

PEOPLE HAVE been racing cars on specially designed public circuits (tracks) almost since cars were invented. The first race on a special circuit took place in 1894 in France. The Italian track at Monza is one of the oldest racing circuits. It was built for the 1922 Italian Grand Prix. Among the most well-known tracks are Silverstone and Brands Hatch in Great Britain, Indianapolis in the United States, the Nurbürgring in Germany, and Monaco. Millions of people all over the world watch the races at these tracks and on television. The teams and the drivers compete furiously with one another to prove whose car is the fastest. Sometimes the competition can be so fierce it is deadly. Ayrton Senna, a top Brazilian racing driver, died in a fatal crash at Imola in Italy in 1994. In this project, you can build your own race track, specially designed to let your cars build up speed on a steep slope, and race against a partner to see whose car is the fastest.

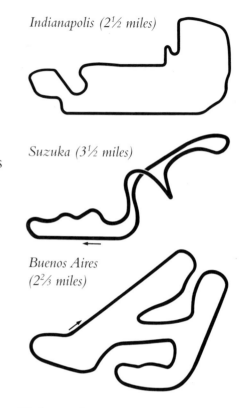

Indianapolis (2½ miles)

Suzuka (3½ miles)

Buenos Aires (2⅔ miles)

TESTING GROUND

You will need: *10in of 3in-diameter cardboard tube, scissors, small paintbrush, blue paint, three strips of colored paper 2½ x 1in, masking tape, two strips of white paper ½ x 3in, pencil, red and black felt-tipped pen, pieces of colored and white paper, toothpicks, 8½ x 11in sheet of stiff red cardboard, ruler, two small model cars.*

Twist and turn

All racetracks, such as those shown above, test the skill of the drivers and the speed and handling of the racing cars. They combine bends with straight stretches. Sharp bends are known as hairpin bends. Most tracks are between 2½ and 3½ miles in length.

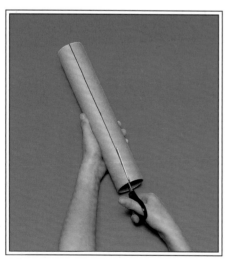

1 Use the scissors to carefully cut the cardboard tube in half along its length. Hold the tube in one hand but make sure you keep the scissor blades away from your hands.

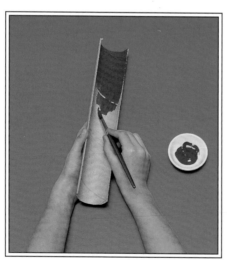

2 Use the paintbrush to apply a thick coat of blue paint to the inside of both halves of the tube. To give a strong color, paint a second coat after the first has dried.

3 Use masking tape to stick the ten narrow strips of colored paper together. Tape them along their widths to make a flexible bend. This joins the racetrack together.

PROJECT

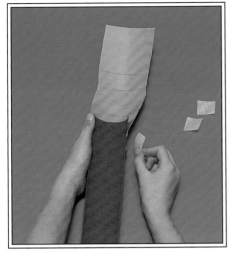

4 Now take the flexible bend you have made from strips of paper. Tape it to one end of one of the painted halves of the tube. Use small pieces of masking tape.

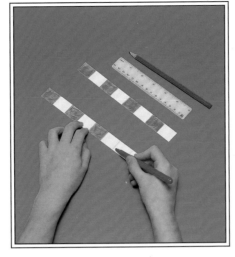

5 Use a pencil to mark eight equal ½in blocks on both of the strips of white paper. Color in alternate red blocks with a felt-tipped pen to make striped crash barriers.

6 Color in a 1½ x 3in piece of paper with ½in black and white squares. Cut the other paper pieces into pennants (forked flags). Tape the flags to toothpicks.

7 Cut three 3in-wide strips from the sheet of stiff cardboard. Use scissors to cut a semicircle out of the top of each of the strips.

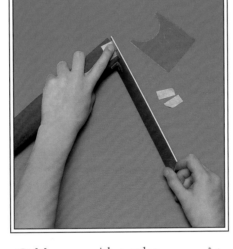

8 Measure with a ruler and cut the three strips to varying heights of 8in, 5½in and 2¾in. Tape them to the underside of half of the tube, fitting them on at the semicircle shapes to support the half tube in a gradual slope.

9 Tape the second half of the tube to the end of the flexible bend. Put in the crash barriers. Now you are ready to roll your toy car down the death-defying slope of your racetrack. Make another racetrack with a friend and you can race each other's cars.

Popping the cork
Race winners Canadian Jacques Villeneuve and Frenchman Jean Alesi celebrate by showering each other with champagne at the Luxembourg Grand Prix in 1997.

COLLECTING

THE CARS that were made many years ago have not been forgotten. They are known as veteran (made before 1905), Edwardian (1905–19), vintage (1919–30) and Classics. Enthusiasts (people with a special interest) all over the world collect and maintain old cars. They value them for many reasons, such as the great care that went into making them, their design, their engine power and their rarity. Clubs such as the AACA (Antique Automobile Club of America) and FIVA (*Fédération Internationale Véhicules Anciens*) exist for the collectors of old American and European cars. There are also specific clubs for owners of particular models of car. Owners like to meet up and compare notes on maintaining their vehicles. Their clubs organize tours and rallies in which owners can drive their cars in working order.

Annual get together
Veteran cars (built before 1905) parade along the sea front in Brighton, England. The London-to-Brighton veteran car run has been held every year (except during wartime) since 1904. It celebrates cars being driven without someone with a red flag walking in front to warn of their approach.

Who stole the roof?
Early vehicles were built on the frames of horse-drawn wagons, so they had little protective bodywork. Drivers and their passengers had to wrap up well when driving.

Room for two?
Frenchman Louis Delage built cars of great engineering skill. The engine of this 1911 racing model was so big that there was little room for the driver. The huge tube in the hood carried exhaust gases to the back of the car.

High roller

The Rolls–Royce Silver Ghost is one of the great early vintage cars. It was first built in 1906. Almost 8,000 were made before production finally stopped in 1925. By that time, fewer people were able to afford such large, expensive cars. Individual buyers could have the car's specification and equipment altered according to their own needs. Several Silver Ghosts were produced as armored cars to protect top British Army generals during World War I.

Mighty midget

The 1930 MG Midget was a powerful small car and clearly deserved its name. The Midget was the first car that the MG company sold in large numbers. Its success allowed the firm to expand and become more widely known.

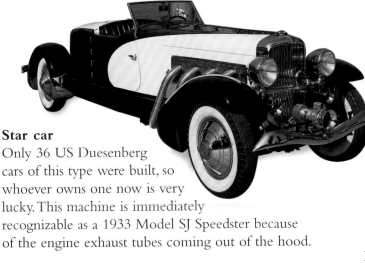

Mint condition

The owners of old cars have to give a great deal of loving care to the car engines. Keeping an original MG Midget engine running demands patience in finding spare parts, maintaining old metal and making regular tests.

Star car

Only 36 US Duesenberg cars of this type were built, so whoever owns one now is very lucky. This machine is immediately recognizable as a 1933 Model SJ Speedster because of the engine exhaust tubes coming out of the hood.

In demand

A 1930s racing car combines style and power, qualities that still give Alfa Romeo its strong reputation. Collectors today value racing cars of the past just as much as old passenger cars. The Italian car maker Alfa Romeo has been building fast cars since 1915.

Starry Ferrari

The Italian company Ferrari is one of the world's greatest car makers. Owning a Ferrari has always been seen as a symbol of wealth and success, so the cars are favorites with movie stars and sportspeople. This 166 Ferrari is from the late 1940s.

OFF-ROAD VEHICLES

Seaside fun
Driving on beaches is difficult because wheels can sink into the wet sand. Vehicles for driving on beaches are built to be very light, with balloon tiiires to spread the vehicle's weight over a wide area.

MOST CARS are designed for driving on smooth roads. There are specialized vehicles, however, that can drive across rough terrain such as mud, desert and stony ground. Usually called off-road vehicles (ORVs) or All-Terrain Vehicles (ATVs), cars of this kind often have four-wheel drive, large tires and tough suspension. They stand high off the ground and have strong bodywork. The earliest ORVs were the US Jeep and the British Land Rover. The Jeep, made by Ford and Willys, was developed during World War II. It was designed to travel across roads damaged by warfare. The Land Rover, built by the Rover company in the late 1940s, was based on the idea of the Jeep. It was intended for farmers who have to drive across difficult terrain. The Land Rover proved useful in all parts of the world where roads were poor or non-existent. Traveling off-road is still a necessity in many places. In recent times, it has also become a leisure activity for drivers who like to test their driving skills on difficult terrain.

Tough cookie
At the start of World War II the US Army developed a vehicle with a sturdy engine, body and framework. The wheels were at the corners for stability over rough ground. The GP (General Purpose) vehicle became known as the Jeep.

No traffic jams
The Lunar Rover, carried to the Moon by *Apollo 17* in 1971, was powered by electricity. The low gravity of the moon meant that it would not sink into soft ground. A wide track and long wheelbase stopped it from turning over if it hit a rock.

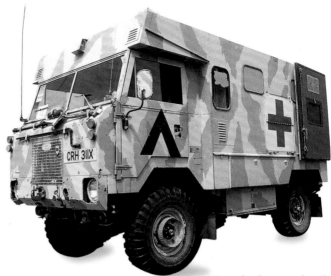

Angel of mercy

Vehicles such as Jeeps help doctors to take medical aid to people living in remote areas where there are few roads. These four-wheel drive vehicles can cross shallow rivers and rough terrain. A specially strengthened underbody protects against damage from water.

Hospital on wheels

Aid agencies such as UNICEF and *Mèdecins Sans Frontières* use specially adapted trucks equipped as mobile hospitals. They help to save lives in times of war and natural disaster. Heavily reinforced bodywork protects patients and easily damaged medical supplies.

Electric caddies

A typical game of golf involves traveling 3 miles or more. Golfers need an easy way to carry heavy golf clubs around the course. Golf carts are simple, light vehicles powered by electricity. They have enough battery life to carry golfers and their clubs from the first to the last hole on the course.

FACT BOX
• The 6,820 mile Paris-Dakar-Cairo Rally is one of the world's best-known off-road races. Founded in 1978 by the French driver Thierry Sabine, the year 2000 race had 600 team members driving 200 motorcycles, 141 cars and 65 trucks.

Get tracking

Half-tracks played an important part in World War II, and still do in modern warfare. They have tracks at the rear to allow them to travel over very broken surfaces such as roads filled with shell holes and debris. The wheels at the front give half-tracks an added mobility that tanks do not have.

Big boss

Large, high, off-road cars such as the Mitsubishi Shogun and commercial SUVs grew increasingly popular from the 1980s. They had four-wheel drive, which made driving on rough ground much easier.

CUSTOM-BUILT

SOMETIMES SERIOUS car enthusiasts decide to adapt a standard model. They might alter the engine to make it run faster, or change the body to make it look different. Cars specially adapted like this are known as custom cars. Custom cars have become very popular since the 1950s, particularly in the United States. The wheels may be taken from one kind of car, the body from a second, the mudguards and engine from others, and the different parts are combined to make a completely original car. The end result can be dramatic. These unusual cars have many different names, such as mean machines, street machines, muscle machines and hot rods. Racing custom cars is a popular activity. Stock cars are custom cars built especially for races in which crashes often occur. Drag racers are incredibly fast and powerful cars built for high speed races over short distances.

Water baby
Surf's up and the muscle machine is on the beach. This cool dude has placed big, wide tires on a sportscar body to spread the car's weight on soft sand. He has been busy with a paintbrush, too, adding flames to his body paint.

Made to measure
This car is a mixture of styles. The driver's cab and steering wheel have been made to look like those in a veteran car. The modern engine is chrome-plated, with all the parts visible. The exhaust-outlet tubes resemble those from a 1930s racing car. The front wheels are bigger than the rear ones.

Soft furnishings
Some people change the insides of their cars to create a truly luxurious look. They replace the standard equipment, for example, with soft leather seats, padded dashboards and chrome-covered gear shifts.

Smokin' steady
The grille on the hood of a customized hot rod is the turbocharger. It can boost the engine to speeds of 250mph. When the car brakes at high speed, its tires make lots of smoke because they are burning from friction with the road.

PROJECT

FLUFFY DICE

You will need: *cuboid box at least 5in square, two 8½ x 11in sheets of white paper, masking tape, scissors, 8-in length of string, 32-in square of furry fabric, pencil, bradawl, glue, circle stencil.*

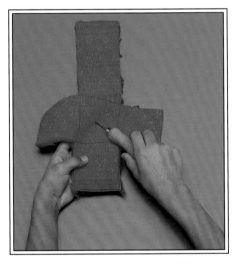

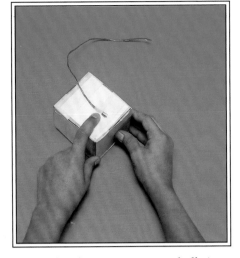

1 Stick white paper around all six surfaces of the box with tape. Use a small piece of masking tape to stick 1¼in of the end of the length of string to one side of the box.

2 Place the fabric furry-side down. Place the box at one edge and draw around it. Then roll the box over and draw around it again. Do six squares like this to form a cross.

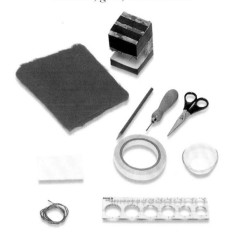

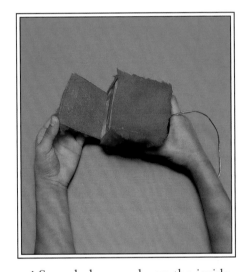

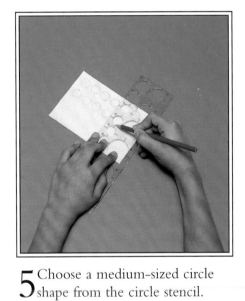

3 Cut out the cross shape. With a bradawl, carefully make a hole in the fur. Place the box face down on the fur where the string is attached. Pull the string through the hole.

4 Spread glue evenly on the inside of each square of the fabric, one at a time. Press the glued material squares onto the box faces.

5 Choose a medium-sized circle shape from the circle stencil. Using a pencil, draw 21 of the same circles onto the piece of white paper.

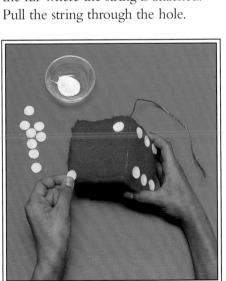

6 Cut out the circles. Glue them onto the furry side of the fabric. Put six dots on one face, five dots on the next, then four, three, two and finally one dot. You could use a real dice to see the correct arrangement.

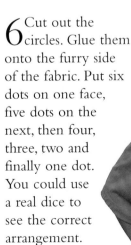

7 Make a second die and hang them in the car for fun. Put them where they will not distract the driver. They should not hang on the windows.

UNUSUAL DESIGNS

CARS ARE often adapted (have their design changed) to suit different needs, or just for fun. Three-wheeled cars, a kind of microcar, are cheap to run and take up less road space than the conventional four-wheeled cars.

Amphibious vehicles that can operate on land and water were built in World War II for fighting. Since then, specialised German, British and Chinese manufacturers have gone on building small numbers of these cars for use in regions with many rivers.

Movie studios often create sensational special effects around cars that appear to have special powers. Then there are the real but wacky cars, made by people who want to create cars that defy the imagination. These have included cars that split down the middle, cars that are covered in fur, and cars that look like sofas and hot dogs.

Frog face
The microcars produced in in the 1950s and 1960s were for driving in towns. This 1959 Messerschmitt had a tiny engine and was just 9ft long. Even so, it had a top speed of 60mph. The top of the car swings over to allow the driver entry. The car was also very cheap to run. It used only a quarter of a gallon of petrol every 15 miles, almost half the fuel consumption of a modern car.

Garden car
This car may look like a garden shed, but in order to travel on a public road it needs to conform to all the regulations of the road. It will have passed an annual inspection for safety and road worthiness. Headlights, turn signals and seatbelts are all installed.

Supermarket beep
A giant supermarket basket has been constructed and installed with a car engine. This vehicle is strictly for fun. Lacking basic safety features such as proper seats, lights and bumpers, it is not allowed to be driven on public roads.

Only in the movies

The 1977 James Bond film, *The Spy Who Loved Me*, featured a car that behaved as though it was also a submarine. It was a British Lotus Elite car body specially altered to create the illusion.

Magic car

Ian Fleming, the creator of James Bond, also wrote a book about a magic car. This became the 1968 film *Chitty Chitty Bang Bang*. The car was an old one that the book's hero, Caractacus Potts, discovered in a junkyard. After restoring it, he discovered it could fly and float.

FACT BOX

• One of the amphibious vehicles used in World War II was called a "duck" after the initials DUKW given it by the manufacturer General Motors. It had six wheels and moved through the water powered by a propeller.

• Microcars, such as the BMW Isetta and the Heinkel Trojan, were also known in the 1950s and 1960s as bubble cars because of their round shapes and large window spaces.

• Race tracks such as Le Mans in France, and Monza in Italy, hosted races in the 1950s and 1960s at which microcars such as the British Berkeley and the Italian Fiat Bianchina raced against each other.

Replica style

This 3-wheeler Triking, a modern replica (copy) of a 1930s Morgan, is a kit car that has been put together. The owner is supplied with all the different body panels and engine parts, and builds the complete car. Kit cars are cheaper than production-line cars, because the costs of assembly and labor are saved.

Web-toed drivers

Cars that can cross water are useful, especially in places where there are rivers but no bridges. Between 1961 and 1968, the German Amphicar company made almost 4,000 amphibious cars. They could reach a speed of 7mph in the water, pushed along by a Triumph Herald engine and two small propellers. On land they could reach 70mph.

COOLING SYSTEM

THE EXPLOSIONS in a car's engine, and the friction caused by its moving parts, create a great deal of heat. If the heat were not kept down, the engine would stop working. The metal parts would expand, seize up and stop. To cool the engine, water from a radiator is pumped through chambers in the cylinder block. The moving water carries heat away from the hottest parts of the engine. The radiator has to be cooled down too. A fan blows air onto it, to cool the water inside. The fan is driven by a belt from the engine crankshaft pulley. This project shows you how to transfer the energy of turning motion from one place to another. It uses a belt to move five reels. In the same way, some of the turning motion of an engine is transferred by a fan belt to the fan.

Rear engine

The air-cooled rear-engined Volkswagen Beetle was designed with an aerodynamic front and no need for a front-mounted radiator. Instead, the engine is cooled by a fan driven by a fan belt, like the one shown here. Engines of this kind are useful in cold climates, where low temperatures can freeze water in radiators.

FAN BELT

You will need: *ruler, 6½-in square of thin cloth, scissors, five spools of thread, 8½ x 11in wooden board, glue or glue stick, pencil, five flat-headed nails 1½in in length, hammer, 3ft length of 1in-wide velvet ribbon, sticky tape, pair of compasses, five pieces of 6in-square colored card, five wooden skewers.*

1 Using the ruler, measure five 1in-wide strips on the thin cloth. The height of the spools of thread should be more than 1in. Use the scissors to cut out each strip.

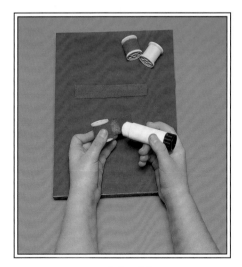

2 Wrap one of the fabric strips around each of the five spools of thread. Glue each strip at the end so that it sits firmly around the spool and does not come loose.

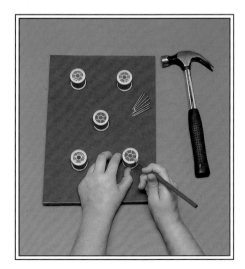

3 Place the spools on the wooden board as shown above. Trace the outlines with a pencil. Put the nails through the center of the reels and hammer them into the board.

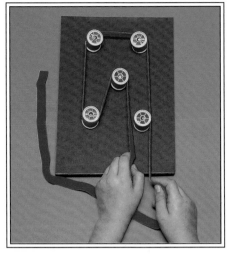

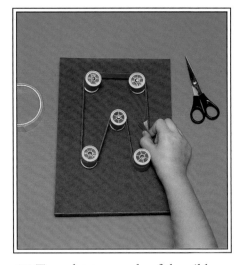

4 Wind the ribbon around the spools with the velvet side against four of the spools. Cut the ribbon at the point where you can join both ends round the fifth spool.

5 Tape the two ends of the ribbon together firmly. Make sure that the ribbon wraps firmly around all of the five spools, but not so tightly that it cannot move.

6 Use the pair of compasses to draw circles about 2¾in in diameter onto the pieces of colored cardboard. Then draw freehand spiral shapes inside each circle.

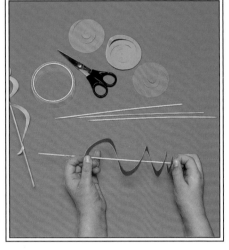

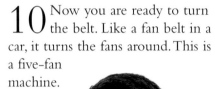

10 Now you are ready to turn the belt. Like a fan belt in a car, it turns the fans around. This is a five-fan machine. You can add more fans if you like.

7 Use scissors to cut each spiral out of each of the pieces of colored cardboard. Start from the outside edge and gradually work your way in along the lines of the spiral.

8 Tape one end of the spiral to the end of a skewer. Wind the other end of the spiral around the skewer stick a few times. Tape it close to the opposite end of the skewer.

9 Put a small amount of sticky tape on the end of each skewer. Then place each skewer into one of the empty holes in the top of each spool.

ENVIRONMENTAL MATTERS

Cars are convenient, but their effect on the environment causes concern. The manufacture, and the driving of cars both use up precious natural resources such as metals and oil. The emissions (waste gases) that gasoline cars produce pollute the atmosphere. One of them, carbon monoxide, is thought by many scientists to be contributing to problems such as global warming (the warming of the world's climate because of gases trapped in the atmosphere).

Although the environmental problems associated with cars are many, car makers have made many improvements to their models during recent years. Cars are much lighter than they used to be, so smaller amounts of raw materials are needed to make them. Because they are lighter and their engines are more efficient, they can drive many more miles per gallon of fuel than previously. In many countries, the emission of carbon monoxide into the atmosphere is actually lower now than twenty years ago, despite their being many more cars.

Costly accident

The gasoline that cars burn is extracted from oil pumped out of the ground or from under the sea. The oil is transported in enormous ships to refineries where the gasoline is extracted. Occasionally, a tanker sinks or springs a leak. When this happens, oil seeps into the ocean and forms a slick on the surface, killing and injuring fish and birds.

FACT BOX
• Ford launched the Ford Fiesta in 1976, and the Ford Ka in 1998. Both are small compact cars. But the exhaust gases of the 1976 Ford Fiesta contained fifty times more pollutants such as carbon monoxide and nitrogen oxides than the 1998 Ford Ka.

Route guidance

Traffic police may gradually be replaced by computerized route guidance technology called Telematics. In-car navigation systems and traffic messaging (radio messages on traffic conditions) enable drivers to use the best route. This can reduce travel times, and gasoline consumption, by 10 percent.

Going nowhere fast

There are too many cars in the world. Traffic congestion is a common experience for many. Transportation experts are trying to link public transportation with car use to reduce the problem. For example, park-and-ride programs allow drivers to park near a town center, then catch a free bus into the center.

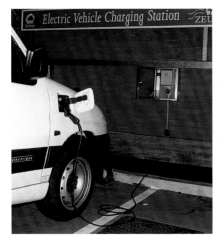

Plug-in car

Electric cars create much less pollution than gasoline cars. They run off electricity stored in batteries. The batteries need to be recharged regularly by being plugged into the main electricity supply. In parts of the United States such as California, drivers can find recharging stations in public places. Seven hours of charging will allow a car to travel a distance of about 100 miles.

On the junk pile

Most of the materials used in cars can be recycled. Car companies are using more and more recycled materials in their new cars, such as old batteries to make new batteries, and plastic parts to make new plastic-based parts. However, it is still very expensive to recycle the metal, so many old cars end up on junk piles.

Rubber bounces back

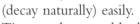

The treads (gripping patterns) on tires wear away until the tire is too smooth to grip the road. Car owners throw away the old tires and buy new ones. Like metal and plastic, rubber does not biodegrade (decay naturally) easily. Tires can be reused by being shredded and turned into tiny chips of rubber. These can be melted down to make asphalt to cover roads.

Lights in the smog

Fumes from gasoline cars cause smog over the city of Los Angeles. This is dangerous to people's health. Scientists are constantly researching alternative fuels. CNG (compressed natural gas) cars, which are already on sale, produce 20 percent less emissions than gasoline cars.

BRAKING SYSTEMS

CARS HAVE two types of brakes. Parking brakes lock the rear wheels when the car is standing still. They are controled by the handbrake lever inside the car. Brakes for when the car is moving are usually made of steel discs fixed to each wheel. They are called disc brakes and are controled by the brake pedal inside the car. The disc brakes attached to the car's road wheels work just like the model disc brake in the project. Putting the brakes on too sharply when a car is moving can cause a skid, when the wheels lock and the tires slide on the road surface.

Antilock braking systems (ABS), now used in many cars, measure the road surface conditions and stop the car going into a skid. This is done by making the disc brakes come on and off very quickly, so that the wheels cannot lock.

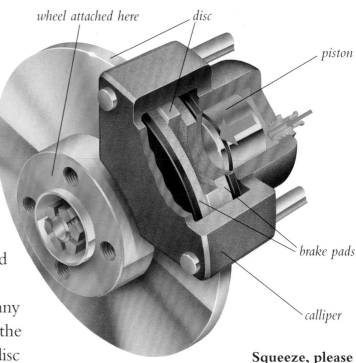

wheel attached here   disc

piston

brake pads

calliper

Squeeze, please

The disc brake unit's disc is attached to a turning hub This is bolted to the road wheel. When the driver presses the brake pedal, fluid is squeezed down a tube to the piston on the side of the disc brake. The piston presses together two pads, one on either side of the disc, gripping it firmly and stopping it from turning. As the disc slows, so does the car wheel.

Ready, steady, go

A stock car (modified standard car) accelerates from stop very quickly. The driver builds up the power in the engine. When the engine is near full power, the driver quickly releases the brakes. Because the wheels suddenly start spinning incredibly quickly, the tires roar and whine against the hard ground, and burn with the heat of the friction (rubbing) against the road. The burning rubber turns into smoke which billows in white clouds around the rear wheels.

Water sports

Rally drivers have to deal with extreme conditions such as dirt tracks, mud, snow and water. Powerful brakes help them to keep control of the cars. After going through water, a rally car's brakes would be wet. This makes them less effective because there is less friction. The brake pads slip against the wet disc. The driver has to press the brake pedal with a pumping action to get rid of the water.

DISC BRAKE

You will need: *scissors, 14in length of fabric, circular cardboard box with lid, masking tape, pencil, 8in length of ½in-diameter wood dowel, glue, 3 x 4½in piece of medium sandpaper, 2½ x 4in wooden block, two plastic cups, insulation tape.*

1 Use the scissors to cut a 14in long strip from the fabric. You may have to use special fabric cutting scissors if ordinary scissors are not sharp enough.

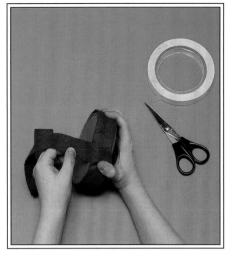

2 Take the strip of fabric you have cut out and wrap it around the rim of the circular cardboard box. Secure it firmly in place with small pieces of masking tape.

3 Make a hole in the center of the box's lid with a pencil. Twist the pencil until it comes through the bottom of the box. Now gently push the wood dowel through both holes.

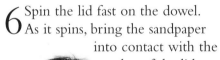

4 Spread lots of glue onto the sandpaper's smooth side. Wrap the sandpaper carefully over the top of the wood block, pressing to stick it.

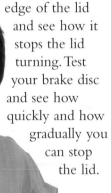

6 Spin the lid fast on the dowel. As it spins, bring the sandpaper into contact with the edge of the lid and see how it stops the lid turning. Test your brake disc and see how quickly and how gradually you can stop the lid.

5 Stand two plastic cups upside down on a flat surface. Rest either end of the wooden dowel on each cup. Cut two small pieces of insulation tape. Use them to attach each end of the dowel firmly to the cup tops.

SAFETY ISSUES

TRAFFIC ACCIDENTS are a constant danger. As the number of cars on the roads increased in the first half of the 1900s, the number of accidents to pedestrians and drivers increased also. During the last 50 years, ideas were put forward to reduce the scale of the problem. Gradually, most countries have decided that a driver must pass a test in driving skills. Governments have created safety regulations for road builders and car makers to follow. In many places, drivers and passengers are required by law to wear seat belts, and driving while under the influence of alcohol is forbidden in most countries.

New cars often have built-in safety features such as car body parts that resist crushing, and airbags that inflate to lessen the impact of collisions. Emergency road services deal more quickly with injured people. All these advances mean that in many countries there are now fewer road deaths than there were 20 years ago, even though there are more cars.

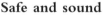

Safe and sound

If a car traveling at the relatively slow speed of 20mph stopped suddenly, a child could be thrown forward and injured. To prevent this, a child can be strapped into a specially designed chair that is attached securely to a car seat. It also stops the child from distracting the driver.

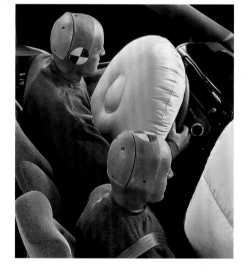

Bags of life

Experts who test cars for safety use crash-test dummies that react just like human bodies. These dummies are being protected by airbags, which were introduced into European production-line cars by Volvo in the 1980s. Airbags act as a kind of life-saving cushion, protecting a person from being thrown into the dashboard or the seat in front. The airbags inflate with gases as soon as sensors detect the first moment of a collision.

Not a care in the world

In the early days of motoring, people were much less aware of road safety as there were very few cars. In this 1906 drawing, a rich young man-about-town leans over the back of his car seat. He does not have to worry about where he is going because he has a chauffeur to drive him. Yet even the chauffeur is careless and narrowly avoids hitting a pedestrian in front of the car.

Pain in the neck

When a car stops suddenly, a person's head is jolted forward and then sharply backward. This can cause damage to the neck called whiplash. It often results in serious injury. Car manufacturers have invented seats that slide backward and then tilt. The pictures show (1) the seat in normal position, (2) the seat sliding back, and (3) the seat's backrest tilting over. Combined with the headrest at the top, this seat design helps reduce whiplash.

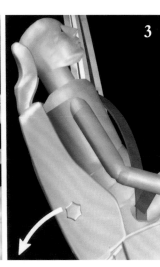

Traffic control

Before traffic control measures were introduced, accidents were common. In 1914, the first electric traffic light was installed in Cleveland, Ohio. Traffic lights control the flow of cars through road intersections.

Grand slam

When cars collide with each other at high speed their bodywork (outer metal shell) smashes and twists. Safety engineers test the strength of a car's bodywork by hitting sample cars with powerful robot sledges. Wires attached to the car detect information about safety weak points. This information is used to improve the safety of materials and designs used in cars.

Major obstruction ahead

When a large truck tips over and spills its cargo, it creates all kinds of problems. Fire crews rescue anyone who is trapped in a vehicle, and medical teams treat any injured people. The police and fire crews direct the removal of the spilled cargo. Heavy cranes are needed to shift the truck. Although drivers are diverted to other routes, traffic jams build up that can stretch for long distances.

GOOD DESIGN

AR MAKERS use large teams of people to create their new cars. Stylists, design engineers and production engineers combine with the sales team to develop a car that people will want to buy. Before the new car is announced to the public, models are made. A quarter-sized clay model is tested in a wind tunnel to investigate the car's aerodynamics (how air flows over its shape). Finally, a prototype (early version) of the car is built and tested for road handling, engine quality and comfort.

Painting on wheels
An old Mini Minor has been painted in exciting bright designs. A car's paintwork is called its livery.

Sleek and shiny
CAD (computer-aided design) software allows car designers to create a three-dimensional image of a new car design that can be looked at from any angle.

MODEL CAR

You will need: *two 8½ x 11in sheets of cardboard, pair of compasses, ruler, scissors, glue, brush, bradawl, 6in square piece of colored cardboard, pliers, four paper clips, two 4in lengths of ½in diameter wood dowel, masking tape.*

Wire basket
Three-dimensional, wire-frame (see-through) computer images allow designers to see how the shapes of the car fit together.

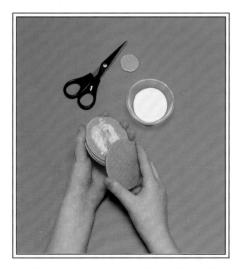

1 Draw and cut out four 1in and eight 2½in diameter cardboard circles. Glue the 2½in circles together to make four wheels. Glue a 1in circle to the center of each wheel.

2 Use the bradawl to make a hole in the center of each wheel. Cut four ¼in strips of colored cardboard. Wrap one each around the wheel rims. Glue the overlapping ends.

3 Push straightened paper clips into the holes and bend the outer ends with pliers. Attach the wheels to the two pieces of dowel by pushing the paper clips into the ends.

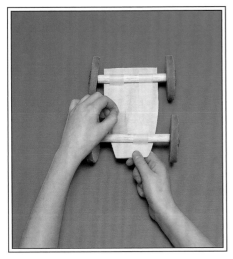

4 Cut a piece of cardboard to 3¼ x 6in. Trim one end to make it 2½in wide. Tape the two axles to the board, one at each end. Leave space for the wheels to rotate freely.

5 Cut a piece of cardboard 3¼ x 14in. Double it over and bend it into a cab shape. Tape the two loose ends together. Stick the bottom of the cab shape to the car base.

6 Cut two cardboard shapes 6in long and 4in high. Trim them with the scissors to the same shape as the side of your car cab. Attach the sides to the cab with sticky tape.

DECORATE
YOUR CAR

You will need: *two colors of acrylic paints, medium paintbrushes, pencil, three 4 x 6in sheets of colored card, a piece of white cardboard, two colors of felt-tipped pens, scissors, glue.*

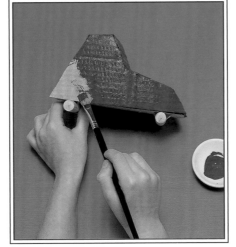

1 Remove the wheels from your car. Paint the sides and top of the cab with one of the two colors of paint. Paint two coats and leave to dry.

2 Draw exciting designs for the sides of the car, and a driver to go behind the windshield. Color them in with the felt-tipped pens.

3 Let the paint dry for a couple of hours. Cut the designs out of the cardboard. Glue them to the sides and back of the car. Paint the wheels with the color of paint not yet used.

4 Replace the wheels when they are dry. Now your car looks just like a real street machine. Cut photographs of cars from magazines for ideas for new designs.

FRICTION AND OIL

W HEN THE parts of an engine move, they touch and create friction (rub against one another). The more quickly and often they move, the more friction there is. This makes the engine parts grow hot, but if they become too hot they expand and no longer fit properly. When this happens, the parts jam against one another and the engine seizes up.

Oil, a slippery liquid, lubricates the car engine. It is stored in a part of the engine, from where it is pumped onto the moving parts. Eventually the oil gets dirty with soot and dirt from outside. The dirty oil must be drained, and clean oil put in at regular intervals. Ball bearings help other moving parts of the car turn against each other. The project shows you how marbles can behave like ball bearings to reduce friction.

Oil giant
Car ownership grew steadily in the 1930s. This created a big demand for new car products. People wanted to keep their cars running smoothly and safely. Most of all, car owners needed engine oil that was always high quality, wherever and whenever they bought it. Oil companies spent a lot of money on advertising, telling people that their oil was the best.

Sea changes
Oil rigs drill deep into the sea-bed to find crude (natural) oil. Car lubricating oil is made from this. Pumps in the rig draw the crude oil up from the sea-bed into pipes leading to refineries on land. Impurities are removed from the crude oil in the refineries. This makes it light enough to use in car engines.

Extra Jag
High-performance sports cars such as the Jaguar E-Type of the 1960s need a particularly light oil. Otherwise their powerful engines will not run smoothly. The E-Type engine in this car has six cylinders (most car engines have four). They generate the power needed to accelerate to a top speed of 150mph. Over time a thick oil would clog the oil ways, leading to friction and wear and tear of many engine parts.

PROJECT

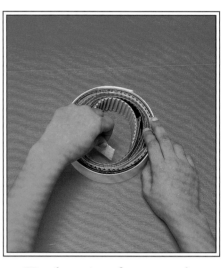

Oil guzzler
Large luxury cars
need a lot of oil.
This 1958 Lincoln
Continental has a huge
eight-cylinder engine to
lubricate. During the 1950s, oil
was very cheap. American car makers had less reason to think about
the costs of running cars as carefully as they have in more recent years.

Beetle's brother
Between 1955 and 1974,
Karmann produced the Karmann
Ghia cabriolet for the car maker
Volkswagen. It has a special body
on the chassis (frame) of a
Volkswagen Beetle. Like the
Beetle, it has a rear engine.

BALL BEARINGS

*You will need: 8½ x 11in sheet of stiff
cardboard, scissors, sticky tape,
five ⅜ x 8in strips of corrugated
cardboard, 16 glass marbles.*

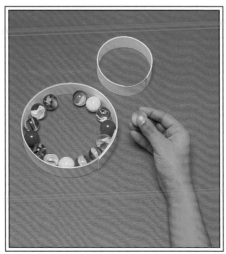

1 Cut two strips of stiff cardboard,
both ¾in wide. The first one
should be 8in long and the second
4in long. Make both into circle
shapes. Tape the ends together.

2 Use the strips of corrugated
cardboard to line the inside of
the larger cardboard circle. Put all
five strips in, and make sure that they
are packed very closely together.

3 Place the smaller circle inside. Try
to turn it against the corrugated
cardboard. The corrugations create
friction so it is not easy to turn the
smaller circle.

4 Take the smaller circle and the
corrugated strips out of the large
circle. Now line the inside of the
larger circle with the marbles until
there are no gaps between them.

5 Place the smaller circle inside
the larger one again. Turn the
small circle. It moves very easily. The
smooth surface of the glass marbles
creates much less friction.

CLASSIC MODELS

DIFFERENT PEOPLE collect different kinds of cars. Those who are looking for style collect classic cars (at least 20 years old). Often the cars come from the 1950s, 1960s and 1970s. Owners take pride in the exceptional design and quality of the vehicles. For example, Rolls-Royces of any era look distinctive, and their engines and other mechanical parts were made with unusual care and the very best materials. High-performance classic sports cars such as the 1954 Mercedes-Benz Gullwing, the 1968 Aston Martin DB4, the 1960s Ford Mustang and the 1988 Porsche 959 are popular too.

Collectors of classic cars often belong to special clubs. The clubs help them to find the spare parts needed for their cars, and to meet people who are interested in the same models. Motor museums such as the Museum of Automobile History in the United States, the National Motor Museum in the UK and the Porsche Museum in Germany exhibit classic cars for people to look at and enjoy.

One of the greats
Few sports cars are as eagerly collected as the 1949 Jaguar XK120. It combines high speed with good looks. Its six-cylinder engine has double overhead camshafts (to control the valves in the cylinder heads). It can reach speeds of up to 120mph.

Bumper beauty
American car makers of the 1950s such as Cadillac created cars that shone with large areas of chrome (shiny metal). Bumpers and radiator grilles were molded into streamlined shapes to catch the eye.

Up, up and away
The Mercedes-Benz 300SL sports car was built by hand, so only 1400 of them were ever made. The car has one very striking feature. Its passenger and driver doors open upward from the roof of the car. The unusual design gave the car its nickname "The Gullwing," because the open doors look like a seagull. It is not very easy to get in and out of the car. Once inside, the driver and passenger sit close to the ground. The engine of the Gullwing was also set very low, to make sure that the driver could see over the top of the long hood.

Air-cooled cool

The 911 series Porsche Carrera was first made in 1964. The Porsche first appeared in 1939, as a higher-powered, streamlined, variation of the Volkswagen Beetle. Like the Beetle, the Porsche engine was air-cooled. Then, in 1997, the firm produced its first water-cooled car, the 928.

FACT BOX

• The classic Jaguar E-type was Britain's fastest production-line car in 1961. Its top speed was 150mph.

• The 1968 Ferrari 365GTB4 Daytona is still one of the world's fastest cars. It has a top speed of 176mph.

• A 1926 Bentley 3-liter four-seat tourer was auctioned for $153,000 in 2000.

Lucky devil

Italian car maker Lamborghini produces the classic cars of tomorrow. They are are among the world's most exotic and expensive cars. This 1990 Diablo (devil) can accelerate to 60mph in just four seconds.

Classic car, classic film

The 1997 film comedy *Austin Powers* used many different examples of 1960s style. They all helped to recreate the fun-loving, swinging image of that period. In this scene, the hero of the film, played by Mike Myers, is standing up in the seat of a 1960s Jaguar E-Type. The bullet shape of this car is a classic design of the period.

Classic performance

The British car maker Jaguar made many classic models in the past, such as the XK120 and the E-Type. The cars it makes today are also of top quality and performance. This 155mph XKR convertible's engine is supercharged to give extra power.

Super-streamlined

Modern sports car maker Marcos designs cars such as the Mantis that are destined to become classics of the future. They have luxurious interiors and powerful engines to match any of the old greats. The streamlining on the front of this Mantis gives the car a look that stands out from other sports cars.

FUEL CONTROL

THE CONTROLLED flow of fuel into a car's engine is very important, because it affects how the car performs. If there is too much fuel and not enough air, the engine will flood with gasoline and won't start. If there is not enough fuel, the engine will run in a jerky way. The mixing of fuel and air occurs inside the carburetor. A piston goes down as a rod, called a camshaft, opens a valve to let the fuel and air mixture in. The valve closes and the piston goes up, compressing (squeezing) the fuel and air mixture. The spark plug fires to ignite the fuel mixture, pushing the piston down again. The piston rises again and the exhaust valve opens to release the waste gases.

The project shows you how to make a model that works in the same way as a camshaft. It opens one valve and then, as it closes the first valve, a second valve opens.

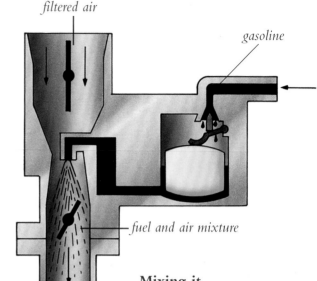

filtered air

gasoline

fuel and air mixture

Mixing it

In cold weather, engines need more fuel to get started. In some cars the driver pulls out a choke. This causes the carburetor to increase the amount of fuel in the fuel and air mixture. Many modern cars have automatic chokes. Internal computers work out the exact mixture of fuel and air that will suit the weather conditions.

In search of power

Very powerful cars such as the Lamborghini Diablo need to generate a lot of energy to accelerate (increase speed) quickly. They have 12 cylinders in their engines, burning much more fuel than an ordinary four-cylinder car. The burned fuel creates a large amount of exhaust gas. The Diablo has four exhaust pipes at the rear of the car. Most ordinary cars have only one exhaust pipe.

ROCK AND ROLL CAMSHAFT

You will need: *scissors, 2½in square stiff cardboard, masking tape, cardboard tube with plastic lid, pencil.*

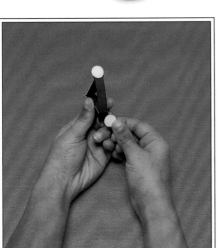

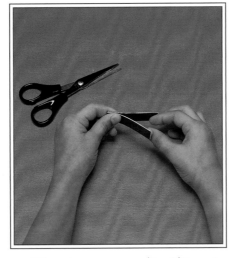

1 Use scissors to cut a ½ x 2½in strip from the stiff cardboard. Double it over in the center. Hold it with your fingertips. Bend the two ends of the cardboard away from one another.

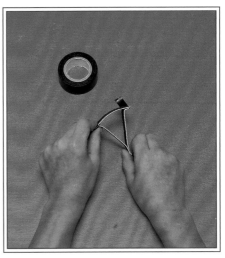

2 Cut a ½ x 1½in strip from the original piece of cardboard. Use masking tape to fix the card strip to the bent bottom ends of the first piece. This makes a triangle.

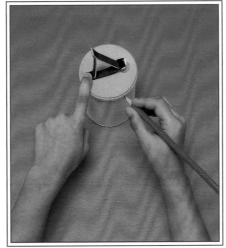

3 Use the scissors to cut out two small circle shapes from the original piece of card. Use masking tape to secure them to the bottom piece of the triangle you have made.

4 Put the triangle on top of the cardboard tube. The circles should touch the plastic lid. Mark where the circles sit on the lid with a pencil.

5 Using the scissors, carefully cut around the pencil marks you have made in the plastic lid of the tube. These form an inlet and an outlet.

6 Now you can rock the triangle back and forth to cover and uncover the two holes one after another. This is just how a camshaft opens and shuts the inlet and outlet valves in a car's cylinder.

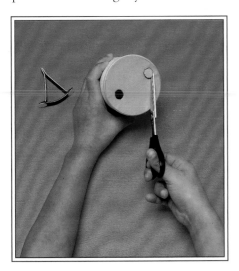

HOME FROM HOME

THE GREAT advantage of setting off on an adventure by car is that you can go where you want, when you want. It is even possible to travel to places where there may be no towns or people. Once you're there, however, what do you do when you want to go to sleep at night? One solution is to drive a special car such as a multi-purpose vehicle (MPV) or a recreational vehicle (RV). They are built to provide sleeping space. Smaller ones have car seats that will lie flat to make a bed. Larger RVs have cabins with built-in bunks, kitchens and sitting areas. They may also have televisions, music systems, microwave ovens and all the high-tech equipment that can be found in a conventional house. The interiors of top-of-the-range RVs can be built according to the buyer's preferences.

Long way from home
Long-distance truck drivers, who drive thousands of miles every year, often travel through regions where there are very few towns or villages. At night the driver finds a safe place to park, then sleeps in a built-in bunk on a shelf behind the driver's seat.

Time for a drink
Rolls-Royce built the 1960 Phantom as a touring car for people who wanted to travel to the countryside and eat when they arrived. The small seats fold down when the car is moving and pull up in front of the bar when the car is stopped. Cars such as this were often driven to outdoor events such as horse races, where eating a picnic from a car is a tradition.

Open-air life
Campers are mobile living units that can be towed from place to place by cars. Towing a camper requires a lot of extra power from the car, so larger vehicles are the most suitable. Drivers have to keep their speed down when pulling a camper, because the camper could easily flip over.

PROJECT

SCENTED AIR FRESHENER

You will need: *7oz water, mixing bowl, 7oz all-purpose flour, wooden spoon, baking tray, pencil, bottle of essential oil, paintbrush, four colors of acrylic paint, 17½in length of string.*

1 Pour the water into a mixing bowl. Stir in the flour slowly with a wooden spoon. Continue to stir until the paste thickens into a dough mixture that you can mold.

2 Place the dough mixture in the baking tray. Mold the dough into a bell shape that bulges out at the bottom. Roughly shape a roof at the top and wheels underneath.

3 Wet the rough shape so it is easy to mold a design on it. Smooth your fingers over the top area to make a windshield. Shape the wheels more accurately.

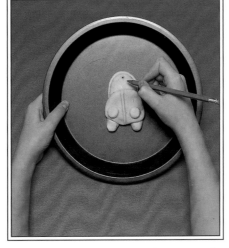

4 Make small holes in the car and one larger hole in the top. Sprinkle essential oil in the holes. Bake in an oven for 45 minutes at 300°F.

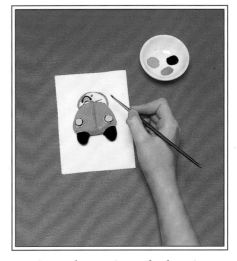

5 Once the car is cool, place it on a sheet of paper. Paint the hood first, then the details, such as a driver's face. Add lines around the headlamps.

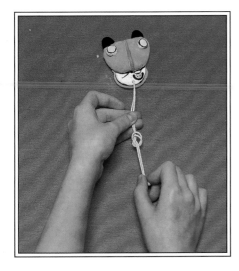

6 Allow the paint to dry. Thread the piece of string through the hole in the top of the car's windshield. Double the string back and knot it to make a noose.

7 Your air freshener is all ready to go in a real car. Now you can put it on the dashboard, hang it from the back of a seat or put it on the shelf in front of the rear window. It will make any car smell fresh and clean.

FUEL CONSUMPTION

The amount of gasoline a car uses depends on the weight of the car, the speed it is traveling and the size and efficiency of the engine. Pressing on the accelerator pedal lets more fuel flow into the engine's cylinders, speeding the car up. Most ordinary cars have four cylinders. A few extremely economical cars have two cylinders, and some powerful sports cars have six or even eight. Today, cars of all engine size are designed to use as little gas as possible. This is because the oil from which gasoline is made is much more expensive than it was in the 1950s and 1960s. The average modern car can travel 15km or 20km on a quarter of a gallon of gas. Gas guzzlers such as the American Cadillac Fleetwood could only drive 2½ miles on a quarter of a gallon of gas.

Roaring oldie
Super Street hot rodders often take the bodies of old cars and combine them with modern parts. The 1950s car body here has been joined to big tires by a complicated suspension system. Some hot rodders use special chemical fuels such as ethanol and nitromethane. When they burn, they get much hotter than gasoline. The extra heat helps them to accelerate to very high speeds.

FACT BOX
• Rising oil prices in the late 1970s led to the creation of gasohol, a mixture of lead-free gasoline and ethanol. Ethanol can be made from plants such as grain and potatoes.

• Traces of the metal lead in car exhaust fumes are harmful to health. It is thought that many people suffered lead poisoning. Now, lead-free gasoline has been developed and is widely available.

Where's the car?
Members of the Eddie Jordan pitstop crew swarm over the Jordan 199 at the Australian Grand Prix in 1999. In the center, a team member holds the hose that forces fuel into the car's gas tank at high pressure. Up to 25 gallons of fuel can be pumped into the car in about 10 seconds. Speed is essential. Every second in the pit lane is equal to about 200ft lost on the track.

Two-carb Caddy

The Cadillacs of the 1950s are reminders of a time when petrol was cheap and car makers could make big, heavy cars. In the 1970s, the price of oil rose dramatically, so petrol became much more expensive. The 1955 Cadillac Fleetwood had two carburetors, even though most cars built at that time would have had just one. The second carburetor was needed because the Fleetwood used so much petrol.

Pink thunderbird

The sleek rear fins and supercool spare-wheel casing made the 1957 Ford Thunderbird a car that people remembered long after Ford stopped making the model. This restored T-Bird is equipped out as a convertible. When the cars were first sold, buyers were given both a hard top and a convertible top. They could fit whichever one they wanted. In 1998, the 1957 Thunderbird's good looks earned it a Lifetime Automotive Design Achievement Award from the Detroit Institute of Ophthalmology in the United States.

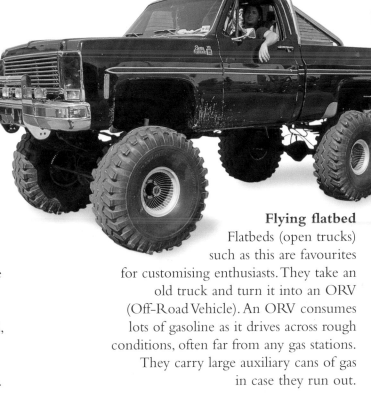

Twice as much

Cars that use a lot of gasoline may have two or even four exhausts. Twin exhausts extract waste gases from the engine in a more efficient way than a single exhaust could, which allows the engine to perform more efficiently too.

Flying flatbed

Flatbeds (open trucks) such as this are favourites for customising enthusiasts. They take an old truck and turn it into an ORV (Off-Road Vehicle). An ORV consumes lots of gasoline as it drives across rough conditions, often far from any gas stations. They carry large auxiliary cans of gas in case they run out.

SPEED RECORDS

IN MORE than a hundred years of car building, cars have reached faster and faster speeds. In 1899, the Belgian inventor Camille Jenatzy was the first person to drive a car faster than 60mph. The car, designed by Jenatzy himself, ran on electricity. In the same year, Sir Charles Wakefield created his Castrol Motor Oil company. The company awards the official trophy for the land-speed record to drivers who break the record. The trophy was first won in 1914 by the Englishman L. G. Hornsted. He reached a speed of 125mph in a car from the German car maker Benz. Since then 38 other people have broken the record. The last person to succeed was the British RAF Tornado pilot Andy Green, on 13 October 1997. His car, powered by two jetplane engines, broke the sound barrier (sound travels at a speed of 760mph), reaching 761mph.

Satisfaction at last

Between December 1898 and April 1899, there were no less than six attempts to beat the land-speed record. All of them were made by drivers in electric cars. The fastest, in April, was the Belgian Camille Jenatzy who reached 65mph. He called his car *La Jamais Contente* (Never Satisfied) because he had already tried to set the land-speed record twice before.

Gas-powered wheels

Finding a long, flat, hard surface to travel on is very important when trying to set a speed record on land. Donald Campbell thundered across the Lake Eyre Salt Flats in Australia in 1964. He reached a speed of 400mph in his gas-turbine powered car Bluebird. He was following in the footsteps of his father Malcolm, who set nine land-speed records.

Golden goer

The Golden Arrow set a land-speed record of 190mph on March 11, 1929. The enormous, streamlined car was powered by a Napier-Lion airplane engine. It flashed along the hard, white sand at Daytona Beach in Florida. The driver was Major Henry Seagrave. After setting the land-speed record, Seagrave went onto set the world water-speed record.

Goodbye, Mr Bond

In the 1974 Bond film *The Man with the Golden Gun*, the character James Bond performs many death-defying feats. His car takes at least as much punishment as the Secret Service Agent himself. To fly across the river, the car would have had to be traveling at 125mph when taking off from the ramp.

Expensive record

The Black Rock Desert in Nevada was the scene for another record-breaking attempt in 1983. On this dried lake bed, in blistering desert heat, Richard Noble set a new record of 631mph. He was driving the specially made jet-engine powered Thrust 2. Making a speed record attempt costs a lot of money. The advertisements plastered all over the car are for businesses that donated money for this record attempt.

Head for the horizon

Ever since commercial films started to be made in the early 1900s, car chases have formed part of the action. The cars are usually driven by stunt men and women specially trained in fast driving. In the 1991 film *Thelma and Louise*, the two heroines are chased by dozens of police cars. In the end, the two women drive over the edge of a cliff.

Supersonic car

In 1997 Andy Green drove the Thrust SSC at an incredible 761mph. He did not just set a new world land-speed record, he traveled faster than the speed of sound (760mph). Until then, speeds greater than that of sound had only been possible in flight. Andy was used to the speed because he was a jet pilot for the British Royal Air Force.

ROADS AND HIGHWAYS

BEFORE THE 1800s, most roads were just earth tracks. Some roads in cities and towns were made of stone and wood blocks, which gave a rough ride. Macadam roads (roads covered in a hard layer of tiny stones) were a great improvement in the 1800s, but with the invention of cars at the end of the 1800s, new road surfaces were needed. Roads made of asphalt (a mixture of bitumen and stone) and concrete offered the hardness and smoothness that cars needed to travel safely and quickly.

The first highway was completed in 1932 in Germany, between Cologne and Bonn. As car ownership grew during the second half of the 1900s, road building programs followed. Some people think there are too many roads. They protest against the building of more roads because they want to protect the countryside.

Multilane moves
Some highways are called freeways in the United States. Car ownership and use has grown relentlessly, and the freeways have grown too. In the last 30 years some freeways have increased in size from four lanes to 12 lanes, and even to 16 lanes on some stretches.

Pay as you go
The enormous costs of building highways can be partly paid for by charging drivers a toll (payment for using a road) when they travel on the new roads. The road owners set up barriers through which a car must pass to drive onto the road. Drivers crossing the Queen Elizabeth Bridge in Dartford, England stop at toll booths to buy tickets that allow them to drive over the bridge.

Keep calm
Traffic calming is the name given to the different ways of slowing down traffic speed. Building speed bumps (bumps in the road) is one example of traffic calming. The speed humps force drivers to slow down in areas where there is a lot of housing. Slower car speeds help to prevent accidents.

Going places

Modern countries need well-built roads so that goods and people can travel easily between cities and towns. This is Interstate 35W approaching the city of Minneapolis. It is part of the vast interstate highway system that links the entire United States.

Major to minor

Road networks are often much easier to understand from the air. A cloverleaf links two major highways. Long curving roads such as these allow drivers to switch between major roads without having to stop at a junction. The roads that link up major roads are called access roads.

Night guide

Small glass reflectors called Catseyes help drivers to see the road at night. The Catseyes are set at regular intervals in the middle of the road. They gleam brightly when a car's headlights shine on them. The British inventor Percy Shaw invented the device in 1933, after noticing how a cat's eyes shine at night.

The long and winding road

There are still many narrow old roads in remote areas. They twist and turn for miles through beautiful countryside. There is much less traffic on country roads, and they offer an enjoyable test of driving skills. Four-wheel drive vehicles handle particularly well on the tight corners and steep slopes.

Road construction ahead

Modern roads carry a lot of traffic and need constant repair and maintenance. They cannot simply be shut down while that happens. Instead, some lanes are closed for repair while others remain open. The long lines of plastic cones on this stretch of highway have restricted traffic to one lane on one side and two lanes on the other side.

HOOD ORNAMENTS

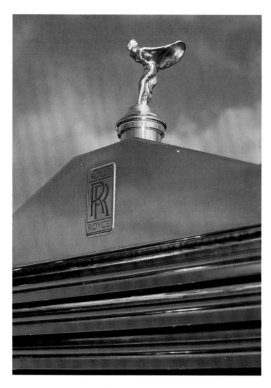

CAR MANUFACTURERS take pride in the work that goes into the machines that they make. They put badges or symbols on their cars to show which company made the car. The badges are usually found on the car hood, where they are easy to spot. There are many different car makers all over the world, and they each make a different badge. The instantly recognizable designs of the most prestigious companies, such as the Silver Lady on Rolls-Royces or the three-spoked circle on Mercedes cars, suggest elegance or power. Other celebrated symbols are the rearing horse on the front of cars made by the Italian Ferrari company, and the VW symbol used on Volkswagen cars. Sometimes these badges are called mascots, perhaps because car makers see them as a symbol of good luck. When people identify a car's badge, they immediately know the name of the car maker. In this project, you can make your own car mascot to symbolize the kind of car you like.

Leading lady

All Rolls-Royce cars carry a winged figure hood ornament on the hood. It is called The Spirit of Ecstasy and was created by the sculptor Charles Sykes. The figure first appeared on Rolls-Royce cars in 1911. In modern Rolls-Royces, the hood ornament folds down backward into the hood in an accident to avoid injury.

HOOD HIGHLIGHT

You will need: 8½ x 11in sheet of cardboard, pencil, scissors, masking tape, bradawl, glue, matchstick, newspaper, fork, 9oz all-purpose flour, 7oz water, can of silver spray paint, fine paintbrush, black paint.

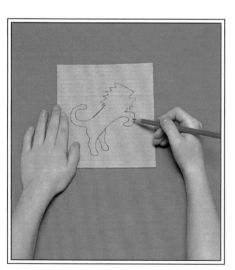

1 Cut a piece measuring 8 x 6in from the cardboard. Use a pencil to draw the outline of the shape you want to put on your car hood on the cardboard sheet.

2 Use the scissors to cut roughly around the badge shape. Then cut around the outline accurately. Be careful not to cut off any of the detail in your drawing.

3 Cut three square pieces from the cardboard, one 2in, one 2½in and one 2¾in. Tape the smallest on top of the next largest and those on top of the largest as a solid base.

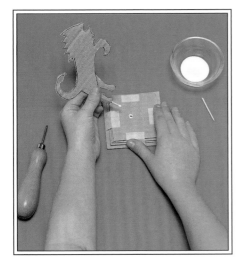

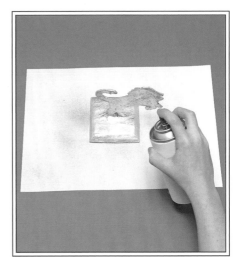

4 Make a hole in the center of the base with the bradawl. Put a glued matchstick in the bottom of your badge. Insert it into the hole in the base so that the badge stands upright.

5 Tear strips of newspaper. Mix flour and water with a fork, to make a thick paste. Dip the paper in the mixture. Apply the wet paper to the badge in three layers.

6 When the newspaper is dry, spray your badge with spray paint. Be careful to point the can downward, away from you. Put a piece of paper under the badge.

7 Use the paintbrush to apply black lines on the badge where you want to show more detail. For example this one shows detail of the lion's mane, tail and paws.

Speeder's shield

The badge on Porsche cars is like a coat of arms from medieval times. In the past, important people made decorations on shield shapes to tell others who their ancestors were and where they came from.

8 Your finished hood ornament could form the start of a great collection. You could copy all your favourite hood ornament. There are many more to choose from.

Roar of power

Jaguar cars have used the model of the leaping jaguar as their hood ornament for many years. More recent models do not have the statuette on the hood. They have been declared illegal because they could cause injury to pedestrians in an accident.

THE FUTURE

THE CARS of the future already exist, but only as the still-secret designs of car makers. The use of in-car computers will be one of the main ways in which cars will change. These already control engine performance, navigation aids and air temperature. In future, a computer chip may apply the brakes automatically when the car in front is too close, or flash up HUDs (Head Up Display) messages on the windshield about road conditions ahead.

Designers and engineers will continue to develop fuel-efficient cars (ones that use as little gasoline as possible), such as the Toyota Echo. They will also look at the potential of alternative power sources such as electricity, natural gas (a gas found under the ground), solar power (power from the sun's energy) and hydrogen (a gas in the earth's atmosphere). Of all the many developments that will occur, one is almost certain. There will be even more cars on the roads.

Hot item

Cars powered by energy from the sun (solar power) would be better for the environment than petrol engine cars. Photo-electric cells on the back of the car turn energy from the sun's rays into electricity. This energy is stored in batteries inside the car. The batteries then supply power to the engine. At the moment this method can only store enough energy to power small cars. Scientists are trying to find a way to use solar power in bigger vehicles.

FACT BOX

• The US car manufacturer General Motors is developing a car that will change its shape from a sedan to a pickup truck by means of voice-activated commands spoken by the driver in the front seat.

• Car makers are building concept (future idea) cars in which each seat has its own LCD (liquid-crystal display) screen. Passengers will be able to send and receive e-mail, browse the internet, make phone calls and read maps.

Take me home

GPS (Global Positioning System) navigation aids are already installed in high end cars. A radio aerial in the car sends a signal to one of the 24 GPS satellites that orbit the earth. The satellite sends a signal back to the car giving its exact position on the earth. The data is sent to a computer that reads maps stored on a CD-ROM. A small screen on the dashboard of the car displays a map of the road network and the position of the car on the map. If the driver inputs the destination, the screen displays the best route.

Neat package

Car makers produced classic microcars such as the BMW Isetta in the 1950s and 1960s. In the future, they will continue to make very small cars. They are ideal for short trips in built-up areas. The number of cars in towns and cities continues to grow. Extra-small vehicles such as the Smart car could be the answer to parking problems. It is so short (8ft) that it can park not just along the edge of the road, but hood-on with the sidewalk.

Snappy mover

Research has shown that on most trips, the average number of people who travel in a car is two. Car makers now know that two-seater cars like the one shown here make a lot of sense for many drivers. Less metal is needed to make them, they use less fuel, and they are cheaper to buy. A car as small as this is also much easier to maneuvre in the tight spaces of modern cities.

Three-wheel dream

One-person cars seem an obvious answer to many traffic problems. They are not always a hit with drivers, however. The British inventor Sir Clive Sinclair produced the electric-powered Sinclair C5 in 1985. The vehicle was not very popular, and was soon taken out of production.

Future taxi

Will the four-wheel yellow cabs of New York today be replaced by three-wheel taxis in the future? The 1992 science-fiction film *Freejack* showed great imagination in guessing what the taxicabs of tomorrow might look like.

AIRCRAFT AND FLIGHT

More than any other form of transportation, aircraft have been inspired by the natural world. The very first flying machines, as well as the jumbo jets and supersonic warplanes of today, all have design features gained from studying birds and insects in flight. Here, you will find out the technological secrets of powered flight by looking at all the different types of aircraft, past and present. You can follow some of the challenges that have faced pioneers throughout the history of aviation, and understand how mastering the power of flight has made the world a much smaller place.

AUTHORS

Peter Mellett and John Rostron

CONSULTANT

Chris Oxlade

WHAT IS FLIGHT?

THINK OF flight and you may think of birds and insects, paper airplanes and airplanes, bullets and footballs. All of these can move swiftly through the air, but are they all really flying? To answer this question, imagine you are launching a paper airplane into the air. It glides away from you and finally lands back on the ground. Now throw a ball in exactly the same way. It hits the ground much sooner than the paper airplane. We say that the paper airplane was flying, but the ball was not. This is because bullets, footballs, stones and arrows are all projectiles. They do not really fly because they have nothing to keep them up in the air. Birds, aircraft, rockets and balloons do fly – they stay off the ground longer than something that is simply thrown.

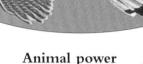

Animal power

Birds, insects and bats all have wings. These animals use their wings to hold themselves up in the air and move along. Muscles provide power for take-off.

Balloons

This balloon is filled with a gas called helium that is seven times lighter than air, so the balloon floats upward, just like a cork floats upward in water. Blimps are also filled with helium to keep them airborne. Before airplanes were invented, lighter-than-air craft, such as these, were the only way people could make a sustained flight.

Spaceflight

The space shuttle is launched into space by powerful main engines and booster rockets. It uses smaller engines, as part of the orbital maneuvring system, to increase speed, in order to reach an orbit about 185mph above the Earth. The force of Earth's gravity acts like a tether, keeping the shuttle in orbit, while the shuttle's speed prevents it from falling back to the ground.

Airplanes

Like birds, airplanes have wings to hold them up in the air, but they also have engines. Engine power is needed to help them take off from the ground and push them through the air. Most long-distance airplanes fly at great heights because as air becomes less dense with height, drag is reduced so less thrust is needed to maintain speed. So the power and fuel needed to push them through the air is much less than at ground level. More fuel is needed during take-off as engines work at maximum thrust to gain height as quickly as possible.

Gliders

Since gliders have no engines, they have to be towed into the air by small airplanes or by machines on the ground. The towline is then released and the gliders' wings hold them up. In still air they will glide slowly back to the ground in a gentle spiral. The pilot controls the glider's flight by searching for rising air currents, called thermals, and by altering the shape of the glider's wings. Most gliding is done in a hilly landscape where the hills cause the air to rise. By using these air currents, a glider pilot can keep his plane aloft for many hours, so long as these rising currents persist.

Flying a kite

A kite is lifted into the air by a blowing wind. A long string called a tether holds the kite at an angle to the wind. The air rushes against the kite, pushing it upward and keeping it in the air. If the wind drops or the tether breaks, the kite will fall back to the ground.

BIRDS IN FLIGHT

M USCLE-POWERED flight is very hard work. In the past, many people have tried to fly by flapping artificial wings but no-one has succeeded. Birds, however, are very light and powerful compared to us, and are perfectly designed to stay up in the air. Birds' wings are covered in feathers – one of the strongest and lightest natural materials known. The airfoil shape of their wings provides lift, while tail feathers help with steering and braking. Birds flap their wings hard to take off and climb into the air, and need enormous flight muscles to provide enough power for flight. These muscles account for nearly a quarter of the weight of some birds, for example eagles. To make sure plenty of blood is pumped to the muscles as they work, birds also have a large, fast-beating heart. If humans were to fly, they would need a chest the size of a barrel, arms 10ft long, legs like broom handles, and a head the size of an apple – as well as thousands of feathers!

barb

Light as a feather
Every feather has a hollow tube running down its center. Microscopic hooks lock each barb together so that air cannot pass through.

Eagle in flight
A soaring bird such as a vulture or an eagle has spread-out feathers with slots in between. Each feather acts as a tiny airfoil, lifting the bird as it flies through the air.

primary feathers

Flying feathers
The large primary flight feathers on the end of each wing produce most of the power for flight. These feathers can be closed together or spread apart to control flight. Smaller feathers on the inner wing form the curve that provides lift and are known as secondary flight feathers. The innermost feathers keep the bird warm and shape the wing into the bird's body, helping to prevent turbulence in flight.

secondary feathers

On the wing

This sequence of pictures shows how an owl flies through the air. A bird's wings bend in the middle as they rise upward and the feathers open to let air pass through the wings. On the powerful downstroke, the primary flight feathers slice through the air and the feathers close up again. This pushes the air down and back and pulls the bird upward and forward.

flight feathers

wing bone

flight muscles

breastbone

A bird's body

Flight feathers are connected to thin bones at the end of each wing. Bird bones are light – most are hollow and filled with air. The large flight muscles are anchored to the breastbone at the front of a bird's chest.

Deadly speed

Peregrine falcons are the fastest animals in the world. They fold back their wings to reduce drag, then dive at their prey at speeds up to 220mph. The force of the impact breaks the victim's neck instantly.

HOW BIRDS FLY

Move your hand across and back in a tank of water, with the palm flat. Now tilt your thumb side downward as you move it across. You can feel the forces pushing against your hand.

L OOK AT a large bird, such as a goose, in the sky. Can you describe how its wings are moving? Flying birds do not simply flap their wings up and down. Their wings are not stiff and flat – instead, each wing has a joint like an elbow in the middle. This joint allows the wing to twist upward on the downstroke and downward on the upstroke. The feathers on the part of the wing corresponding to your hand are called the primary or flight feathers. On the downstroke, the front edge of the hand is tilted downward, so that the effect of the air flow is to generate a forward thrust as well as to produce lift. On the upstroke, the front edge is tilted upward. One effect of this is to produce a downward force (called anti-lift), but it also produces forward thrust. Thrust propels the bird forward.

As you bring your hand back, tilt the thumb side upward. The forces are now pushing in different directions. In each case, a force pushes the thumb-edge forward.

A BIRD OF YOUR OWN

You will need: *sheets of stiff paper, sticky tape, scissors, glue stick.*

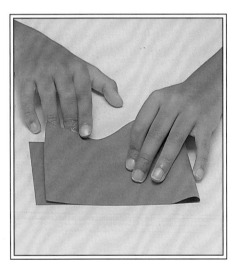

1 Start by making the bird's short legs. Fold one piece of paper in half lengthwise. Fold it again several times until the paper is about 1in across.

2 Fold the strip of paper in half, as shown, and make a fold at each end for the feet. Tape the feet to your work surface to help keep your model stable.

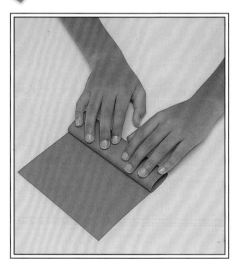

3 To make the body of your bird, roll a piece of paper into a tube and secure the edge with adhesive tape. Use some more tape to attach the body to the legs.

PROJECT

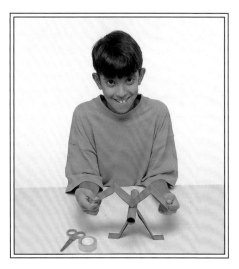

4 To make the wings, fold a piece of paper twice lengthwise so that it is about six times longer than it is wide. Fold it into a W shape.

5 Stick the wings onto the body. You have now made a model bird. To mimic how a bird flies, hold one wing tip in each hand.

6 Move your hands in circles – one going clockwise, the other counterclockwise. At take-off, a bird's wings make large, round circles.

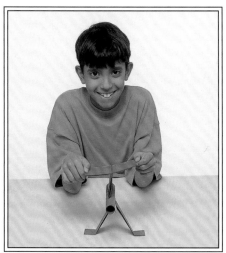

7 During the upstroke, notice how the bird's wings bend in the middle. Some birds raise their wings so high at the top of the upstroke that they bang together.

8 During the downstroke, the wings become flatter. To see how a bird's wings move when the bird is flying level, place your hands farther apart and move the wings in small, flat circles.

AMAZING FLYING ANIMALS

BATS ARE the only animals that can fly, apart from birds and insects. They have wings that can push downward to create lift. Unlike most birds, most bats are nocturnal – they fly at night and sleep in the day. Some other animals can glide through the air, but cannot control or power their flight with flapping wings. Instead, animals such as flying frogs, sugar gliders, lizards, snakes and squirrels glide down. They jump outward from high places like trees and cave walls, moving forward through the air as they parachute downward. These animals usually have loose flaps of skin attached to their bodies. The flaps of skin act like the envelope of a parachute, catching the air and enabling controlled descent. Flying fish escape from their enemies and predators just below the ocean surface by sailing through the air above. Their gliding flight only lasts a few seconds, but it is faster than the fish's swimming speed.

Wings and fins

Flying fish swim very fast, close to the surface of the water. With wing-shaped fins stretched out, they leap upward and forward into the air, thrashing the water with their tails until they reach take-off.

Parachute tactics

Flying frogs have enormous webbed feet. They use their feet as parachutes when they jump down from trees in search of insects. They alter the shape of their feet to control their flight. There are sticky pads on their toes to help them climb. Using these pads, they can cling to the smoothest leaves and branches in the rainforest.

FACT BOX

• Some flying fish can glide along at 30mph for several hundred yards. The longest recorded flight for a flying fish lasted 90 seconds and covered more than ½ mile.

• Flying foxes are actually a type of large fruit-eating bat. There are more than 2,000 species, or types, of bat living in the world.

• Flying snakes are able to flatten their bodies to help them glide from tree to tree.

• Some flying frogs jump from a height of 130ft. They glide along, covering about 100ft in only 8 seconds.

• The colugo, or flying lemur, can easily glide for at least 325ft between trees.

Life-saving spines

A flying lizard has flaps of skin along each side of its body. These are supported by spines hinged to the ribs. When danger threatens, the spines stick out and the lizard glides away.

Tree gliding

Flying squirrels have folds of thin skin between their front and rear legs. They glide from tree to tree by stretching out their legs to spread the skin wide.

Smooth as honey

Sugar gliders (*Petaurus breviceps*), are small mammals that sail through the rainforests of Queensland and New Guinea. They eat sweet sap (sucked from trees) and nectar (from flowers).

Flexibility

A bat's wing is a sheet of flexible skin stretched between its fingers, the side of its body and the back of its legs. Bats can alter the shape of their wings much more than birds. They can twist and turn like acrobats in the air as they chase insects for food. The largest bats have wingspans up to 6½ft, but weigh only 2¼lb.

WINGS AND LIFT

HOWEVER MUCH you flap your arms up and down like a bird, you cannot take off because you are not designed to fly. Humans are the wrong shape and their muscles are not strong enough. Birds have wings and powerful muscles that enable them to fly. Flapping provides a force called thrust, which moves a bird forward through the air. A bird's wings are a special shape, called an airfoil. In an airfoil, the top side is more curved than the underneath. This helps to keep a bird up in the air, even when its wings are not flapping.

When an airfoil wing moves through the air, it creates an upward push. This push is a force called lift. It counteracts the weight of the object (due to the force of gravity), which pulls an object down toward the ground. There are many different shapes and sizes of birds, gliders and airplanes, but they all have airfoil wings.

If you blow across a sheet of paper it reduces the pressure of the air above the paper. The stronger pressure beneath lifts the paper up.

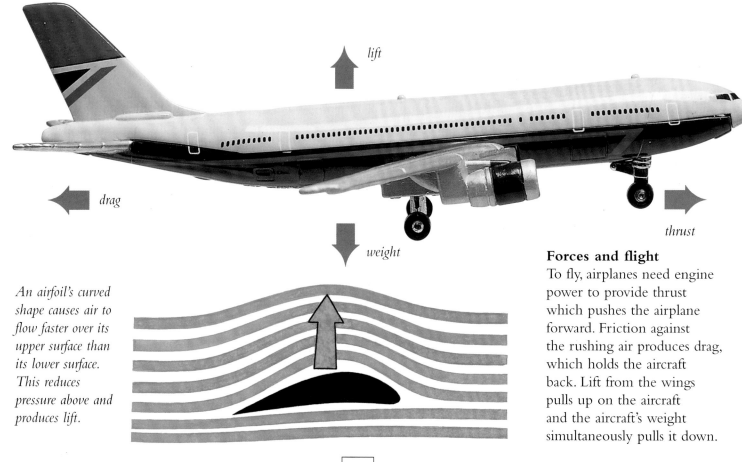

lift

drag

thrust

weight

An airfoil's curved shape causes air to flow faster over its upper surface than its lower surface. This reduces pressure above and produces lift.

Forces and flight
To fly, airplanes need engine power to provide thrust which pushes the airplane forward. Friction against the rushing air produces drag, which holds the aircraft back. Lift from the wings pulls up on the aircraft and the aircraft's weight simultaneously pulls it down.

Wings and soaring

A Lammergeyer can soar through the air without flapping its wings. As its wings slice through the air, the force of lift pushes up on them. The faster the bird's speed, the greater the lift. It is able to glide like this for many hours provided that it can maintain speed. Many seabirds can use the updraft near cliffs for this. Birds of the open ocean, such as the albatross, use variable air currents near the water surface, where the wind is slowed by contact with the water.

Rotation

Helicopters have long thin airfoil wings called rotor blades. Powerful engines whirl the blades to produce lift. Helicopters can hover, or fly forward, backward and sideways, as well as straight up and down. The pilot can position the angle of the blades to control lift and make the helicopter go in any direction. Because the rotor blades are continually spinning in one direction, the helicopter tends to rotate the other way. Most helicopters have a small propeller at the end of their body to help prevent this. Large helicopters may have a set of rotor blades at each end of the aircraft.

Taking off

Most airplanes need long runways to take off. They speed along, faster and faster, until the lift pushing up is greater than the weight pulling down, allowing them to leave the ground.

AIR RESISTANCE

WHEN YOU are swimming, you push your way through the water. All the time, the water is resisting you and slowing you down. In the same way, things that fly have to push their way through the air. Air also clings to their surfaces as they rush through it. The result is a backward pull called drag, or air resistance. Drag is the force that works against the direction of flight of anything that is flying through the air. The amount of drag depends on shape. Fat, lumpy shapes with sharp edges create a lot of drag. They disturb the air and make it swirl about as they move along. Sleek, streamlined shapes have low drag and hardly disturb the air as they cut smoothly through it so they fly fastest of all.

Whatever the shape, drag increases with speed. Doubling the speed creates four times the amount of drag. The result is that drag limits how fast aircraft, birds and insects can fly, increasing the amount of thrust needed.

Trapped air
Parachutes fall slowly because air is trapped beneath them. They are deliberately designed to have very high drag.

When an aircraft is in flight, the angle the wings make to the airflow is called the angle of attack. If the angle of attack is increased, the amount of lift also increases – but so does the drag.

angle of attack

If the angle of attack becomes too great, lift drops suddenly. The smooth flow of air over the wing is broken, creating turbulence, increasing drag and reducing lift.

turbulence

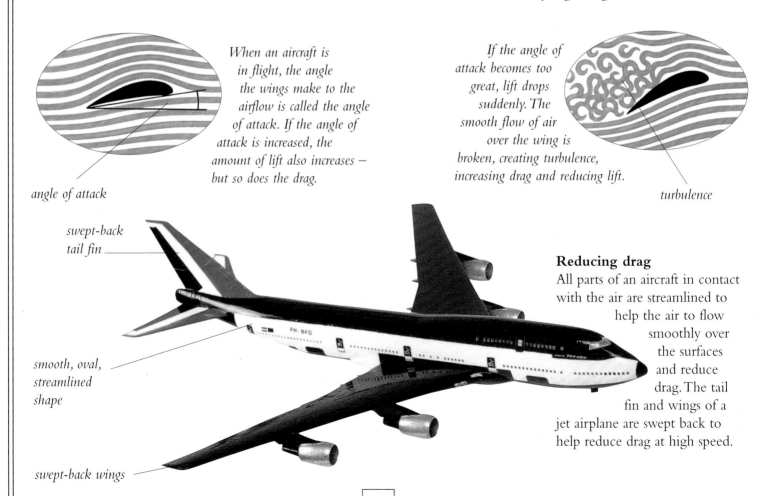

swept-back tail fin

smooth, oval, streamlined shape

swept-back wings

Reducing drag
All parts of an aircraft in contact with the air are streamlined to help the air to flow smoothly over the surfaces and reduce drag. The tail fin and wings of a jet airplane are swept back to help reduce drag at high speed.

Coming in to land

Birds must slow down before they land. This owl has tipped up its wings so that the undersides face forward. It has also lowered and spread out its tail feathers to act as a brake. Drag increases suddenly, lift decreases and the bird drops to its landing place.

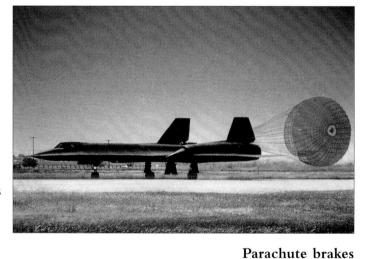

High speed

The Concorde can fly at a speed of over 1,250mph. Its wings are swept back to reduce drag to a minimum. If its wings stuck straight out they would be ripped off at this speed.

Parachute brakes

The Lockheed SR-71 lands at over 215mph. A parachute helps it slow down, as ordinary brakes on its wheels would take too long.

Down to earth

Coming in to land, an airplane uses flaps on its wings to increase lift at low speeds. During flight, these flaps are retracted (pulled in) to reduce drag.

207

SHAPED BY DESIGN

THINK OF a sleek canoe moving through water. Its streamlined shape makes hardly any ripples as it passes by. Streamlined shapes also move easily through air. We say that they have low drag, or air resistance. Angular shapes have more drag than rounded ones. For effective streamlining, think about the shape of fast-moving fishes, which have to be very streamlined. A fish such as a tuna has a blunt front end, is broadest about a third of the way along, then tapers toward the tail. This is more streamlined than a shape with a pointed front end and thicker at the other end because it creates least drag as it moves through water. It splits the water cleanly, allowing it to flow along each side of the tuna to rejoin without creating turbulence. In these experiments, you can design and test your own streamlined shapes, or make a model parachute with high drag to make it fall slowly.

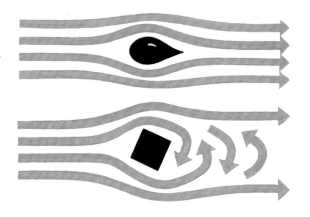

How it works
Air flows in gentle curves around the streamlined shape (top). Angles or sharp curves break up the flow and increase drag.

star   *square*   *teardrop*

Shape race
Make different shapes (*as shown on the right*) from balls of modeling clay all the same size. Race your shapes in water – the most streamlined shape should reach the bottom first.

Splash down
How much of a splash would you make diving into a pool? This diver's carefully streamlined shape will help her cut cleanly through the water to dive deeply.

MINI PARACHUTE JUMP

You will need: *felt-tipped pen, a large plate, thin fabric, scissors, needle, cotton thread, sticky tape, plastic spool.*

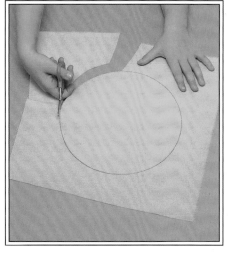

1 Use the felt-tipped pen to draw around the plate on the fabric. Using the scissors, carefully cut out the circle to make what will be the parachute's canopy.

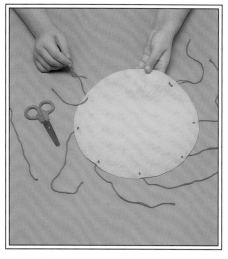

2 Make about eight equally spaced marks around the edge of the circle. Use a needle to sew on one 12in long piece of cotton thread to each point you have marked.

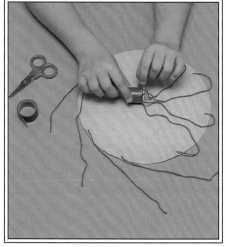

3 Use sticky tape to secure the free end of each thread to a spool. Make sure you use a plastic spool, as a wooden one will be too heavy for your parachute.

Holey parachute

Parachutes today have a hole in the center. This one brought two *Apollo 17* astronauts safely to land in the Pacific Ocean. The hole ensures that the air escapes evenly instead of at the sides, which would cause swinging.

4 Let your parachute go from as high up as possible. As it falls, the canopy will open and fill with air. The larger the canopy, the slower the parachute will fall.

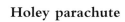

GLIDING AND SOARING

WATCH A small bird as it flies. It flaps its wings very fast for almost the whole time. Large birds, however, often glide with their wings stretched out flat and unmoving. They can do this because their large wings create enough lift to keep them up in the air without flapping. Soaring birds, such as albatrosses and condors, glide for hours hardly moving their wings at all. They gain height by using thermals (rising columns of hot air) over the land and sea. Gliders are aircraft that do not have engines. Instead they have long, thin wings, similar to those of soaring birds. They are pulled along by small aircraft or by winches on the ground, until the lift generated by their wings keeps them airborne. Glider pilots also seek out thermals to lift their aircraft up.

Long, thin wings

A glider is towed into the air attached to a cable. Its long, thin wings give maximum lift and minimum drag for their size. If a glider flies level in still air, drag forces slow it down and the wings lose their lift. So, to keep up speed, a glider flies on a gradual downward slope.

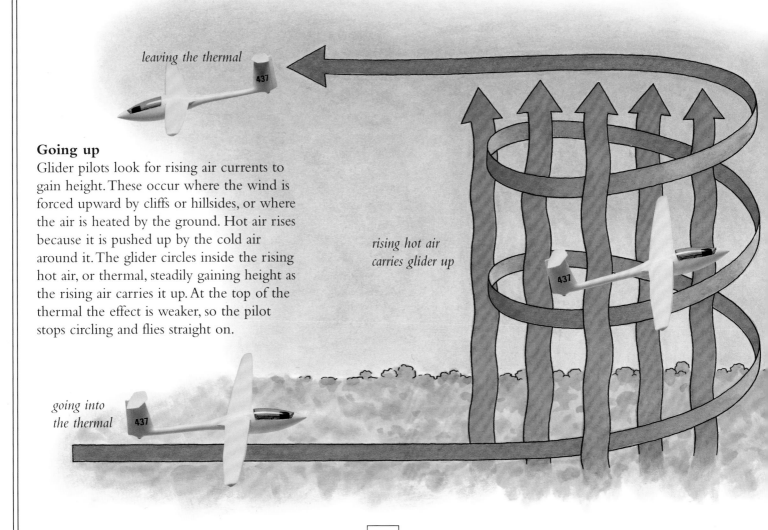

leaving the thermal

Going up

Glider pilots look for rising air currents to gain height. These occur where the wind is forced upward by cliffs or hillsides, or where the air is heated by the ground. Hot air rises because it is pushed up by the cold air around it. The glider circles inside the rising hot air, or thermal, steadily gaining height as the rising air carries it up. At the top of the thermal the effect is weaker, so the pilot stops circling and flies straight on.

rising hot air carries glider up

going into the thermal

Flying high
The wing shape of a paraglider is made by air blowing into pockets on its leading edge. The pilot steers from side to side and can ride up thermals.

Wingspan
Albatrosses have long narrow wings. This wing shape helps them to glide for enormous distances on air currents blowing over the open ocean. Albatrosses have the longest wingspan of any bird, measuring over 10ft from tip to tip.

Cockpit dials
This picture shows the inside of a glider's cockpit. The dial at left gives forward air speed. The middle dial shows the rate of climb or descent (how fast the glider is going up or down). The last dial on the right shows the glider's altitude (height above the ground).

Hang-glider
A hang-glider is made from strong, thin material stretched over a framework of aluminium poles and is very light. The material on the hang-glider's wing is stretched into an airfoil shape to produce lift. To steer the hang-glider, the pilot moves a control bar forward to climb and backward to dive. Hang-gliders are often launched by the pilot simply jumping off the edge of a cliff where an updraft of air will provide the necessary lift. Because of the pilot's all-round vision, hang-gliders are used for aerial surveys and observation.

KITES AND SAILS

WIND IS moving air that pushes against anything standing in its path. You can fly a kite because it is held up in the air by the force of the wind pushing against it. A string, called a tether, joins the kite to the person flying it and holds it at the correct angle to the wind. You can feel tension in the tether pulling on your hand. The tension is the result of the wind blowing against the kite and lifting it up. If the tether broke, the kite would no longer be held at the correct angle and it would fall to the ground or blow away. When there is no wind, a kite can still be made to fly by pulling it through the air. A simple kite like the one below will also need a tail. This tail provides extra drag and ensures that the kite always faces into the wind at the correct angle so it can create lift. Traditionally, kite tails have many tassels along their length. These also add to the drag and mean that the tail does not need to be so long.

Open mouthed

Windsock kites may be flown from poles during festivals. They have open ends to catch the wind. Like all kites, they only fly when the wind blows against them.

Flying a kite

What makes a kite fly? Wind is deflected downward when it blows against a kite. This pushes the kite upward and creates lift. The tether keeps the kite at an angle to the wind (the angle of attack) with the nose higher than the tail. The kite's surface deflects the air downward. In a good breeze, a kite's weight is very small compared to the forces of lift and drag.

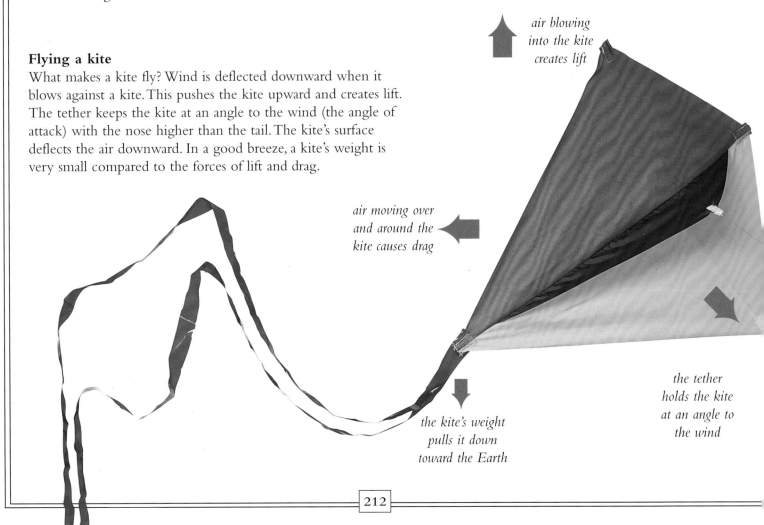

air blowing into the kite creates lift

air moving over and around the kite causes drag

the kite's weight pulls it down toward the Earth

the tether holds the kite at an angle to the wind

Flat kite

The oldest and simplest kite is the plane surface, or flat, kite. It has a simple diamond shape and a flat frame. Kites like these have been flown for thousands of years. Flat kites look very impressive strung together to make a writhing pattern in the sky.

Box kite

A square box kite is more complicated to make than a flat kite. Its shape makes it more stable and gives it better lift. It does not need a tail to keep it upright. Box kites can be a combination of triangles and rectangles. Large box kites have been used to lift people off the ground in the past.

Parasail

A parasail is a kite that lifts a person into the air. It does not rely completely on the wind, but instead it is towed behind a boat or a car. A parasail looks like a parachute that has been divided into different parts, called cells. As the parasail is pulled along, air flows into each separate cell, inflating it to make a shape that creates lift. Parasails usually fly about 165 miles above the ground.

LET'S GO FLY A KITE

FOR MORE than 3,000 years, people have been making and flying kites. The first ones were made from cloth or paper attached to a light wooden or bamboo frame. As time went by, the essential but simple secret of building a good kite was discovered. It must be as light as possible for its size, so that it catches as much wind as possible. Some kites can fly in remarkably gentle breezes. Their surfaces are wide so that the breeze has a large area to push against. Their low weight means that only a small amount of lift is enough to make them take off into the sky.

The Chinese have for long made some of the most elaborate and colorful kites of all. In Tibet and some other Himalayan regions, kite-flying is often a part of religious festivities. Competitions to see whose kite flies or looks best are now organized in many countries around the world. The kite design shown in this project has been used for many hundreds of years. Try flying it first of all in a steady wind. You might have to experiment with the position of the bridle and the length of the tail.

MAKE A KITE

You will need: *pen, ruler, two bamboo stakes (one about two-thirds as long as the other), string, scissors, sticky tape, sheet of thin fabric or plastic, fabric glue, colored paper.*

1 To make the frame, mark the center of the short stake and mark one-third of the way up the long stake. Tie the stakes together crosswise at the marks with string.

2 Tape string around the ends of the stakes and secure it at the top. This will stop the stakes from moving and it will also support the edges of your kite.

3 Lay the frame on top of the sheet of material or plastic. Cut around it, 1½in away from the material's edge. This will give you enough to fold over the string outline.

4 Fold each edge of the material over the frame and stick the edges down firmly with fabric glue (or sticky tape if you are making the kite from plastic). Let the glue dry.

5 Tie a piece of string to the long stake, as shown – this is called the bridle. Tie the end of the ball of string to the middle of the bridle to make the tether.

6 To make the tail, fold sheets of colored paper in zigzags. Tie them at about 10in intervals along a piece of string that is about twice as long as the kite. Glue or tie the tail to the bottom tip of the kite.

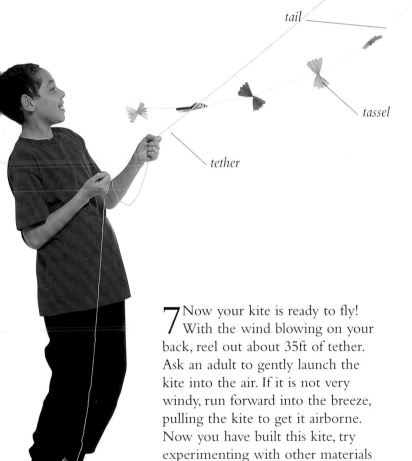

bridle

tail

tassel

tether

7 Now your kite is ready to fly! With the wind blowing on your back, reel out about 35ft of tether. Ask an adult to gently launch the kite into the air. If it is not very windy, run forward into the breeze, pulling the kite to get it airborne. Now you have built this kite, try experimenting with other materials and shapes to find which work well.

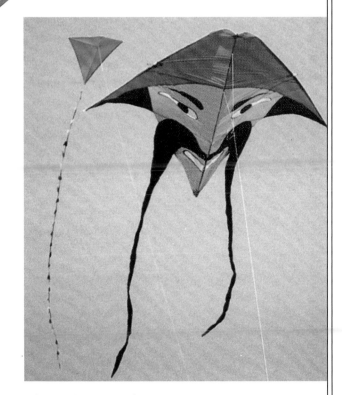

Flying faces
This kite has been made to look like a face with a long trailing moustache. Highly decorative designs can make the simplest kite look very effective.

LIGHTER THAN AIR

Hot stuff
A candle heats the air around it. Even after you snuff out the flame the smoke is carried upward by the hot air.

Oil slick
Watch how oil floats on water because it is less dense than air. The water surrounding the oil pushes upward on it. This push is called upthrust. Try this with a glass of water and a teaspoon of cooking oil.

OIL FLOATS on water because it is the lighter and less dense of the two liquids. A bottle full of oil weighs less than the same bottle full of water. Water pushes upward on the oil with a force called upthrust. A similar process happens when smoke rises from a fire. Hot air is less dense than the cold air around it and is forced up by the cold air. It floats upward, taking the smoke with it.

A hot-air balloon is simply a huge bag full of hot air. It experiences upthrust from the cold air around it. The balloon takes off because the upthrust is greater than its own weight pulling it down. Blimps are also lighter than the air around them. Modern blimps are filled with a gas called helium, which is seven times lighter than air. The hot air in a balloon gradually escapes or cools down, however, so the pilot needs to regularly produce more by burning gas underneath it. The hot gases from a single gas cylinder can carry several people for half an hour.

FACT BOX
• The first ever balloon passengers were not humans but a sheep, a duck and a chicken, in 1782, at the Court of Versailles, in Paris. They were sent up to make sure it was safe to travel by this new form of transportation.

• The first untethered balloon flight took place over Paris on November 21, 1783. It lasted only 25 minutes but reached 1,650ft.

• Marie Elisabeth Thible became the first woman aeronaut. On June 4, 1784, she flew in a balloon over Lyon, France.

• One of the largest blimps was the German *Hindenburg*, at 800ft long. In 1937, it burst into flames on landing, killing 35 people.

The first aviators

In 1783, French brothers Joseph and Jacques Montgolfier built an enormous paper balloon and lit a fire on the ground beneath it. The air inside the balloon gradually cooled after take-off. The balloon sailed into the sky, safely carrying two people into the air for the very first journey by hot-air balloon. By 1784, refined versions of their balloon could carry six people.

Hanging baskets

Modern hot-air balloons are as tall as an eight-story apartment block. They are made of nylon and can carry about five people in a basket hanging underneath. All hot-air balloons can only go where the wind blows them. This means pilots must have a landing site arranged downwind before setting off!

Danger

Blimps in the 1930s were huge, being designed to carry passengers across the Atlantic in luxury. They were filled with hydrogen gas that easily burst into flames, making the airships very dangerous. Today airships use helium.

Modern blimps

Unlike a hot-air balloon, this blimp uses helium to float. It also has engines and propellers to drive it. The pilot steers by moving fins on the tail.

PROJECT

HOT AIR RISING

HOT AIR BALLOONS rise into the sky because the air inside them is lighter than the air outside. The main part of the balloon is called the envelope. Hot air rises into the envelope from gas burners stored just beneath the envelope but above the basket. The number of gas cylinders stored in the basket depends on the journey time. The envelope fills with about 2½ tons of hot air – about the weight of two cars. This hot air pushes cold, more dense air around the balloon, out of the way, producing enough upthrust to lift the balloon, its passengers and bottles of gas off the ground.

You can make and fly a model hot-air balloon to see it rise in exactly the same way. However, do not attempt to fill your balloon using flames of any sort. Modern hot-air balloons are made of flame-resistant fabric so that they do not melt or catch fire, especially during the process of filling the balloon with hot air. The best material for a home-made balloon is colored tissue paper. You can easily produce hot air without using flames by using a hair dryer.

A super challenge
Virgin *Challenger* is capable of flying journeys of thousands of miles. Once the balloon is high into the atmosphere, the strong winds of a jet stream (fast moving, high altitude winds) carry it along.

Stabilize a balloon
Try adding modeling clay to the string of a helium balloon until the balloon hangs steady. The force downward (weight) now equals the force upward (upthrust).

Gas burners
Roaring gas burners heat the air. The hot air rises to fill the balloon's envelope, which takes more than half an hour. When the envelope is full, the balloon is launched by untying ropes that hold it to the ground.

PROJECT

BALLOONING AROUND

You will need: *pencil, cardboard, ruler, scissors, sheets of tissue paper, glue stick, hair dryer.*

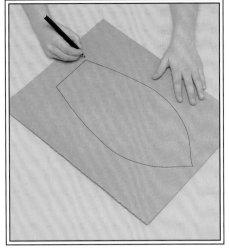

1 Draw a petal-shaped template on card and cut it out. The shape should be 12in long and 5in across with a flat bottom edge.

2 Draw around your template on seven pieces of tissue paper. Be careful not to rip the paper with the tip of your pencil.

3 Use the pair of scissors to carefully cut out the shapes you have drawn. You should now have seven petals that are all the same size and shape.

5 To fly your balloon, hold its neck open and fill the inside with hot air from a hair dryer. After ten seconds, switch off the hair dryer and let go of your balloon to launch it into the air.

4 Glue along one edge of a petal. Lay another petal on top and press down. Open out and attach another petal in the same way. Keep going until the balloon is complete.

WHAT'S IN A WING?

THE SMALLEST microlight aircraft carries one person and weighs less than 220lb. The largest passenger jet carries over 500 people and weighs nearly 400 tons. Whatever the size or shape, all airplanes have wings in common. Wings provide the lift they need to hold them in the air. The shape of the wings depends on how fast and high an aircraft needs to fly.

Narrow wings can reduce the amount of drag, and so are better for high-speed flight. Drag can also be reduced by having swept-back wings. However, wings like this are not as efficient when taking off and landing. To carry heavy loads, the airplane needs high lift which is provided by a large wing area. Passenger and cargo planes have broad (medium-length) wings, slightly swept back. All wings have moving parts to help the airplane land, take off, slow down and change direction.

Triplane
This aircraft is called a triplane because it has three sets of wings. Early planes needed more sets of wings to provide enough lift as their speed was slow. Some very early planes were built with five or more sets of wings, but they were never successful.

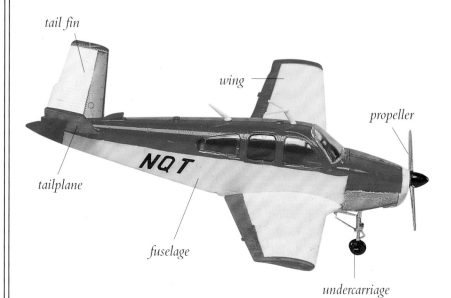

The parts of an aircraft
Each of the main parts of a small aircraft labeled here plays a part in helping the aircraft to take off, fly level, change direction and land. The body of the aircraft is called the fuselage and the landing wheels are called the undercarriage. On many aircraft, the undercarriage folds up inside the body of the aircraft during flight to reduce drag. Hinged control surfaces on the tail and the wings are used to steer the aircraft from left to right as well as up and down.

Piper Cadet
Most airplanes today are monoplanes. A monoplane has one set of wings. The wings of small planes such as this Piper Cadet stick straight out from the aircraft's body, because at speeds of only a few hundred miles per hour they do not need to be swept back, and this way they provide the greatest lift. These planes fly only short distances at a height of a no greater than half a mile.

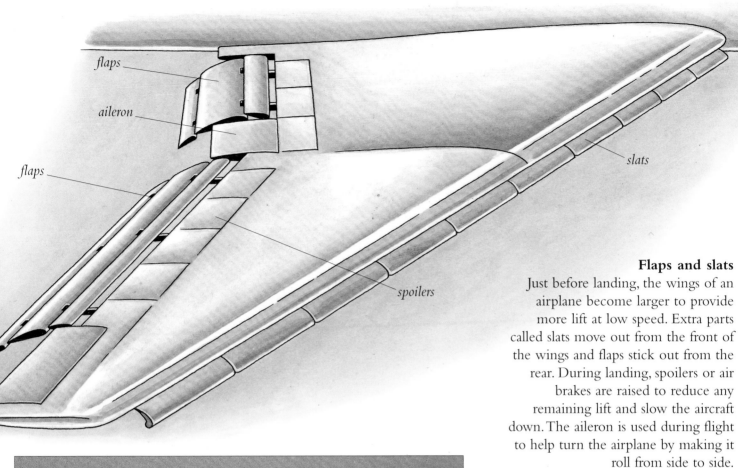

flaps

aileron

flaps

slats

spoilers

Flaps and slats
Just before landing, the wings of an airplane become larger to provide more lift at low speed. Extra parts called slats move out from the front of the wings and flaps stick out from the rear. During landing, spoilers or air brakes are raised to reduce any remaining lift and slow the aircraft down. The aileron is used during flight to help turn the airplane by making it roll from side to side.

Boeing 747
Wide-bodied jets, such as this Boeing 747, fly high and fast. Large wings provide enough lift to carry nearly 400 tons, more than a third of which is the aircraft's fuel. The wings are tapered and swept back to keep drag low when flying at 620mph. Swept-back wings reduce lift, so a high take-off speed is needed, but by reducing drag they also reduce fuel consumption. Even so, in one hour, a Boeing 747's engines burn 2,125 gallons aviation fuel, which is enough to run a family car for six years.

Swing-wings
Some military aircraft can move their wings. For high-speed flight, wings are swept backward in a low-drag triangle shape. To provide lift at lower speeds, the wings are swung forward.

TAKING FLIGHT

To MAKE a car turn left or right, all you have to do is turn the steering wheel. To steer a light aircraft, you must move two sets of controls, one with your hands and one with your feet. Moving these controls alters the control surfaces on the plane's wings and tail. Control surfaces are small hinged flaps that affect how air flows around the plane. There are three main types of control surface. Ailerons are attached to the rear edge of each wing. Elevators are mounted at the rear of the tailplane and the rudder is at the rear of the tail fin.

The pilot can also control flight by engine power – more power increases speed and so increases lift. So, an accelerating aircraft flying level will steadily gain height.

In a large or fast aircraft, controls are operated either electrically or hydraulically. The pilot can send electrical signals to small motors which operate the controls, or they can be hydraulically controlled by pumping fluid along pipes inside cylinders to operate them.

Double power

Biplanes have two sets of wings. They are strong, agile and easy to fly and are often used as trainer planes or in acrobatic displays. Biplanes with open cockpits and wings braced with wires and struts were the most common airplane design until the 1930s. Then, monoplanes (with single wings) replaced them in almost all functions.

Control surfaces

To turn the aircraft (yaw), the pilot turns the rudder to one side. To make the aircraft descend or climb (pitch), the pilot adjusts the elevators on the tailplane. To roll (tilt or bank) the aircraft to the right or left, the ailerons are raised on one wing and lowered on the other.

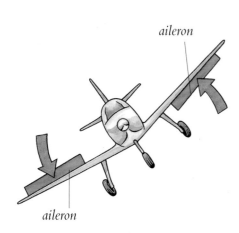

aileron

aileron

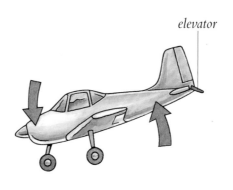

elevator

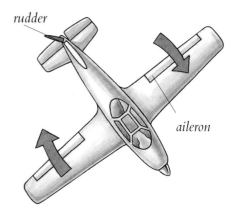

rudder

aileron

Roll

The ailerons operate in opposite directions to each other to tilt the aircraft as it turns. When one aileron is raised, the other is lowered. The wing with the lowered aileron then rises while the wing with the raised aileron automatically drops.

Pitch

The elevators on the plane's tail are raised or lowered to alter the pitch of the plane. Lowering the elevators causes the aircraft's nose to drop, putting the plane into a dive. Raising them causes the aircraft to climb.

Yaw

The rudder works with the ailerons to adjust the yaw. When the yaw is swivelled to one side the aircraft moves to the left or the right. Whichever way it points, the aircraft's nose (at the front) is turned in the same direction as the yaw.

Bank on it

When an aircraft turns, it moves rather like a cyclist going round a corner. It banks as it turns, which means that it leans to one side with one wing higher than the other. This means that some of the lift from the wings is used to turn the aircraft.

In the cockpit

Inside the cockpit of a modern airplane, the pilot moves throttle levers to control engine power. The control column and pedals move the control surfaces. Dials and gauges give information such as fuel consumption, flight direction, altitude and how level the plane is flying.

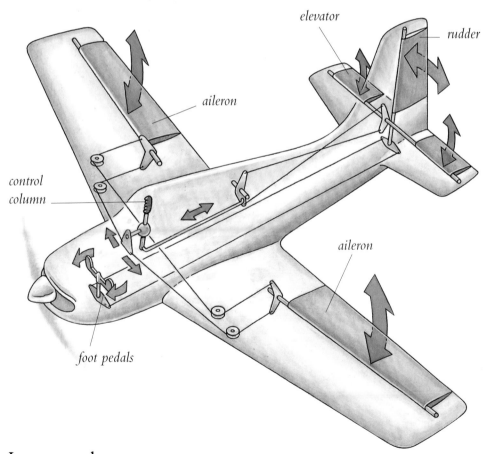

elevator

rudder

aileron

control column

aileron

foot pedals

In command

To control the aircraft, the pilot moves the control column from side to side to operate the ailerons. Moving the control column backward or forward operates the elevators. The foot pedals move the rudder from side to side.

FACT BOX

• Many flight terms are borrowed from terms used on board ships, including yaw, pitch and roll, port (left) and starboard (right).

• It takes an airplane one minute and nearly 1¼ miles of airspace to reverse its course.

• A cruising airliner loses 3 tons in weight every hour as fuel is used up.

• Many aircraft use computer-controlled autopilot systems. These fly the aircraft automatically from one place to another.

• To control a helicopter, the angle of the rotor blades is adjusted. This allows the aircraft to hover, go straight upward, forward, backward or even sideways.

MODEL PLANES

Paper airplanes
You can make model planes with nothing but paper. They can vary from a simple airplane to a glider with separate wings and a tailplane. To make a successful paper plane, you need to use stiff paper (not cardboard), so that it will hold its shape. You can also cut ailerons in the rear edges of the wings to adjust the flight as described in the project below.

WE HAVE seen how the control surfaces on the wings and the tail of an aircraft work – they change the way air flows over the aircraft, allowing the pilot to steer the aircraft in different directions. Working together, the ailerons and rudder make the plane turn to the left or right. Moving elevators on the tail make the nose of the plane go up or down. Although a model is much smaller than a real full-size aircraft, it flies in exactly the same way.

The scientific rules of flying are the same for any aircraft, from an airliner weighing 350 tons to this model made from pieces of paper, sticky tape and a drinking straw. Making this model plane allows you to see how control surfaces such as the aileron, rudder and elevators work. The flight of any plane, including your model, is sensitive to the angle of the controls. They need be only a slight angle from their flat position to make the plane turn. Too big an angle will make the model unstable.

GLIDE ALONG

You will need: pencil, set square, ruler, paper, scissors, glue, sticky tape, drinking straw, paper clip.

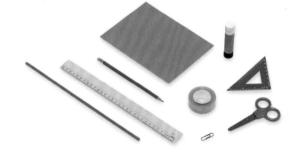

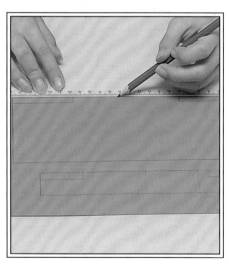

1 Draw two paper rectangles, 9 x 4in and 8 x 1½in. Mark ailerons 2½ x ½in on two corners of the larger one. Mark two elevators 1½ x ½in on the other. Cut them out.

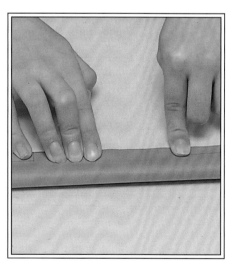

2 To make the wings, wrap the larger rectangle over a pencil and glue along the edges. Remove the pencil and make cuts along the ½in lines to allow the ailerons to move.

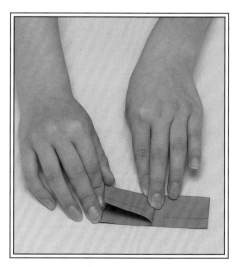

3 To make the tail, fold the smaller rectangle in half twice to form a W. Glue its center to make the fin. Cut along the two ½in lines. Make a ½in cut on the fin to make a rudder.

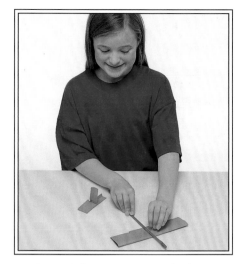

4 Use sticky tape to attach the wings and tail to the straw (the plane's fuselage or body). Position the wings about one quarter of the way along the fuselage.

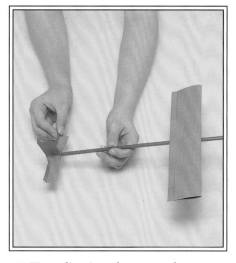

5 Try adjusting the control surfaces. Bend the elevators on the tail up slightly. This will make the plane climb as it flies. Bend the elevators down to make it dive.

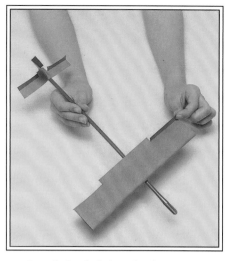

6 Bend the left-hand aileron up and the right-hand aileron down the same amount. Bend the rudder to the left. This will make the plane turn to the left as it flies.

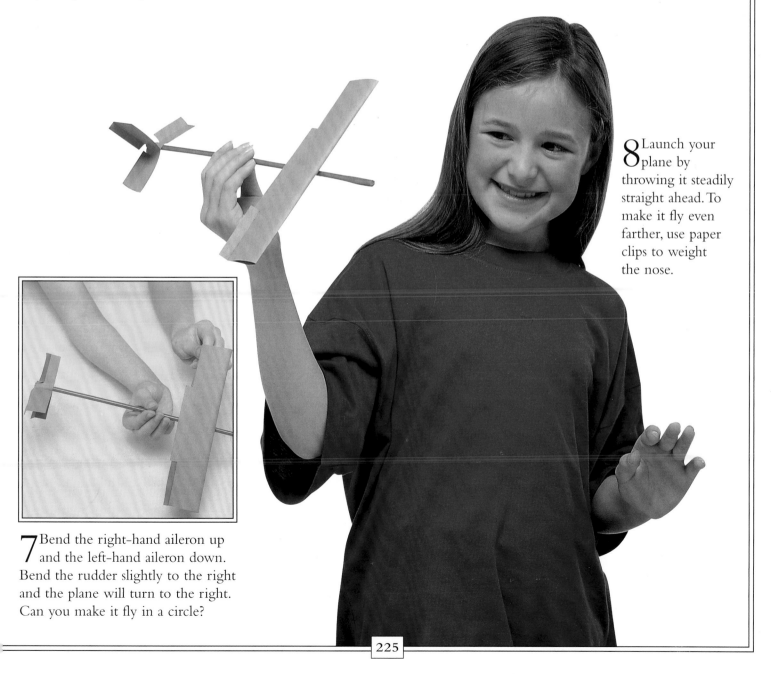

8 Launch your plane by throwing it steadily straight ahead. To make it fly even farther, use paper clips to weight the nose.

7 Bend the right-hand aileron up and the left-hand aileron down. Bend the rudder slightly to the right and the plane will turn to the right. Can you make it fly in a circle?

PROPELLERS

ALL AIRCRAFT need thrust to push them through the air. A propeller whirling at high speed creates thrust. Propellers have two or more blades, each of which is shaped like a long, thin airfoil wing. The blades generate lift in a forward direction as they move through the air. Modern propellers have variable-pitch blades, which means the pilot can alter the angle at which they bite into the air. Changing the pitch of a propeller is like changing gears on a bicycle. For take-off, the front of the blades point forward and the engine spins very fast to generate maximum thrust. Less thrust is needed when cruising, so the blades are set at a sharper angle and the engine spins more slowly. This arrangement gives the most economical use of fuel.

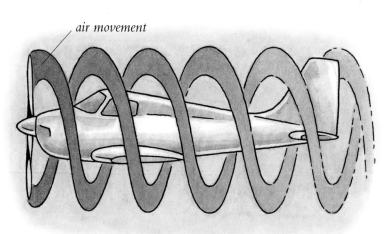

air movement

Air strike
Propellers screw their way through the air, in the same way a screw goes into wood. For this reason, aircraft driven by propellers are often known as airscrews. As the propeller turns, the blades strike the air and push it backward. This produces thrust and moves the aircraft forward.

DH-88 Comet

Early racers
Sir Geoffrey De Havilland designed many early aircraft. The De Havilland DH-88 Comet took part in a race from England to Australia in 1934. It is shown here after it was restored for the fiftieth anniversary of the race. Each propeller is driven by a separate engine. Each one is like a huge car engine and is fueled by gasoline.

Wooden propellers
The first airplanes had propellers made from layers of wood that were glued together. The pilot would spin the propeller by hand to start the engine. This was a very dangerous job because there was a chance that the pilot might be hit by the fast-spinning propeller.

Microlight

If you attach an engine-driven propeller to a hang-glider, the result is a microlight. The engine in this microlight aircraft develops about the same power as a small family car. The twin-bladed propeller is less than 3¼ft across. It pushes the plane along at around 40mph. Microlight aircraft are often used for survey work in remote parts of the world. The aircraft can be carried by road and then launched to survey areas far from the road.

Training planes

The Piper Seneca has four seats, so it can carry a pilot and three passengers. Aircraft like these are typically used for learning to fly. Like a car, they can be equipped with dual controls for teacher and student. The propellers each have two blades. They are twisted at an angle like the blades of a fan. As the propellers spin, the blades force air backward.

Piper Seneca

Lockheed Hercules

Heavy-duty carriers

This aircraft carries military supplies. Each propeller has four variable-pitch blades. The propellers are driven by a turboprop engine, a type of jet engine in which the hot gases drive a turbine, which in turn drives the propeller. There is also some thrust provided by the fast-moving exhaust gases.

PROPEL YOURSELF

To and fro
A boomerang is a special form of spinner. Each of the two arms is an airfoil shape. When it is thrown correctly, a boomerang will fly in a circle, eventually returning to the thrower.

PROPELLERS WORK in two different ways. When a propeller spins, it makes air move past it. At the same time, the moving air makes the propeller spin. Propeller-driven aircraft use this effect to produce thrust. These projects look at propellers working in these two ways. In the first you can make a simple paper propeller called a spinner. As the spinner falls, moving air rushes past the blades, making it revolve. This acts just like the fruits and seeds of maple and sycamore trees which have two propeller blades. As they drop from the tree, they spin and catch the wind, and are carried far away.

In the second project, you can make a spinning propeller fly upward through the air. The propeller-like blades are set at an angle, like the blades of a fan. They whirl around and make air move. The moving air produces thrust and lifts the propeller upward. Children first flew propellers like these, 600 years ago in China.

IN A SPIN

You will need:
thin paper, ruler, pencil, scissors, paper clip.

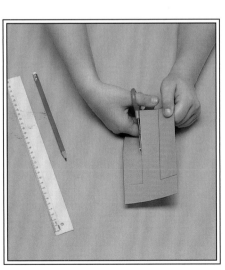

1 Take a piece of paper, 6 x 3½in, and draw a T shape on it, as shown in the picture above. With a pair of scissors, cut along the two long lines of the T.

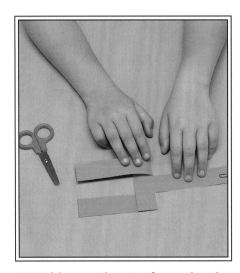

2 Fold one side strip forward and one backward, as shown above, making two blades and a stalk. Attach a paper clip to the bottom. Open the blades flat.

3 Now drop the spinner - what happens? Before dropping it again, try giving each blade a twist to make your spinner spin round faster.

PROJECT

LET'S TWIST

You will need: *thick cardboard, ruler, pair of compasses, protractor, pen, scissors, ½in sheet of cork, bradawl, 3¼in length of ⅛in-diameter dowel, model glue, spool, string.*

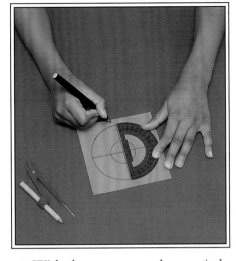

1 With the compasses, draw a circle about 4in across on the cardboard. Draw a smaller circle ¾in across in the center. With the protractor, draw lines across the circle, dividing it into 16 equal sections.

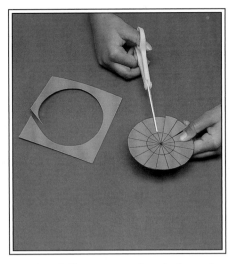

2 Carefully cut out the circle and along the lines to the smaller circle. Twist the blades sideways a little. Try to give each blade the same amount of twist, about 20 to 30 degrees.

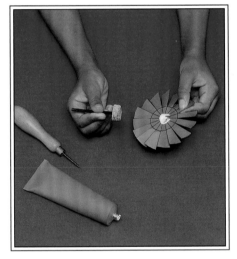

3 Make a hole in the center of the cork sheet with a bradawl. Put glue on the end of the dowel and push it into the hole. Stick the cork in the middle of the propeller.

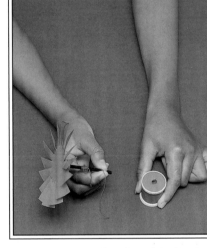

4 When the glue has dried, wind a long piece of string around the dowel. Drop the dowel into the spool launcher. You are now ready for a test flight.

5 Pull steadily on the string to whirl the propeller around. As the end of the string comes away, the blades produce enough thrust to lift the spinning propeller out of the launcher and into the air.

JET ENGINES

Most large modern aircraft are driven by jet engines. They fly faster than airplanes with propellers because they can fly high where the air is thin and drag is less. Jet engines have huge fans inside them that suck in air and compress it. Fuel burns in this air and produces a roaring jet of hot gases that blasts from the rear of the engine, producing thrust. Even more powerful turbojet engines are fitted to some fighter aircraft, but they are noisy and use enormous amounts of fuel.

Passenger jets use turbofan engines that have an extra-large fan at the front of the engine. This fan produces most of the thrust by forcing air around the engine so that it joins up with the jet of exhaust gases at the rear. This surround of cooler air helps to muffle the roar of the jet.

Jet stream
An octopus uses jet propulsion to move along. It sucks in water and squeezes it out through a small hole. The jet of water pushes it along.

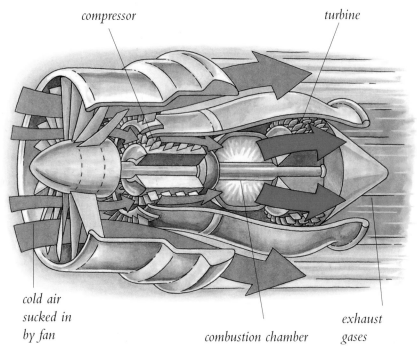

compressor

turbine

cold air sucked in by fan

combustion chamber

exhaust gases

A turbofan engine
Jet engines are naturally tube-shaped because of the shape of the workings inside. Fast-spinning fans compress air into the engine. Fuel burns in the air and heats it. The exhaust gases spin the turbine, a set of blades that drives the compressor. Gases are forced out of the engine at over 6,550ft per second and at 1,832°F. The blast of hot gases, together with the surrounding cold air, pushes the engine, and the aircraft, forward.

Inside a jet engine
A model of an aircraft's jet engine is shown with its protective casing removed so that the internal parts can be seen. The air is drawn into the engine from the left. The blades in the compressor unit then increase the air pressure before the fuel is passed further into the engine and ignited.

Lockheed Blackbird

Executive jet

A small commuter jet can reach speeds of 500mph – nearly as fast as a large airplane. It is designed with the engines on the tail, rather than under the wings. The high tailplane avoids jet exhausts.

Reconnaissance

The Lockheed SR-71 Blackbird reconnaissance plane is powered by turbojet engines. In 1974, one flew from New York to London in 1 hour, 54 minutes – a still unbroken record of 2,065mph. In the 1970s and 1980s, these airplanes were designed to fly fast and at high altitude specifically for the use of the US Air Force to take aerial photographs of enemy territory.

Turboshaft engine

This helicopter is powered by a type of jet engine without a stream (jet) of gases. Most of the energy from the engine turns the rotors providing the thrust needed to keep it airborne. Only a tiny bit of energy pushes the helicopter forward.

Jumbo jet

The Boeing 747 was the first wide-bodied jet airplane. It can carry 400 or more passengers. Since it was introduced in 1970, it has made international jet travel commonplace.

Turboprop engine

The Vickers Viscount was one of the first and most successful passenger aircraft powered by jet engines that turned propellers. It was widely used in the 1950s and could carry 60 passengers.

ZOOM THROUGH THE AIR

A JET engine produces thrust from a roaring jet of super-hot gas. Its construction looks complicated, but the way it works is very simple. A powerful jet of gas moving in one direction produces thrust in the other direction. Imagine you are standing on a skateboard and squirting a powerful hose forward. Jet propulsion will push you backward. This reaction has been known about for nearly 2,000 years, but it was not until the 1930s that it was applied to an engine.

In the first experiment, you can make a jet zoom along a string. The jet engine is a balloon that produces thrust from escaping air. The second project shows you how to make a set of blades called a turbine. It uses hot air to turn the blades. These projects may seem very simple, but they use the same scientific principles that propel all jet airplanes through the air. When doing the turbine project ask an adult to light the candles.

Water pressure
As the fruit of the squirting cucumber ripens, the contents become liquid. More water is drawn into it so that the pressure inside increases, like a balloon. Eventually it breaks off the stem and shoots away, squirting the seeds behind it.

BALLOON JET

You will need: long, thin balloon, scissors, sticky tape, drinking straw, string.

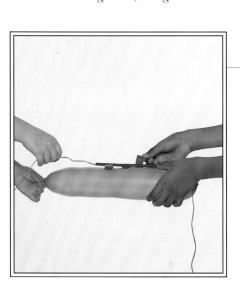

1 Blow up the balloon and, while a friend holds the neck, tape the straw to its top. Thread the string through the straw and, holding it level, tie it to something to keep it in place.

2 Let go of the neck of the balloon. A stream of air jets backward and produces thrust. This propels the balloon forward along the string at high speed. Bring the balloon back, blow it up and try another flight.

PROJECT

TURBINE LIGHTS

You will need: *aluminum foil pie dish, scissors, pair of compasses, protractor, ruler, straight pin, 3¼in length of ⅛in diameter dowel, masking tape, bead, spool, non-hardening modeling material, plate, four votive candles, matches.*

1 Cut out the bottom of a large foil pie dish as evenly as possible. Make a small hole in the center with the point of the pair of compasses.

2 Mark a smaller circle in the center. Mark 16 equal sections as in the spin project and cut along each one to the inner circle. Try to use just one scissor cut along each line.

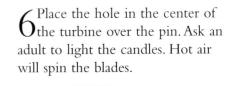

6 Place the hole in the center of the turbine over the pin. Ask an adult to light the candles. Hot air will spin the blades.

3 Angle the blades by holding the inner tip and twisting the outer edges 20 to 30 degrees. The center of the inner tip should be flat, in line with the centre of the disk.

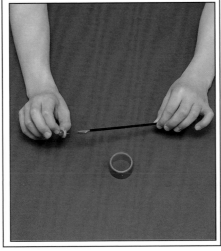

4 Tape the head of the pin to one end of the dowel. Place the bead on the pin. This will allow the turbine to spin freely.

5 Put the dowel in the spool and press the spool into the modeling material in the center of the plate. Place the four candles on the plate around the spool.

FASTER THAN SOUND

THE SOUND barrier is like an invisible wall that travels in front of a speeding aircraft. As an airplane flies, it sends out pressure waves through the air that are like the ripples streaming from a boat. The waves move away from the aircraft at the speed of sound. When the aircraft is traveling at this speed, the waves cannot outrun it. They build up and compress the air in front of the aircraft.

To fly faster than the speed of sound, the aircraft must fly through this barrier of dense air and overtake it. Wartime pilots, whose planes flew close to the speed of sound in a dive, reported that there seemed to be something slowing them down. The aircraft goes through the sound barrier with a jolt because drag suddenly increases and decreases again. Shock waves spread out and can be heard on the ground as a rumbling sonic boom. This boom represents all the sound energy that otherwise would be spread out in front of the aircraft, all arriving at once. We hear it as a rumble because of the distance it has traveled.

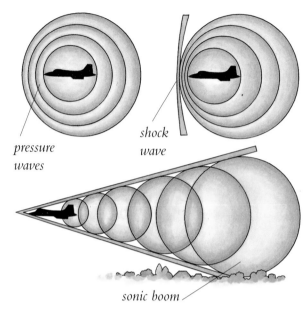

pressure waves

shock wave

sonic boom

Under pressure

As an aircraft flies along, it sends out pressure waves. At the speed of sound, a shock wave builds up in front of the aircraft. As the aircraft accelerates through the sound barrier, the shock wave breaks away to be heard on the ground as a sonic (sound) boom.

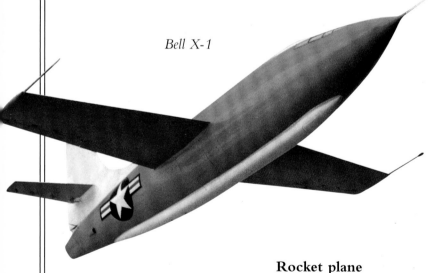

Bell X-1

Rocket plane

In 1947, the rocket-powered Bell X-1 was the first aircraft to travel faster than the speed of sound. The thin air at great heights reduces friction, but would not provide a propeller-driven engine with the oxygen in the air that it would need to burn its fuel. A rocket motor was needed for this.

Bombshell

The Bell X-1 rocket plane was dropped from a B29 bomber at 20,000ft. This was the highest that a propeller-driven engine could reach. As the pilot accelerated and climbed to a height of 42,500ft, the aircraft broke through the sound barrier.

Pilot's-eye view

A large transparent canopy gives the pilot a good field of view. Fighter pilots need an array of computers in the cockpit to cope with the enormous amounts of information they need to fly their jets safely.

Jet fighter

The Mirage flies at more than twice the speed of sound. It climbs almost straight upward, speeding faster than a rifle bullet. It can reach the same height as a cruising airliner in about one minute. The Mirage is used by air forces around the world. There are different models for use as fighters, fighter bombers or for reconnaissance.

Making waves

The wave created by the front of a boat (pushing through the water) is caused by the same process as the shock wave of a supersonic aircraft. The boat is traveling faster than the natural speed of the wave at the water's surface. The denser the air (or water), the quicker sound can travel through it. So speed of sound is greatest at sea level, where the air is most dense.

FACT BOX

• The speed of sound is described as Mach 1. The actual speed can change, according to air temperature and density. Sound travels faster in warm air. At sea level (68°F), Mach 1 is 760mph, but at 39,000ft (−58°F) Mach 1 is 657mph.

• Subsonic speeds are below Mach 0.8 (jumbo jets). Transonic speeds are between Mach 0.8 and Mach 1.2 (breaking the sound barrier). Supersonic speeds are between Mach 1.2 and Mach 5 (Concorde and fighter jets). Hypersonic speeds are above Mach 5 (the space shuttle during re-entry).

• The first supersonic civilian aircraft to fly was the Russian Tupolev Tu-144 on the last day of 1968, two months before the Concorde.

Breaking the sound barrier

The Concorde is the world's only supersonic passenger aircraft. It cruises at 13,500mph, over twice the speed of an ordinary airplane, and can cross the Atlantic Ocean in just over three hours. Its engines, however, are noisy and use a lot of fuel.

GOING UP

W ATCH A BIRD taking off. It flaps its wings and up it goes! A modern airplane must hurtle down a runway as fast as a racing car. It has to travel up to 2 miles to reach take-off speed, when its wings lift it off the ground. Some special types of aircraft are designed to take off and land on a single spot. These are called Vertical Take-Off and Landing aircraft (or VTOL for short). Examples include the Harrier jump jet and an early prototype, nicknamed the *Flying Bedstead* because of its very peculiar appearance.

Helicopters are VTOL aircraft, but they are slow compared to airplanes and use a lot of fuel. Other aircraft are designed to use very short runways a few hundred meters long. They are called Short Take-Off and Landing aircraft (STOL). They can fly from inner-city airports or from remote airstrips in fields or deserts. Modern aircraft for use on aircraft carriers are now VTOL or STOL fighter planes. For this reason, the flight deck of modern aircraft carriers is much shorter than that of earlier ships. However, these aircraft still use up more fuel than conventional planes.

Up and away
The *Flying Bedstead* from the 1950s was built to experiment with ideas about vertical flight. Moving nozzles directed the thrust from a jet engine. Experiments with this machine helped finalize the design of the Harrier jump jet.

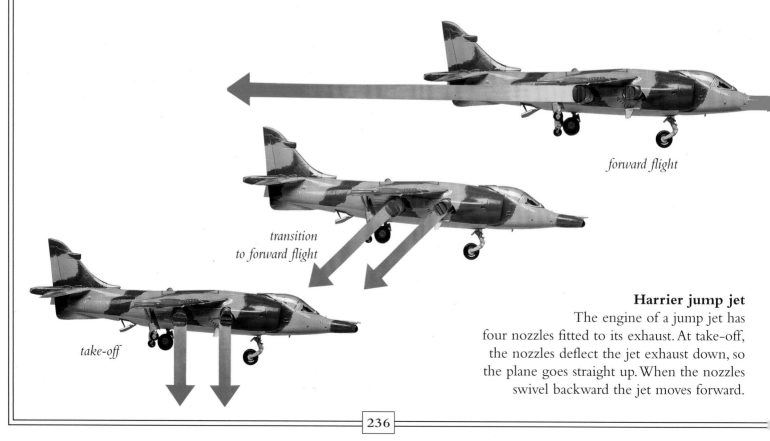

forward flight

transition to forward flight

take-off

Harrier jump jet
The engine of a jump jet has four nozzles fitted to its exhaust. At take-off, the nozzles deflect the jet exhaust down, so the plane goes straight up. When the nozzles swivel backward the jet moves forward.

De Havilland Dash

This aircraft is used on short runways in cities. It has four extra-quiet engines and can carry up to 54 passengers. Its large wings provide plenty of lift and are set high on its body to keep the propellers clear off the ground. The Dash can take off on a runway just 2,300ft long.

Autogyro

The autogyro is a cross between an airplane and a helicopter. The helicopter-type rotor is not driven by the engine. During flight, rushing air spins the rotor which provides most of the lift to keep the autogyro up in the air.

Bell-Boeing Osprey

The Osprey is known as a tilt-rotor aircraft. The giant propellers are called proprotors. These are mounted at the tips of the wings and tilt upward for take-off, like a helicopter. For forward flight, the proprotors swing into the propeller position of an airplane. The Osprey can fly about three times as far as a helicopter on the same fuel load.

Landing on water

Some modern aircraft carriers are much shorter than World War II carriers. They carry short take-off and landing planes such as the Harrier jump jet which need the ski-jump ramp at the bow, for almost vertical take off. Some carriers catapult the planes as they take-off from the bow. Such planes land at the stern and are stopped by wires across the deck.

STRANGE AIRCRAFT

MANY AIRCRAFT have strange shapes. The Belluga looks like an enormous, fat dolphin with wings. The fabric used to make the wings of a pedal-powered aircraft is so thin that light shines through it. In each case, an aircraft's appearance is due to its being designed for a particular purpose such as speed or transportation. The Belluga is designed to carry large items which will not fit into the cargo hold of an ordinary cargo airplane. The wings of pedal-powered aircraft are covered in thin plastic films to make them ultralight.

The people who design new planes are called aeronautical engineers. They can design planes for all sorts of different purposes – to carry enormous loads, to fly super-fast, or even to fly non-stop around the world. All aircraft, however, have certain common requirements – they all must be able to take off, fly straight and level, and to land safely. Most aircraft are a compromise between many conflicting factors. They need to carry loads, fly fast and be efficient. Some aircraft have mostly been designed to be as effective as possible in just one of these ways at the expense of the others.

On the lookout
The *Optica* observation plane was designed for low-speed flight and to give a clear view. It is used to observe such things as problems with traffic flow or crop growth.

Pedal power
Gossamer Albatross was the first pedal-powered aircraft. It was made of thin plastic stretched on ribs only ¼in thick to make it light enough for a strong man to operate.

World traveler
In 1986, *Voyager* took nine days to fly Americans Jeana Yeager and Dick Rutan non-stop around the world without refuelling. Each wing of the specially built plane was four times the length of the fuselage, providing the greatest lift with the lowest drag.

Invisible fighter

The F-117 "stealth" fighter is made up of flat, slab-shaped panels and special materials. These scatter beams from enemy radars and make the plane almost undetectable. Ordinary aircraft reflect radar beams straight back so they can be spotted. The F-117's low, flat shape reflects radar waves in directions other than back to the receiver, while special paint absorbs some of the radar waves.

A whale of a plane

The Belluga transport plane can carry almost 25 tons of cargo in its 26¼ft-high hold. The Belluga is enormous, but it has the streamlined shape of a dolphin to help reduce drag. The hold is so enormous that it can carry a set of airliner wings from their manufacturers to the assembly point.

Sun strength

Solar Challenger was the world's first solar-powered aircraft. It flew across the English Channel in July 1981, in 5 hours and 23 minutes. Weighing 130lb, it is still the lightest powered aircraft. Solar cells on the wings change sunlight into electricity. An electric motor drives the propellers. A solar powered plane, based on the same ideas, has flown non-stop around the world.

Splash down

In areas near forests like this one in Canada, firefighting planes are used to carry water from the ocean or a lake to put out forest fires. Some use an enormous flexible bucket suspended below the plane to pick up the water. Others, like this one, scoop the water directly into the body of the fuselage.

FACT BOX

• In 1907, one of the first British powered flights was made in a bizarre-looking multiplane known as the *Venetian Blind*. It had nearly 50 sets of wings.

• The aircraft with the longest wingspan was a flying boat, the *Spruce Goose*. Designed by eccentric millionaire Howard Hughes, it had a wingspan of over 320ft. It made its first and only flight in 1947.

• A flying wing is an airplane with no tail or fuselage. The cabin and engines are inside the wing. The Northrop B-2 stealth bomber is an example of a flying wing.

PROJECT

SPEEDING THROUGH WATER

WINGS CAN also work underwater. Some boats have underwater wings called hydrofoils. As the boat speeds along, the airfoil-shaped hydrofoils lift it out of the water. The hull of the boat is now travelling in the air, so drag is greatly reduced. Hydrofoil boats can travel at 60mph, over three times as fast as an ordinary boat. Hovercraft seem to fly across the sea, just a few inches above the surface. Powerful fans blow air down through a rubber skirt to provide a cushion of air. This cushion cuts down the friction between the hovercraft and the water below. Propellers drive the hovercraft forward at up to 75mph.

Many birds and even a few insects fly underwater. Penguins are birds that cannot fly in the air but can move so rapidly underwater that they can leap out of the water and even onto ice floes a yard or more above the surface. They don't flap their wings up and down to swim, but use a rowing action. Birds that can fly both above and below the water include the auks, such as puffins and guillemots.

Sea skimming
Hydrofoils lift the hull of this craft completely clear of the water. At rest, it floats on the water like a normal boat. A small hydrofoil lifts a large boat because water is more dense than air and so slower speeds create more lift.

HOW A HYDROFOIL WORKS

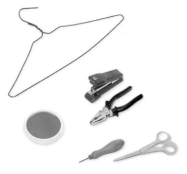

You will need: *the lid of a margarine tub, scissors, stapler, bradawl, pliers, coat hanger wire (ask an adult to cut out the bottom section).*

3 Make sure that the hydrofoil moves freely on the wire. Try moving your hydrofoil in air – it will not lift up because air is far less dense than water. Pull it through water and it will rise up the wire. Water moves quicker over the hydrofoil than beneath it, reducing the pressure above. The higher pressure below pushes up the hydrofoil.

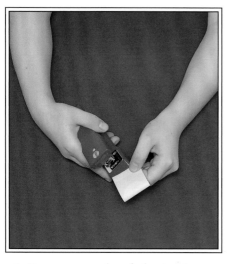

1 Cut a rectangle of plastic, about 2 x 4in, from the lid of the margarine tub. Fold it in half. Staple the ends together ½in in from the back edge.

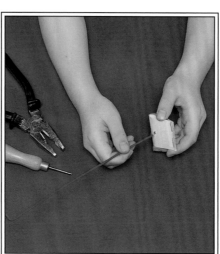

2 Use a bradawl to make two holes in the front of the hydrofoil ½in away from the folded edge. Use pliers to bend 1½in of one end of the wire. Slide the hydrofoil on to the wire.

HOW A HOVERCRAFT WORKS

You will need:
polystyrene tray, pencil, balloon,
balloon pump, button.

1 Use a pencil to poke a hole through the middle of the polystyrene tray. The hole should be about ½in across.

2 Blow up the balloon with the pump. Push its neck through the hole. Keep pinching the neck of the balloon to stop the air escaping.

3 Keep pinching with one hand, using the other hand to slip the button into the neck. The button will control how fast the air escapes.

4 Place the tray on a table. Air escapes steadily from under the tray's edges, lifting it up between ⅛ and ¼in. Give the tray a gentle push and it will skate along.

Water spray
A hovercraft's rubber skirt is the black part just above the water. You can see how the air cushion makes the water spray about. Four large propellers drive the hovercraft in any direction. Hovercraft work best if the water is not too rough. They are used for travel along rivers and lakes, but some are still used on the sea.

FLYING THROUGH SPACE

S PACE ROCKETS rely on jet propulsion to fly. A stream of hot gases roars out from the tail end and the rocket surges forward. Deep under the sea, octopuses rely on jet propulsion to escape from their enemies. They squirt out a jet of water and shoot off in the opposite direction. This project shows you how to make and fly a rocket that uses jet propulsion. The thrust of a rocket depends on the mass of propellant it shoots out every second. Water is a much better propellant than hot gas because it is so much heavier. Follow these instructions carefully and your rocket could fly to over 80ft above the ground. You may need adult help to make some parts of this rocket and to launch it. When you are ready for a test flight, set your rocket up in an open space, well away from trees and buildings. This rocket is very powerful – you must not stand over it while it is being launched. Wear clothes that you do not mind getting very wet!

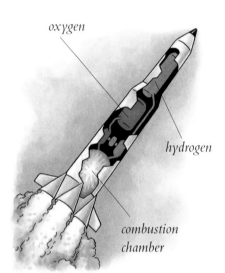

oxygen

hydrogen

combustion chamber

Inside the rocket
Liquid hydrogen and liquid oxygen are pumped into the combustion chamber. The hydrogen burns furiously in the oxygen. The exhaust produces immense thrust.

Satellite launch
Rockets with powerful engines can carry satellites into orbit 200 miles or more above the Earth's surface.

MAKE A ROCKET

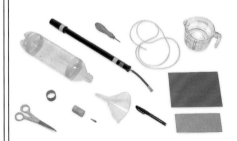

You will need: *cardboard, pen, colored cardboard, scissors, plastic bottle, strong sticky tape, funnel, bottle of water, cork, bradawl, air valve, plastic tubing, bicycle pump.*

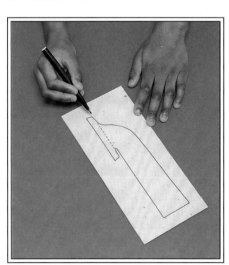

1 Rockets have fins to make them fly straight. Draw out this fin template (it is about 8in long) onto plain cardboard and use it to cut out four fins from colored cardboard.

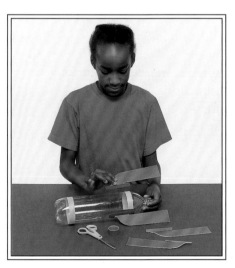

2 Decorate your bottle to look like a rocket. Fold over the tab at the top of each fin. Use long pieces of strong sticky tape to firmly attach the fins to the bottle.

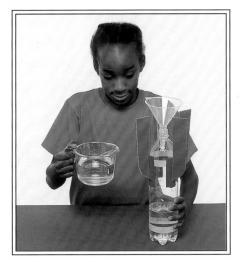

3 Use the funnel to half-fill the bottle with water. (The water is the propellant. Compressed air above the water will provide the energy that makes the thrust.)

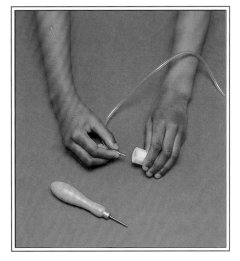

4 Use the bradawl to drill a hole through the cork. Push the wide end of the air valve into the plastic tubing. Push the valve through the hole in the cork.

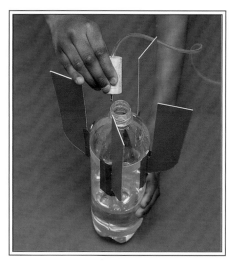

5 Hold the bottle with one hand and push the cork and the valve into the neck of the bottle using the other hand. Push it in firmly so the cork does not slide out too easily.

7 Stand the rocket on its tail fins. Start pumping. Bubbles of air will rise up through the water. When the pressure in the bottle gets high enough, the cork and water will be forced out and the rocket will fly upwards.

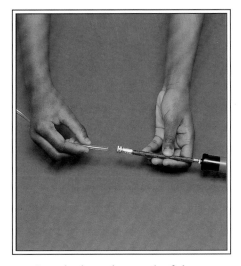

6 Attach the other end of the plastic tubing to the bicycle pump. Turn your rocket the right way up – you are now ready to launch your rocket outside. Look for a launch site well away from trees and buildings.

FLY INTO THE FUTURE

BIRDS HAVE been flying for more than 30 million years. Humans took to the air in kites 700 years ago, in balloons only in the 1760s, and in airplanes 100 years ago. Now the air is full of aircraft of all descriptions. You can fly half-way around the world in less than 24 hours. Some planes fly three times faster than sound. When you look up into the sky in ten years' time, what will you see? Engineers are developing new and more powerful engines, new materials that are lighter and stronger than metal, and strange new wing shapes to help aircraft fly ever faster and higher. Whatever happens, human flight will continue to develop, probably at heavy cost to the health of our environment and the birds and animals who share it. However, efforts are now being made to reduce the damage.

Jumbo jet
This Boeing 747–400 can carry up to 567 passengers. It is the double-decker version of the 1970s jumbo jet. Plans for a super jumbo, the 747–600X, include an on-board fitness center and a cinema.

Up, up and away
The Roton is still under development. It claims to be an entirely new approach to space flight. It will use a turbo-driven propeller to rise into the upper atmosphere. It then becomes rocket-powered. On landing the process is reversed.

Horizontal take-off
An artist's impression shows HOTOL, an aircraft that takes off and lands horizontally, riding piggy-back to a height of 50,000ft on the *Antonin 225*, the world's largest airplane. The HOTOL then launches into space using rocket engines. Traveling at Mach 5, it could fly from the UK to Australia in under four hours.

FACT BOX
• A Russian experimental plane, called the Aquatain, has been designed to gain extra lift by skimming across the surface of the ocean. The craft is reported to use much less fuel than a conventional aircraft.

• All new airplanes have to meet strict environmental rules governing noise levels and emissions that might further damage the sensitive ozone layer.

• Modern cockpits use advanced systems to reduce the pilot's workload. Holographic displays and keyboards project data on to a see-through screen. Optical fibers carry signals at the speed of light to the aircraft's control surfaces.

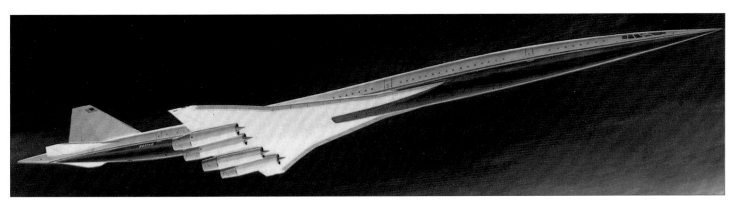

High speed civil transportation

Although modern airplanes are very efficient, they still contribute enormously to the pollution of the upper atmosphere. Flying at Mach 3, this airliner may one day carry 200 passengers from New York to Tokyo in about three hours. Cruising above 60,000ft, it will have low polluting engines that will not damage the ozone layer.

Space plane

Aircraft can travel extremely fast in space because there is no air to create drag. This model shows what the X-30 space plane might look like, flying at speeds up to Mach 5 through the edge of space to reach its destination. The plane does not have to reach escape velocity (68mps) as spacecraft do. It can fly to the edge of the atmosphere reaching Mach 5, then cruise through space in an arch, descending again at the end of the journey. At such high speed, extremely thin air on the borders of space provides enough lift to keep it up.

Experimental plane

The X-29 aircraft refuels in mid-air from a large tanker plane. The X-29 has unusual swept-forward wings. These give high lift and low drag making the plane very maneuvrable. Tests with the X-29 may lead to new designs for passenger planes. The swept-forward wings bear a strange resemblance to *Sharovipteryx*, one of the earliest gliding reptiles. This species differed from other gliders in that the wing was supported by the hind limbs. Scientists studying this fossil think that it also had extended flaps at the front, as in the X-29.

GLOSSARY

A

accelerator pedal A pedal beneath the driver's foot used to control the flow of fuel to a car engine.

aileron A movable flap on the trailing (rear) edge of an aircraft wing.

air pollution A situation in which the air we breathe is poisoned by gases such as the carbon monoxide emitted by cars.

airbag A cushion that automatically inflates in a crash, protecting a car driver and his or her passengers from serious injury.

airbrake A mechanism that will slow a vehicle down using air resistance.

air-cooled An engine-cooling system in which the heat of the engine is carried away by air.

airfoil An object, such as a wing, that is shaped to improve efficiency of movement through air.

alloy A mixture of metals.

amphibious car A car that travels both on land and in the water.

anchor A device that is dropped overboard to stop a ship from drifting.

angle of attack In aviation, the angle between the lower surface of an airfoil and the direction in which it is moving.

asphalt A mixture of bitumen (tar) and concrete used to give roads a hard, smooth, weatherproof surface.

autopilot A computerized or mechanical system that senses changes in the direction of a vehicle, such as a ship or plane, and automatically adjusts the controls to maintain the original direction.

B

ball-bearing A hardened steel ball, often arranged with other ball-bearings around a turning surface, used to reduce friction.

bank To incline an aircraft at an angle, as part of a turn. When an aircraft turning left banks, the right wing tip is higher than the left one.

battery A device that contains chemical substances that convert chemical energy into electricity.

bilge pump A means of pumping water that has collected in the bilges, or bottom of the hull, of a ship.

biplane An aircraft with two sets of wings, one above the other.

bogie A unit underneath a locomotive that guides a train around curves in the track. Four or six pivoted wheels are mounted on one bogie.

boiler The part of a steam engine where steam is produced through the action of heat on water in the boiler tubes.

boom A pole to which the bottom of a ship's sail is attached.

bow The front part of a ship or boat.

brake A pad or disc that slows down a moving surface by pressing on it.

bridge The platform from where a ship's officers direct its course.

bubble car The name given in the 1950s and 1960s to microcars such as the BMW Isetta because of their unusual, rounded shape.

buffer A rigid metal structure that absorbs the impact of a train to stop it at the end of the track.

bulkhead A solid, waterproof, airtight wall, ceiling or floor in a ship or aircraft that separates one section from another.

Bullet Trains The nickname for the high-speed, streamlined passenger trains that operate in Japan.

bumper The protective, wraparound metal or rubber barrier that protects the front and rear of a car.

buoy A float used to mark channels or dangerous waters in shipping lanes.

buoyancy tank A tank that can be filled with water to make a submarine sink or filled with compressed air to enable it to rise to the surface.

C

camshaft A device that creates a regular, rocking movement, such as the opening and shutting of a valve on a car cylinder head.

canoe A light, narrow, open boat operated by human-powered paddles.

carbon monoxide A poisonous gas that is a by-product of burning gasoline.

carburetor A unit that controls the fuel mixture entering the combustion chamber in an engine.

carriage The part of a train that carries passengers, also known as a coach or car.

catamaran A boat with two hulls.

catenary An overhead power cable supplying electricity to a locomotive through a pantograph attached to the top of the locomotive.

centerboard A movable plate that can be lowered through the keel of a sailing boat to stop sideways drift when sailing into the wind.

checkered flag A black-and-white, checked flag that is lowered as each car in a race crosses the finishing line.

chrome A shiny metallic finish from the metal chromium used, for example, on car fittings such as bumpers and handles.

classic car A car built after 1930, which is at least 20 years old.

clipper A fast sailing ship with large sails. The popularity of clippers peaked in the mid-1800s.

coachwork The outside body of a car.

cockpit 1) The area around the seat of a pilot in an aircraft (usually at the front) containing the control panel and instruments. 2) The part of a small boat containing the wheel or tiller.

compass An instrument that enables people to find the right direction, especially one with a magnetized needle that swings to magnetic north so that true north can be calculated.

container In transportation, an enormous metal box for carrying goods. Containers can be easily transferred from one means of transport to another, such as from ship to lorry or lorry to train.

convertable A car with a flexible roof that can be folded away into the rear of the car.

convertible A car that can be driven with or without a roof.

coracle A small, oval boat made from the animal skins that are tightly strapped to a wickerwork frame.

coupling A connecting device that joins a locomotive to a carriage or wagon to make a train.

coupling rod A long, metal rod that connects the driving wheels on each side of a locomotive.

cowcatcher A sloping, V-shaped plate attached to the front of American locomotives. Cowcatchers clear cattle and other obstructions from the line.

crankshaft The part of a car that transmits movement from the pistons to the road wheels.

cruise 1) To fly at the most efficient speed and altitude for the design of a particular aircraft. The cruising speed and height is the one that uses least fuel for the distance covered. 2) To travel by boat for pleasure.

custom car A car that has been deliberately adapted by the owner to make it look and drive the way he or she wants.

cut-and-cover construction An early method of building underground tunnels. A large trench is cut into the earth along the line of the tunnel, lined with brick and then roofed over.

cylinder In an engine, a hollow tube in which a piston moves.

D

dashboard The horizontal surface that contains the instruments facing a driver inside a car.

deadweight The difference in the volume of water displaced by a ship when it is loaded and when it is unloaded.

deck A floor or platform in a ship or plane.

density A measure of how tightly the matter in a substance is packed together.

dhow An Indian boat with one or more triangular sails.

displacement The volume of water displaced by a ship when it is afloat.

drag Resistance or force that acts in the opposite direction to motion.

drag racer A car specifically designed to take part in races at very high speeds over short, straight distances.

driveshaft A shaft that transmits power from an engine to the propeller in a ship or plane, or to the wheel in a train or car.

driving wheel The wheel of a locomotive that turns in response to power from the cylinder.

dry dock A dock that can be pumped dry so that the part of a ship's hull that is normally underwater can be repaired.

dug-out canoe A canoe made by hollowing out a log.

E

elevator A movable flap on the tailplane or rear wing of an aircraft that causes the nose to rise or fall.

F

fathom A way of measuring the depth of water in units of 6ft.

flange A rim on the inside of the metal wheel of a locomotive that stops the wheels slipping sideways and falling off the rails.

Formula One A class of racing car that has the most powerful engine specification of all.

four-wheel drive A car in which power from the engine can be transferred to all four wheels simultaneously, not just to either the front or the rear wheels.

freight Commercial goods transported by rail, road, sea or air.

friction A rubbing action between two surfaces that stops or slows movement.

fuel A substance, such as gasoline, that is burned to provide energy.

fuel efficient Designed to use as little fuel as possible while ensuring normal speed and power.

funicular A type of railroad that operates on steep slopes. Two cars move up and down the slope simultaneously as a cable attached to each carriage winds around an electrically powered drum.

fuselage The main body of an aircraft to which the wings and tail are attached.

G

gas 1) A non-solid, non-liquid substance. 2) Short for gasoline (petrol) – the main fuel used to power internal combustion engines.

gasoline A liquid used to power internal combustion engines. Gas is made from oil and is easily burned, making it ideal for use as a fuel.

gauge The width between the inside running edges of the rails of a railroad track. In Britain, the United States and most of Europe, the gauge is 4¾ft.

gear A toothed wheel designed to interact with other toothed wheels to transfer motion in a controled way.

glide To fly through the air in a controled way using air currents (rather than an engine) as the power source.

H

hang-glider A simple gliding aircraft consisting of a wing with a framework beneath for the pilot.

harbor A sheltered port for a ship.

helium The second lightest of all gases, used for filling lighter-than-air balloons.

helmsman The person who steers, or helms, a ship or boat.

hovercraft A vehicle that can travel across land or sea on a cushion of air.

hull The main body or outer shell of a ship.

humpyard An area beside a main rail route where freight cars can be sorted to make a freight train.

hydrofoil A type of boat with wing-like attachments on the bottom of the hull. At high speed, the force created by these foils lifts the boat clear of the water.

hydrometer An instrument for measuring the relative density of a liquid.

I

inner tube A rubber tube filled with air contained inside the tires of bicycles and older cars.

internal combustion The burning of fuel in a closed chamber to generate mechanical power.

J

jet ski A small, self-propelled boat that resembles a scooter.

jib Any triangular sail set before the foremast of a boat.

joystick The control stick of an airplane or other vehicle.

jumbo jet A passenger jet aircraft that can carry several hundred people. It is often wide-bodied, with ten or more seats across.

junk A Chinese sailing vessel.

K

kayak A canoe-like boat with an enclosed cockpit.

keel The narrow point of a hull that runs between bow and stern, and from which the hull is built up.

knot A unit of speed. One knot equals one nautical mile per hour.

L

lateen A triangular sail.

leading truck The pair of leading wheels at the front of a locomotive.

lift Force generated by an airfoil that counters the force of gravity and keeps a flying object in the air.

limousine Luxurious closed-bodied car, featuring a glass partition between the driver and the passengers behind.

liner A passenger ship or aircraft.

locomotive An engine powered by steam, diesel or electricity used to pull the cars of a train.

longship A narrow ship with a square sail used by the Vikings.

lubrication The smoothing of friction between the parts of an engine, usually with oil.

M

maglev train A high-speed, streamlined train that moves as a result of the action of powerful electromagnets.

mast Any vertical spar that supports sails, rigging or flags above the deck of a vessel.

mayday An internationally recognized signal of distress.

microcar A particularly small car, designed for use in cities to minimize traffic congestion.

N (continued from column)

monohull A ship or boat with a single hull.

monoplane An aircraft with a single pair of wings, one either side.

monorail A train that runs along a single rail.

mudguard The wide wing of metal around a car wheel that prevents mud and stones from flying up off the road.

multi-purpose vehicle (MPV) A vehicle that has more than one use, for example, one that has space for passengers as well as goods.

N

navigation The skill of planning and directing the route of a plane, ship or car.

nuclear power Power, usually electrical, produced by a nuclear reactor.

O

oar A long pole with a flattened blade at one end, used for propelling a boat through water.

off-road vehicle (ORV) A car that can drive on surfaces other than smooth, tarmac roads.

oil A thick, black liquid found under the surface of the Earth, from which gasoline and other products are made.

outrigger A framework sticking out from the side of a boat to give the vessel more stability.

oxygen A gas in the Earth's atmosphere. Oxygen is essential for the survival of most animals and plants.

ozone layer The layer of the upper atmosphere, about 12½ miles above the Earth's surface, where ozone is formed. It filters ultraviolet rays from the Sun.

P

paddle A short pole with a flat, broad blade used for propelling a small, light boat, such as a canoe, through water.

paddlesteamer A riverboat powered by giant wheels made up of broad, wooden blades. The blades push against the water as they turn in response to power from a steam engine.

pantograph An assembly attached to the top of some locomotives that collects electricity from an overhead power supply.

parachute A device made of a light material, with a harness attached beneath, to allow a person or a package to descend from a height at a safe speed.

pendolino A train that tilts from side to side, enabling the train to move around curves at higher speeds than non-tilting trains.

periscope A system of prisms or mirrors that allows people, such as submariners, to view things above eye level.

pickup A small truck with a cab at the front and a flat platform over the rear wheels.

pilot A person who flies an aircraft or spacecraft or helps to navigate a ship into harbor.

piston A device that fits snugly inside the cylinders of an engine and is forced to move up and down by the pressure of gas or water. The up-and-down movement is then transferred to the wheels of the vehicle to make them turn.

pitch 1) A change in the vertical direction of flight, either up or down. 2) The angle at which a propeller blade on a ship or aircraft is set.

points Rails that guide the wheels of a train onto a different section of track.

poop deck The raised deck at the stern of a ship.

port 1) The left-hand side of a boat or aircraft when facing forward. 2) A town with a harbor.

production line A way of building machines in which the parts are added, one by one, in a continuous process in a factory.

propel To push or drive forward.

propeller A device with angled blades arranged around a hub. When turning at speed, it propels a plane through the air or boat through water.

prototype The first attempt to build a working model of a machine following the design.

pulley A mechanism for lifting and lowering weights by means of a wheel and a rope or belt.

Pullman A railroad car with luxurious sleeping compartments.

punt A long, flat-bottomed boat.

Q

quay A platform that projects into the water and is used for loading and unloading ships. Also called wharf.

R

rack-and-pinion railroad A railroad that operates on steep slopes. A cogwheel underneath the locomotive engages in teeth on a central rail that runs up the slope.

radar A system for detecting the position of distant objects using high-frequency radio waves.

radiator A container of water from which the water is pumped around an engine to prevent overheating.

raft A simple, flat-water craft, usually made of lengths of wood lashed together.

railcar A driverless passenger vehicle powered by diesel or electricity.

reconnaissance Surveying and searching over an unknown area, especially with a view to guiding others who might follow.

recreational vehicle (RV) A car designed for being driven on rough roads, but not for extreme surfaces such as rocky riverbeds.

resistance A force that acts against an object, causing it to slow down or stop.

rigging The system of ropes and wires that support and control a ship's sails and masts.

roll A sideways, tilting movement of an aircraft or ship.

rolling stock The locomotives, wagons, cars and any other vehicles that operate on a railroad.

rotor A set of angled blades that radiate from a central block and which rotate at speed to form a rotating motor.

rudder A device for controling the direction of a ship or plane. The rudder works by cutting into the flow of water or air.

S

satellite A celestial or artificial body orbiting around a planet or star. Artificial satellites are used for communication, exploration and photography.

sheet In sailing, a controlling rope attached to the lower edge of a sail.

sleeper 1) A horizontal, concrete beam supporting the rails on a railroad track. 2) A railroad carriage providing sleeping accommodation for passengers.

slipway A ramp for launching boats.

sonar A system used to find out the location of underwater objects.

speedometer A dial that displays the speed at which a vehicle is traveling.

spoiler An airbrake formed from a hinged flap on the rear edge of an aircraft wing.

sports car An open or closed car built for performance, usually with two seats.

starboard The right side of a boat or aircraft when facing forward.

steam engine An engine powered by the steam (water vapor) created by heating water.

stern The back part of a ship or boat.

stock car An ordinary car that has been adapted to make it suitable for racing.

stokehole The room containing a ship's boilers.

streamlined A shape that moves through air or water in the most efficient manner, with the least frictional resistance.

submarine A vessel designed for underwater travel.

submersible A small watercraft that can travel on or below the water's surface. Submersibles are used for underwater research, exploration and repairs.

supersonic An air speed faster than the speed of sound.

suspension system The springs and other shock absorbers that cushion the movement of wheels on the ground.

T

tailplane The small, horizontal wings at the rear of an aircraft.

thermal A rising current of air formed when part of the ground surface is heated by the sun.

throttle A valve that regulates the amount of steam or fuel going in to an engine. As a result, the throttle also regulates the speed at which the engine operates and the vehicle moves.

thrust The force that pushes any flying object forwards.

tiller The steering arm in a cockpit that turns the rudder of a boat.

tonnage The space available in a ship for carrying cargo, measured in tons.

trimaran A boat with three hulls.

triplane An aircraft with three sets of wings, one above the other.

tug 1) A small boat used for towing larger boats or oil platforms. 2) An aircraft that pulls a glider into the air.

Tunnel-Boring Machine (TBM) A giant tunnel-making machine that grinds through soft rock, such as chalk, using a giant, rotating, cutting head.

turbine A rotor that is moved by fast-moving gas currents. In aircraft, this air current is generated by burning fuel to produce hot, fast-moving gas.

turbofan A jet engine in which much of the turbine rotation is used to drive a fan that pushes air round the central engine. The thrust comes from the turbine jet exhaust and the fan-driven air.

turbojet A form of jet engine in which the turbine jet provides all the thrust.

turboprop A form of jet engine in which most of the rotation of the turbine is used to drive a propeller that then propels the aircraft.

turboshaft A form of jet engine in which all of the rotation of the turbine is used to drive a rotor which then propels an aircraft such as a helicopter.

turbulence Air movement that consists of tiny wind currents flowing in random directions, with no smooth flow of air.

U

undercarriage The landing wheels of an aircraft. In some aircraft, the undercarriage can be lifted during flight to reduce drag.

upthrust The force that makes a ship float or an aircraft take off.

V

veteran car Any car built before 1905.

vintage car Any car built between 1919 and 1930.

W

welding Joining two pieces of metal together by heat or under pressure.

wind tunnel A large chamber in which powerful drafts of air are blown over a car to test and measure how much air resistance the car shows.

windsock A tubular kite on a short tether that is used to indicate wind direction and strength.

Y

yaw A change in the horizontal direction of flight, either left or right.

INDEX

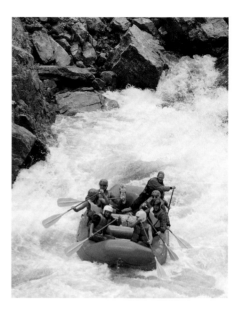

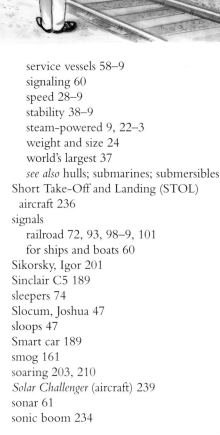

ACKNOWLEDGMENTS

Models

The Publishers would like to thank the following children, and their parents, for modeling in this book – Tyrone Agiton, Mohammed Afsar, Emily Askew, Anthony Bainbridge, Katie Appleby, Sara Barnes, Erin Bhogal, Maria Bloodworth, Joseph Brightman, David Callega, Shaun Liam Cook, Stacie Damps, Aaron Dumetz, Amaru Fleary, Laurence de Freitas, Alistair Fulton, Ricky Garrett, Africa George, Anton Goldbourne, Brooke Griffiths, Francesca Hill, Sasha Howarth, Thomas James, Carl Keating, Eddie Lengthorn, Jon Leming, Gabrielle Locke, Emma Molley, Jessica Moxley, Ifunanya Obi, Nicky Payne, Jamie Pyle, Mai Peterson, Emily Preddie, Zoe Richardson, Elen Rhys, Susy Quirke, Ajvir Sandhu, Jasmine Sharland, Nicola Twiner, Kirsty Wells, Joe Westbrook, Amber-Hollie Wood.

Every effort has been made to trace the copyright holders of all images that appear within this book. Anness Publishing Limited apologises for any unintentional omissions and, if notified, would be happy to add an acknowledgment in future editions.

Picture Credits

b=bottom, t=top, c= centre, l= left, r= right

Ships

Ancient Art and Architecture Collection/M Andrews: page 17bl. Barnaby's Picture Library: pages 16b, 30t, 41c, 69c; /D Coutts: page 63tr. Mary Evans Picture Library: pages 16t, 21c&br, 23t&cl, 52t. FLPA/Celtic Picture Library: page 63tl; /S Jonasson: page 42cr; /P & A Lewis: page 61c; /M Newman: page 56b; /R Tidman: page 42t. Robert Harding Picture Library/A Woolfitt: page 27cr. Michael Holford: pages 17c&br, 18t, 20t, 24t, 32t. Hulton Getty Picture Collection: page 22b. Image Select: page 36t; /C.F.C.L: pages 16c, 24c&b, 27cl, 41c, 42cl, 50b, 60br, 61cl&cr, 65cl, 68t; /Ann Ronan: pages 22t&c, 63b. Kos Picture Source Ltd: pages 13tl, 20bl, 27t, 31tl, 33t, 37b, 46c&b, 53t, 57cl, 59cl, 63cl; /C Borlenghi: pages 13c, 33cl, 57b, 69br; /H Gunn: page 56c; /R Jewell: page 56t; /G Norman: page 33cr; /G M Raget: pages 47b, 61br; /F Taccola: page 62c; /D Williams: pages 37t; 61bl. Military Picture Library: page 51cr; /Crown Copyright: page 52br; /R Adshead: page 51tl; /P Russel: pages 50t&c, 51tr,cl&b. National Maritime Museum Picture Library: pages 12b, 21 t&bl. P&O Cruises: pages 25tl,c&b, 40b. Planet Earth Pictures: pages 13b, 17t, 26c, 53br, 59b; /R de la Harpe 43cr; /N Wu: page 53bl. RNLI: page 65tl; /R Tomlinson: pages 64b, 65tr. Science Photo Library/S Fraser: page 62b; /D Nunuk: page 37cl. Seaco Picture Library: pages 25tr, 36b, 40c. Stock Market: pages 12t, 13tr, 30b, 31tr, 37cr, 38t, 41b, 43cl, 47tr, 57tr, 58t&b, 59t, 64t&c, 68b; /M K Daly: pages 26b, 57tl; /R Soto: page 44t; /T Stewart: page 43t. TRH Pictures: pages 40t, 52bl. Trip: page 68c; /T Bognar: page 20br; /G Hopkinson: page 14c; /D Houghton: page 59cr; /H Rogers: pages 32b, 69t; /R Surman: page 62t; /B Turner: pages 36c, 57cr; 65b, 69bl. Yamaha: page 31bl&br.

Trains

Alvey and Towers Picture Library:90cl, 99tl, 109t, 109cl, 109br, 117c, 125br; Colin Boocock: 93br; Corbis/Morton Beebe, S.F.: 125t; Corbis/Bettmann: 95cl; Corbis/Dallas and John Heaton: 124b; Corbis/John Heseltine: 91bl; Corbis/Jeremy Horner: 102tl; Corbis/Hulton Getty: 108cl; Corbis/Wolfgang Kaehler: 117b; Corbis/Lake County Museum: 73t; Corbis/Milepost 92½: 105tl; Corbis/Paul A. Souders: 93tl; Corbis/Michael S. Yamashita: 95tr, 100b, 114tr; Chris Dixon: 126br; Mike Harris: 125cr, 126bl; Anthony J. Lambert Collection: front cover (br), 72t, 89tr, 91br, 116tl, 123tl; The Illustrated London News: 106t, 106br, 116bl; The Kobal Collection: 120bl, 120br, 121tl, 121tr, 121bl, 121br; London Underground Ltd: 83cr; Mary Evans Picture Library: 80b, 82t, 83t, 83cl, 84t, 84b, 88t, 88c, 90tl, 94tr, 94b, 104cr, 104bl, 108br; Milepost 92½: 72c, 73cl, 73cr, 74t, 76b, 77bl, 77br, 78t, 81cl, 81cr, 85c, 85b, 86t, 88b,89tl, 89cr, 89b, 90cr, 91t, 92t, 92b, 93tr, 93bl, 95b, 99tr, 101t, 101cr, 105cl, 105br, 107tl, 107cl, 110tr, 112bl, 112br, 113t, 113c, 113b, 116br, 118tr, 120tr, 125cl, 126t, 127tl; Millbrook House Ltd: 94c, 96bl; Brian Morrison: 81b; QA Photos Ltd: 107cr; Claire Rae: 123cr; RAWIE: 101bl, 101bc; Science and Society/National Railway Museum: 76t, 104t, 122b, 128t; Science and Society/London Transport Museum: 108tl; SNCF-CAV/Sylvain Cambon: 83b; SNCF-CAV/Jean-Marc Fabbro: 98b.

Cars

Advertising Archive: 168tl. All Sport: 147tr; 147tl; 147cr; 147b; 149bl; 154b; . Agence Vandystadt: 147cr. Art Archive: 135tr; 164bl. The Bridgeman Art Library: 146c. EON Productions: 157tl. Genesis: 152bl. Ronald Grant Archive: 145cr; 157tr; 171tr; 183t; 189b. Hulton Getty: 142tr. Image Bank: 152tl; 162bl; 168c. Jaguar: 170tr; 171bl. The Kobal Collection: 183bl. LAT: 146bl; 180b; 181bl.Don Morley: 133cr; 138tr; 138bl; 141tl; 145tl; 150bl; 151tl; 151tr; 151cr; 151 br; 152cr; 153tr; 154t; 172tr; 180tl; 181br; 181c; 181tr; 182b; 187cr; National Motor Museum: 132br; 153br; 156t; 156b; 164cr; 165cr; 169tl; 171tl; 177cl; 182t; 182c; 183cr; 188br; 189cl. PA News Photo Library: 156bl; 156br. Quadrant: 132tr; 132bl; 133tr; 133cl; 133bl; 133tl; 138cl; 139c; 140br; 141br; 145tr; 150br; 150tl; 151cl; 151bl; 153bl; 154cr; 158tl; 161tr; 161cl; 166tr; 168bl; 169tr; 170br; 172cl; 173tl; 173cl; 173br; 174bl; 176tl; 177cr; 177b; 178cr; 183br; 184bl; 184br; 187bl; Smart Car: 188tl; 188tr. Tony Stone: 138tl; 144bl; 153tl; 153c; 160tl; 160bl; 161tl; 161bl; 161br; 162br; 164cr; 165tr; 165b; 170bl; 177tl; 178tl; 178bl; 184tl; 185tr; 185c. Volkswagen Press: 173tr

Aircraft and Flight

A – Z Botanical /Adrian Thomas: 232tr. Heather Angel: 198bl. The Aviation Picture Library /Austin J. Brown: 237t, 238tr & 200b. Bruce Coleman Ltd: Jane Burton: 198tl; /Alain Compost 199cl; /Michael Kline: 215br; /Gordon Langsbury: 195br; /Hans Reinhard: 207t; /Kim Taylor: 194b, 195tr & 199tr. Mary Evans Picture Library: 200t & c. The Flight Collection: 193t, 203br, 207cl, 210tl, 220br, 221bl, br, 223tr, 226c, 227b &c, 231b, cl, 235c, tl, 236t, 237t, 238br, 239b, cr, 201t, 244t, 245t, bl; /Flight International: 217br; /Peter R Foster: 235tr; /Trent Jones: 235b; /Erik Simonsen: 207cr & 192t; /Keith Wilson: 237br. Genesis: 209bl & 244cl. Image Bank/Paul Bowen: 231tl; NASA: 231tr. NHPA: 194cr: Nature Photographers Ltd /Roger Tidman: 203tl. Oxford Scientific Films: 228tl: Papillio Photographic: 192tr: Popperfoto: 171cl. Science Photo Library /Sam Ogden: 230br. Skyscan Photolibrary: 223tl, 237b: Spacecharts/Robin Kerrod: 192br, 242tl, 244b & 245c. Trip: 238bl; /T. Legate: 208br; /T. Malcolm: 220tl; /R. Marsh: 211bl; /Picturesque/Bill Terry: 207b; /P. Ridley: 213tl; /J. Ringland: 218br; /Streano/Havens: 227tr; /TH-Foto Werbung: 212tl; /Derek Thomas: 217bl. Virgin: 218tr. Stockmarket UK: 193cl, 203cl, 206tr, 211tl, tr, br, 213br, 217tl, 217tr, 199tl, b, 222tl, 226br, 230tr, 231cr, 234bl, 240tr, 241bl, 201bl; /J. Sedlmeier: 201c.

This edition is published by Southwater, an imprint of
Anness Publishing Ltd, Hermes House, 88–89 Blackfriars Road,
London SE1 8HA; tel. 020 7401 2077; fax 020 7633 9499
www.southwaterbooks.com; www.annesspublishing.com

If you like the images in this book and would like to investigate using them for publishing, promotions
or advertising, please visit our website www.practicalpictures.com for more information.

UK agent: The Manning Partnership Ltd;
tel. 01225 478444; fax 01225 478440; sales@manning-partnership.co.uk
UK distributor: Grantham Book Services Ltd;
tel. 01476 541080; fax 01476 541061; orders@gbs.tbs-ltd.co.uk
North American agent/distributor: National Book Network;
tel. 301 459 3366; fax 301 429 5746; www.nbnbooks.com
Australian agent/distributor: Pan Macmillan Australia;
tel. 1300 135 113; fax 1300 135 103; customer.service@macmillan.com.au
New Zealand agent/distributor:
David Bateman Ltd; tel. (09) 415 7664; fax (09) 415 8892

Publisher: Joanna Lorenz
Managing Editor, Children's Books: Gilly Cameron Cooper
Authors: Peter Harrison, Peter Mellett, Chris Oxlade, John Rostron
Consultants: Trevor Blakeley, Peter Cahill, Michael Harris, Chris Oxlade
Additional Text: Gilly Cameron Cooper
Compendium Editor: Leon Gray
Contributing Editors: Rebecca Clunes and Joy Wotton
Assistant Editor: Sarah Uttridge
Designers: Caroline Grimshaw, Michael Leaman, Sarah Melrose,
Caroline Reeves/Aztec Design
Additional Design: Caroline Reeves/Aztec Design
Illustrators: Peter Bull Art Studio, Richard Hawke, Nick Hawken,
Guy Smith, Clive Spong/Linden Artists
Picture Researchers: Gwen Campbell, Liz Eddison, Annabel Ossel
Photographer: John Freeman
Stylists: Marion Elliot and Melanie Williams
Production Controller: Steve Lang

ETHICAL TRADING POLICY
Because of our ongoing ecological investment program, you, as our customer, can have the pleasure and reassurance of knowing that a tree is
being cultivated on your behalf to naturally replace the materials used to make the book you are holding.
For further information about this scheme, go to www.annesspublishing.com/trees

PUBLISHER'S NOTE
Although the advice and information in this book are believed to be accurate and true at the time of going to press, neither the authors nor the publisher can
accept any legal responsibility or liability for any errors or omissions that may be made.

Previously published as *The Illustrated Science Encyclopedia: Transport*

31901047347929